Principles of Ethics

Principles of Ethics:
An Introduction

Paul W. Taylor

Wadsworth Publishing Company
Belmont, California
A Division of Wadsworth, Inc.

ISBN 0-8221-0142-4

Library of Congress Catalog Card Number: 74-83953

Printed in the United States of America

11 12 13 14 15 — 96 95 94 93 92 91

Contents

1   WHAT IS ETHICS?   1
    Ethics and Morality   1
    Descriptive, Normative, and Analytic Ethics   4
    Customary Morality and Reflective Morality   9
    Suggested Reading   11

2   ETHICAL RELATIVISM   13
    Descriptive Relativism   14
    Normative Ethical Relativism   18
    Metaethical Relativism   23
    Ethical Absolutism   26
    Suggested Reading   29

3   PSYCHOLOGICAL EGOISM AND ETHICAL EGOISM   31
    The Distinction between Psychological Egoism
    and Ethical Egoism   31
    Arguments for and against Psychological Egoism   36
    Ethical Egoism   46
    Suggested Reading   53

4   UTILITARIANISM   55
     Two Kinds of Ethical Systems   55
     Utility as the Test of Right and Wrong   59
     Act-Utilitarianism and Rule-Utilitarianism   63
     Are Act-Utilitarianism and Rule-Utilitarianism Incompatible?   68
     Utility and Justice   .   72
     A Defense of Utilitarianism   78
     Suggested Reading   80

5   ETHICAL FORMALISM   82
     Teleological and Deontological Ethics   82
     The Ethics of Immanuel Kant   85
     The Concept of a Moral Agent   93
     Universalizability   95
     Man as End in Himself   105
     The Autonomy of the Will   108
     The Principles of Justice   109
     Suggested Reading   111

6   INTRINSIC VALUE   114
     The Right and the Good   114
     The Concept of Intrinsic Value   115
     Hedonism   121
     Quantity versus Quality of Pleasure   127
     Pleasure and Happiness   129
     Suggested Reading   143

7   MORAL RESPONSIBILITY AND FREE WILL   146
     Excusing Conditions   146
     Determinism and Excusability   150
     Libertarianism   154
     The Compatibilist Concept of Freedom   157
     Soft Determinism and Hard Determinism   160
     The Inescapability of Freedom   163
     The Concept of Moral Responsibility   166
     Suggested Reading   173

8   VALUES AND FACTS   175
          Naturalism and Nonnaturalism   176
          The Naturalistic Fallacy   181
          Noncognitivism   188
          Standards of Evaluation and the Meaning of "Good"   193
          Descriptivism and Prescriptivism   200
          Suggested Reading   204

9   THE ULTIMATE QUESTION   208
          The Demand for a Justification of Morality   208
          The Logic of Moral Reasoning   211
          Is the Ultimate Question an Absurdity?   215
          The Meaning of the Ultimate Question   217
          Two Proposed Answers to the Ultimate Question   220
          The Commitment to Be Moral   225
          Suggested Reading   228

Acknowledgments

This book originated in a series of essays which I wrote for a collection of readings titled *Problems of Moral Philosophy: An Introduction to Ethics* (2nd ed., Encino, California: Dickenson Publishing Co., Inc., 1972). With the publisher's permission I have used here some of the material included in those essays. However, every chapter of the present volume has been conceived afresh and was written as a complete, unified whole. No reference to other writings in ethics is necessary for understanding the concepts and arguments set forth in this book.

A work of this kind, which attempts to give a balanced account of a wide range of problems for a beginning student, is necessarily dependent upon the original thinking of many philosophers, both past and present. I cannot begin to list all the writers whose thought, in one way or another, is fused into the contents of this book. There are simply too many. The bibliography provided at the end of each chapter indicates some of the sources, and my indebtedness to those works is very great indeed. There are a few living philosophers, however, whose ideas have had a particularly large influence on my general approach to ethics. These individuals, to whom I own a special intellectual debt, are: Professor Kurt Baier of the University of Pittsburgh; Professor Richard Brandt of the University of Michigan; Professor R. M. Hare, White's Professor of Moral Philosophy at Oxford University; Professor William K. Frankena of the University of Michigan; and Professor John Rawls of Harvard University.

The entire manuscript of this book was read by the following philosophers, whose criticisms and suggestions helped me to avoid errors of reasoning, clarify certain ideas, and make stylistic improvements: Professors Elizabeth L. Beardsley, Temple University; Ronald E. Benson, Ohio Northern University; Donald Burrill, California State University, Northridge; Romaine L. Gardner, Wagner College; and Ronald D. Milo, University of Arizona, Tucson.

Finally, I wish to express my gratitude to the many fine students I have had the pleasure of teaching at Brooklyn College and at the Graduate School of the City University of New York. They have made a significant contribution to this book by their stimulating discussions in my courses.

Paul W. Taylor

Principles of Ethics

I

What Is Ethics?

ETHICS AND MORALITY

Ethics may be defined as *philosophical inquiry into the nature and grounds of morality*. The term "morality" is here used as a general name for moral judgments, standards, and rules of conduct. These include not only the *actual* judgments, standards, and rules to be found in the moral codes of existing societies, but also what may be called *ideal* judgments, standards, and rules: those which can be justified on rational grounds. Indeed, one of the chief goals of ethics is to see if rational grounds can be given in support of any moral judgments, standards, or rules, and if so, to specify what those grounds are.

Whether actual or ideal, morality has to do with right and wrong conduct and also with good and bad character. Moral judgments are made not only about people's actions but also about their motives or reasons for doing them and about their more general character traits. For example, an action may be judged to be wrong when a person knowingly harms someone, and an action may be considered right if its purpose is to help another in a time of need. An individual's motive for an act may be judged to be bad when his aim is to take unfair advantage of people (even if he falls short of his objective), while someone else's action may be judged to spring from a good motive when he does something out of genuine concern for the well-being of others (even if, through no fault of his own, his action fails to bring about the intended effect). With regard to a person's character traits, if one individual is consistently honest in his

1

dealings with people while another is hypocritical, we may conclude that the first person has good character because he is honest and that the second has bad character because he is a hypocrite.

In all such judgments of actions, motives, and character traits, we are applying moral norms. A moral norm may be either a rule of conduct or a standard of evaluation. That is, it may be a requirement that anyone in certain circumstances should do, or refrain from doing, a certain kind of action. Or the norm may be a standard of evaluation, which we implicitly refer to whenever we decide whether something is good or bad, desirable or undesirable, worthy or worthless. As applied to conduct, standards are used for judging how good or bad are the consequences of a person's actions. It is possible for the same *kind* of action to be wrong in one situation and right in another, because in the first situation the consequences of such an action are bad while in the second the consequences of the same kind of action are good. As an example, consider how an act of lying can be wrong in one case and right in another. If one person harms another by telling a lie, we would ordinarily deem the action wrong. However, in the following situation we would probably judge the same kind of action (telling a lie) to be right: An American abolitionist who is protecting a runaway slave in the cellar of his house tells a lie when a suspicious neighbor questions him about fugitives. We have, then, two sorts of reasons why an action ought or ought not to be performed: (1) that the action is of a *kind* that is required or prohibited by a moral rule, and (2) that the action will, in the given circumstances, have good or bad *consequences* as judged by a standard of evaluation.

Moral judgments of people's motives and character traits are made on the basis of standards of evaluation, not rules of conduct. Thus we judge a person to be morally admirable according to the degree to which he fulfills some ideal of human excellence or virtue. And we think of a person as vicious, ignoble, or despicable insofar as he has motives and character traits we consider morally evil or blameworthy. It is, of course, possible to judge an individual to be morally good because he always strives to act as required by moral rules of conduct and to refrain from actions forbidden by those rules. But even in this case what is being judged directly is not the person's actions but his "will," that is, his aims, motives, and intentions in behaving in certain ways.

It is important to notice that the rules of conduct and standards of evaluation someone uses in his moral judgments need not be the conventionally accepted norms of a society's established moral code. They may, instead, be norms which the individual has chosen for himself after having rejected, wholly or in part, the conventional morality of his society. (See subsection below on Customary Morality and Reflective Morality.) But no matter whether a person has unthinkingly absorbed a set of rules and standards from his social environment or has chosen them himself on the basis of critical reflection, he will implicitly or explicitly use them as grounds for judging right and wrong conduct as well as good and bad character. Insofar as a person tries to live up to the rules and standards he sincerely accepts, they become part of his "philosophy of life," guiding his choices and giving direction to his conduct. They determine his ultimate ends and ideals in life, providing him with reasons for considering some goals to be more worth striving for than others.

When a stable set of rules and standards governs the choices and conduct of most of the people in a given society, we speak of the norms shared by a whole culture. Such norms (which make up the *actual* morality of that people) are embodied in the society's customs, traditions, and laws. They define its moral outlook and give form to its whole way of life. They are reflected in social attitudes of approval and disapproval, and are supported by moral sanctions. These sanctions may be either positive (praise, rewards, expressions of admiration) or negative (guilt and blame, punishments, expressions of condemnation).

We see, then, that moral standards and rules have a special function in practical life. Whether they are chosen by an individual as norms for judging his own character and conduct, or form a society's actual moral code, they serve as action-guides. They are the principles that determine what an individual or group conceives to be moral reasons for (or against) doing one thing rather than another. Thus we can find out what an individual's or group's actual moral norms are by seeing how they morally justify certain actions as being right.

With regard to any moral judgment, standard, or rule, the following questions may be asked: Is it a true judgment, a correct standard, a valid rule? That is, are there good reasons for accepting the judgment as (probably) true, or for using the standard or rule as an action-guide? Or is the judgment (probably) false, the standard unacceptable, the rule unjustified? It is questions like these which we must consider when thinking about ideal morality. They are just as much a part of the subject matter of ethics as are the judgments, standards, and rules of any actual morality. Let us now look more closely at the kind of thinking that is involved in philosophical reflection about morality, whether actual or ideal.

DESCRIPTIVE, NORMATIVE, AND ANALYTIC ETHICS

In the case of actual morality, it is possible to study its data (the specific moral judgments, standards, and rules accepted by a given individual or society) either scientifically or philosophically. Taking first the scientific point of view, we may consider the data as a set of empirical facts to be described and explained by scientific procedures. This can be done whether we focus on the moral consciousness of the individual or on the moral institutions and practices of a culture as a whole.

For a particular individual, his "moral consciousness" consists of his beliefs about what is right and wrong; his feelings of guilt and remorse when he fails to live up to his own moral norms and his sense of self-respect when he does fulfill them; the attitudes he takes toward himself when he holds himself accountable for certain actions, and his attitudes toward others when he considers their actions worthy of praise or blame. It also includes his being inspired or motivated by moral ideals; his exercising willpower and self-control in carrying out what he conceives to be his duty; his commitment to live by certain rules as matters of principle, putting aside all considerations of his own comfort, pleasure, or convenience. It is clear that if a person's morality were different, his whole experience of life would be altered. He would not only behave in another fashion, but would have different thoughts, feelings, attitudes, and desires. In short, he would be another kind of person.

Now since an individual's actual morality is part of his experience of life, it can be studied empirically. His moral judgments can be accurately described and their causes and effects investigated. A psychological explanation can be given to show why a particular person has certain moral beliefs and attitudes and how they influence his behavior. Psychologists can study the origin and growth of an individual's conscience, even relating his moral experiences to unconscious wishes, anxieties, and emotional conflicts of which he is unaware.

Similarly, on the level of society, empirical knowledge about actual morality can be sought and obtained through scientific investigation. Anthropologists, sociologists, historians, and social psychologists have examined the various moral codes of different societies and of diverse epochs. They have studied the moral norms operating in the ways of life of different economic and social classes within a culture. They have observed and explained the presence of "deviants" in a society, people whose norms are at variance with those generally accepted by the culture. They have examined the relationship of moral rules and standards to the social structure and their role in preserving a society's institutions. All these social aspects of actual morality are subject to the techniques of historical research, anthropological "field work," and sociological analysis.

This empirical knowledge of moral phenomena in the life of an individual and in the structure and functioning of a society may be summed up as: *the scientific description and explanation of actual morality.* For convenience, this scientific study of actual morality can be called *descriptive ethics.* It may now be readily distinguished from *the philosophical study of morality,* whether actual or ideal.

Philosophers are interested in actual morality not as a set of facts to be described and explained scientifically, but as the starting point for an inquiry into the possibility of constructing and justifying an ideal morality. Instead of asking, What are the causes for this particular person's accepting such-and-such standards and rules? the philosopher asks, What sorts of reasons (if any) would be good reasons for a person in such-and-such circumstances to accept such-and-such standards and rules? Instead of explaining how a moral practice may serve the interests of a certain class of persons in a given society, the philosopher asks, Are there any moral practices that promote the common good or meet the requirements of social justice; can it be shown that either the common good or social justice is a valid principle for assessing moral practices in any society? Instead of describing what might well be vague, confused, or inconsistent moral beliefs accepted by a given individual at some period in his life, the philosopher examines the logical relationships among different moral judgments and constructs a coherent, internally consistent system of judgments within the framework of certain fundamental principles. (We shall be considering such systems in some detail later in this book.)

In every case, the data of actual morality are of interest to the philosopher only as a starting point for his critical reflection. If he is to be investigating the nature and grounds of *moral* judgments, *moral* standards, and *moral* rules — however ideal they may be — they must have at least some characteristics in common with actual moral judgments, standards, and rules. Otherwise he will not be dealing with morality at all. Furthermore, by understanding how actual moral judgments, standards, and rules come to be accepted by some people and rejected by others; how they change with varying circumstances; how they function as an integral part of a culture's way of life; how they can guide conduct and affect the deliberation and decision-making of individuals; how they are criticized, attacked, and defended in arguments — by understanding these and similar aspects of actual morality, the philosopher is better able to carry out his inquiry into the nature and grounds of ideal morality in an enlightened way.

As he engages in his reflection about ideal morality, what exactly does the philosopher intend to accomplish? His main purpose may be expressed thus: to show how it is possible to construct a consistent system of moral norms valid for all moral agents. A "moral agent" is any being who is *capable* of thinking, deciding, and acting in accordance with moral standards and rules. A moral agent may not always fulfill the requirements of a moral standard or rule; that is, he need not be morally perfect. But he must have the capacity to judge himself on the basis of such a criterion and to use it as a guide to his choice and conduct. To say that a moral standard or rule is "valid for all moral agents" is to say that it is justifiable to appeal to it in judging any moral agent's character and conduct. An ordered set of such standards and rules is sometimes called a "normative ethical system," and the activity of constructing and justifying such a system is known as *normative ethics.*

Many methods of philosophical thinking have been used in normative ethics, and a number of them will be discussed in this book. In all such cases, the philosopher is concerned with whether a rational gound of moral obligation can be established. He examines the ultimate foundations of morality in order to show that a certain set of moral criteria ought to be accepted as the basis for judging the character and conduct of all who possess the capacities of a moral agent. Thus his fundamental aim is not to describe or explain what moral beliefs people actually have, but to inquire into their truth or falsity. As a result of his inquiry, he hopes to be able to answer the question, Is there a set of standards and rules which *any* rational person would be justified in adopting as guides to his life? Normative ethics is simply the systematic, thoroughgoing attempt to answer this question by means of philosophical thought.

In recent years a distinction has been made between two branches of moral philosophy, of which normative ethics is but one. The other branch is known as *analytic ethics* or *metaethics.* Whether these two fields of inquiry can be clearly separated is a matter of current dispute, but it is worthwhile here to consider briefly what the basis of the distinction is held to be. When analytic ethics is considered as an autonomous field of inquiry, it is thought to have an aim of its own that may be contrasted with that of normative ethics described above. The aim of analytic ethics when so conceived may be stated thus: to obtain a clear and complete understanding of the semantical, logical, and epistemological structure of moral discourse. The term "semantical" refers to the *meaning* of words and statements, semantics being the study of what words and statements mean as well as the different kinds of meaning they have. The term "logical" refers to the *relations between statements* in an argument, when someone is trying to show that the conclusion of his argument follows from the reasons he gives in its support. The term "epistemological" refers to *knowledge*, epistemology being that branch of philosophy concerned with the question, What is knowledge and how can it be attained? Since a person might claim to know something as the conclusion of an argument, justifying his claim on the basis of the reasons given in his argument, logic and epistemology are closely connected. As applied to analytic ethics, it will be convenient to consider them together. In general, then, two basic tasks of analytic ethics may be distinguished: first, to analyze the meaning of the terms used in moral discourse, and second, to examine the rules of reasoning and methods of knowing by which moral beliefs can be shown to be true or false. The first task of analytic ethics is a semantical one, the second a logical and epistemological one. Let us consider each in turn.

The aim of the first task is to explain precisely how such terms as "good," "right," "duty," and "ought" function in moral language. When people express their moral convictions, prescribe conduct, appraise character and motives, deliberate about what they ought or ought not to do, and evaluate what they and others have done, they are using moral language. Whether they are thinking out a moral issue for themselves or are discussing it with others, they are carrying on moral discourse. We learn the language of morals in our childhood, and we teach it to our own children when we try to bring them up morally. It is the job of philosophy to make a careful and thorough analysis of the meaning of the words and sentences that make up such language. The final aim is to achieve a full understanding of moral concepts (duty, virtue, responsibility, right action, etc.) and how they function in moral discourse. This first task of metaethics may be designated "conceptual analysis."

The second task of metaethics may be called "the analysis of the logic of moral reasoning." Here the philosopher's job is to make explicit the logical principles which are followed (or are intended to be followed) when people give moral reasons for or against doing an act, or when they try to justify their accepting or rejecting a moral judgment. Just as the philosophy of science attempts to show the logical structure underlying scientific method — the process whereby scientists verify their statements and support their theories by appeal to evidence—so analytic ethics attempts to show how moral beliefs can be established as true or false, and on what grounds anyone can claim to know they are true or false. As we shall see later, there is much dispute, not only about what methods of reasoning are to be used, but even about whether any method is possible at all. Thus this second task of analytic ethics is itself twofold. On the one hand is the question whether there is any such thing as moral truth or moral knowledge. On the other is the question: *If* there is such a thing, how can we gain it? This double aspect of analytic ethics may be brought out in the following list of questions, each pair of which is a way of expressing the basic twofold problem:

Is there a valid method by which the truth or falsity of moral beliefs can be established?	If so, what is this method and on what grounds does its validity rest?
Are moral statements verifiable?	If so, what is their method of verification?
Is there such a thing as knowledge of good and evil, right and wrong?	If so, how can such knowledge be obtained?
Is there a way of reasoning by which moral judgments can be justified?	If so, what is the logic of such reasoning?
Can we claim that the reasons we give in support of our moral judgments are good (sound, valid, acceptable, warranted) reasons?	If so, on what grounds can we make this claim? What are the criteria for the goodness (soundness, validity, etc.) of a reason?

Whenever anyone tries to answer these questions in a clear and orderly way, he is doing analytic ethics. We are now in a position to see a logical relation between analytic and normative ethics. Analytic ethics inquires into the *presuppositions* of normative ethics. If a philosopher constructs a system of moral norms and claims that these norms are validly binding upon everyone, he presupposes that there is a procedure whereby moral norms can be validated and that he has followed this procedure. He claims, in other words, to have moral knowledge and hence assumes that such knowledge is possible. Now it is precisely this assumption that is brought into question in analytic ethics. The very use of such words as "know," "true," "valid," and "justified" as applied to moral judgments is a problem for analytic ethics. Such words are used in normative ethics, but are not explicitly and carefully analyzed. Their analysis is just the task that metaethics sets for itself. It may therefore be argued that metaethics or analytic ethics is logically prior to normative ethics. Metaethical questions must first be answered before the complete development of a normative ethical system can be successfully achieved. It should be noted, however, that these two branches of ethics were not distinguished until midway in the twentieth century, so that the writings of moral philosophers before this time tend to cover both the problems of normative ethics and the problems of analytic ethics. In studying these writings it is always helpful to ask oneself, Is the philosopher making moral judgments and trying to show that they are justified, or is he examining what it means to claim that a moral judgment can be justified? In this way we can make clearer to ourselves exactly what questions the philosopher is trying to answer and so be better able to judge the soundness of his arguments.

We may sum up these introductory remarks about the nature of ethics in the following outline:

I. THE SCIENTIFIC STUDY OF MORALITY (DESCRIPTIVE ETHICS)
   Description and explanation of the moral life of man as manifested in any given individual's moral experience and in any given society's moral code.
II. THE PHILOSOPHICAL STUDY OF MORALITY
   A. Normative Ethics
      Inquiry into the rational grounds for justifying a set of moral norms for all mankind, and the rational construction of a system of such norms.
   B. Analytic. Ethics or Metaethics
      1. Conceptual analysis
         Semantical study of the meaning of words and sentences used in moral discourse.
      2. Analysis of the logic of moral reasoning
         Study of the methods by which moral judgments can be established as true or false, or whether any such method is possible at all.

CUSTOMARY MORALITY AND REFLECTIVE MORALITY

The ultimate purpose of normative and analytic ethics is to enable us to arrive at a critical, reflective morality of our own. Everyone is brought up with some set of moral beliefs, and every society has some moral code as part of its way of life. But an individual may either blindly accept the moral code of his society, or he may come to reflect upon it and criticize it. If he blindly accepts it, we may speak of his morality as "conventional" or "customary." Such an individual might well have strong moral convictions and might well be a good person in that he lives up to his norms. But he remains a child of his culture and lacks the ability to support his convictions by rational argument. Should he suddenly be confronted by others who have moral beliefs contradictory to his own and who hold them with as much certainty as he holds his own, he will feel lost and bewildered. His state of confusion might then turn into a deep disillusionment about morality. Unable to give an objective, reasoned justification for his own convictions, he may turn from dogmatic certainty to total skepticism. And from total skepticism it is but a short step to an "amoral" life — a life without any moral principles at all. Thus the person who begins by accepting moral beliefs blindly can end up denying all morality. Disillusionment and doubt can demoralize him, ultimately leading him to repudiate all moral ideals.

We can think of the process of moral growth as moving away from both complete dogmatism and complete skepticism. Neither of these conditions can provide reasons for or against moral beliefs. They are not the result of philosophical thought. One rests on blind faith in the authority of parents or society; the other is a reaction to deep emotional insecurity when intellectual certainty has been destroyed. The condition of moral maturity is the condition in which an individual has the capacity to be open-minded about his moral beliefs, defending them by reasoned argument when they are challenged and giving them up when they are shown to be false or unjustified. Of course it is possible for a person to conclude, on the basis of his own philosophical reflection about morality, that there is no valid method of reasoning by which moral beliefs can be justified or shown to be unjustified. That is, a person might come to think that all the metaethical questions placed on the left side of the foregoing list must be answered in the negative. But even here he will remain open-minded about his conclusions, always holding them tentatively and always willing to listen seriously to arguments on the other side.

Moral growth occurs, then, as the individual develops the capacity to reason about his moral beliefs. Instead of blindly adopting his society's moral code or being easily shocked by the moral systems of other cultures, he is able to think clearly, calmly, and coherently about any set of moral norms. He learns how to give good reasons for accepting and rejecting such norms, or else he learns the limits of moral reasoning, or why no such reasoning is possible. But whatever might be his conclusions, they are arrived at on the basis of his own reflection. He can then decide for himself what standards of evaluation and rules of conduct to commit himself to.

It is this sort of person — one who can think for himself and make decisions on the basis of his own thinking — who is the true individualist. Even if he ends up with moral norms that happen to be in general agreement with those of his society, they are of his own choosing so long as he can show why he thinks they are the norms he ought to follow. The process of critical reflection, however, will often lead a person to disagree with his society. In this case it is his critical reflection, not his disagreement, that makes him an individualist.

How can the shift from customary morality to reflective morality be accomplished? The answer lies in ethics, the philosophical study of morality. For ethics is nothing but the most systematic and thorough endeavor to understand moral concepts and to justify moral norms. Its supreme goal is to construct a moral order that can stand up to the critical scrutiny of reflective persons. Insofar as each of us tries to develop into a morally mature person, we are engaged in the practice of moral philosophy. We are striving to be clear and rational in our ethical thinking (the specific purpose of analytic ethics) and, if possible, to arrive at the principles of a universally valid moral system (the specific purpose of normative ethics). Thus ethics is not to be thought of merely as an intellectual game. It deals with the most vital issues we shall ever confront in practical life, and it alone can provide an adequate foundation for the moral growth of the individual.

Suggested Reading

Some general books on ethics, recommended for extending and deepening the reader's competence in ethical thinking beyond the level of the present volume:

Baier, Kurt, *The Moral Point of View: A Rational Basis of Ethics*. Ithaca, N. Y.: Cornell University Press, 1958. *Abridged Edition*. New York: Random House, Inc., 1965.*

Brandt, Richard B., *Ethical Theory: The Problems of Normative and Critical Ethics*. Englewood Cliffs, N. J.: Prentice-Hall, Inc., 1959.

Gert, Bernard, *The Moral Rules: A New Rational Foundation for Morality*. New York: Harper Torchbooks, Harper and Row, Publishers, Inc., 1973.*

Nowell-Smith, P. H., *Ethics*. Baltimore: Penguin Books, Inc., 1969.*

Rawls, John, *A Theory of Justice*. Cambridge, Mass.: Harvard University Press, 1971.*

Richards, David A. J., *A Theory of Reasons for Action*. London: Oxford University Press, 1971.

Toulmin, Stephen Edelston, *An Examination of the Place of Reason in Ethics*. Cambridge: Cambridge University Press, 1950.*

*Available in paperback

Wallace, G. and A. D. M. Walker, eds. *The Definition of Morality*. London: Methuen and Co. Ltd., 1970.*

Warnock, G. J., *The Object of Morality*. London: Methuen and Co. Ltd., 1971.*

Some relatively inexpensive collections of essays that cover a wide range of problems in ethics:

Ekman, Rosalind, ed., *Readings in the Problems of Ethics*. New York: Charles Scribner's Sons, 1965.*

Feinberg, Joel, ed., *Moral Concepts*. New York: Oxford University Press, 1970.*

Margolis, Joseph, ed., *Contemporary Ethical Theory: A Book of Readings*. New York: Random House, Inc., 1966.*

Thomson, Judith J. and Gerald Dworkin, eds., *Ethics*. New York: Harper and Row, Publishers, 1968.*

*Available in paperback

II

Ethical Relativism

One of the most commonly held opinions in ethics is that all moral norms are *relative* to particular cultures. The rules of conduct that are applicable in one society, it is claimed, do not apply to the actions of people in another society. Each community has its own norms, and morality is entirely a matter of conforming to the standards and rules accepted in one's own culture. To put it simply: What is right is what my society approves of; what is wrong is what my society disapproves of.

This view raises serious doubts about the whole enterprise of normative ethics. For if right and wrong are completely determined by the given moral code of a particular time and place, and if moral codes vary from time to time and place to place, it would seem that there are no unchanging cross-cultural principles that could constitute an ideal ethical system applicable to everyone. Since the purpose of normative ethics is to construct and defend just such a universal system of principles, belief in the relativity of moral norms denies the possibility of normative ethics. It is therefore important at the outset to examine the theory of ethical relativism.

The question raised by the ethical relativist may be expressed thus: Are moral values absolute, or are they relative? We may understand this question as asking, Are there any moral standards and rules of conduct that are universal (applicable to all mankind) or are they all culture-bound (applicable only to the members of a particular society or group)? Even when the question is interpreted in this way, however, it still remains unclear. For those who answer the question by claiming that all moral values are relative or culture-bound may be expressing any one of three different ideas. They may, first, be making an empirical or factual assertion. Or secondly, they may be making a normative claim. And thirdly, they may be understood to be uttering a metaethical principle. The term "ethical relativism" has been used to refer to any or all of these three positions. In

13

order to keep clear the differences among them, the following terminology
will be used. We shall call the first position "descriptive relativism," the
second "normative ethical relativism," and the third "metaethical relativism." Let us consider each in turn.

DESCRIPTIVE RELATIVISM

Certain facts about the moral values of different societies and about the
way an individual's values are dependent on those of his society have been
taken as empirical evidence in support of the claim that all moral values are
relative to the particular culture in which they are accepted. These facts are
cited by the relativist as reasons for holding a general theory about moral
norms, namely, that no such norms are universal. This theory is what we
shall designate "descriptive relativism." It is a factual or empirical theory
because it holds that, as a matter of historical and sociological fact, no
moral standard or rule of conduct has been universally recognized to be the
basis of moral obligation. According to the descriptive relativist there are no
moral norms common to all cultures. Each society has its own view of what
is morally right and wrong and these views vary from society to society
because of the differences in their moral codes. Thus it is a mistake to think
there are common norms that bind all mankind in one moral community.

Those who accept the position of descriptive relativism point to certain
facts as supporting evidence for their theory. These facts may be conveniently summed up under the following headings:
  (1) The facts of cultural variability.
  (2) Facts about the origin of moral beliefs and moral codes.
  (3) The fact of ethnocentrism.

(1) The facts of cultural variability are now so familiar to everyone that
they need hardly be enumerated in detail. We all know from reading
anthropologists' studies of primitive cultures how extreme is the variation in
the customs and taboos, the religions and moralities, the daily habits and
the general outlook on life to be found in the cultures of different peoples.
But we need not go beyond our own culture to recognize the facts of
variability. Historians of Western civilization have long pointed out the
great differences in the beliefs and values of people living in different
periods. Great differences have also been discovered among the various
socioeconomic classes existing within the social structure at any one time.
Finally, our own contemporary world reveals a tremendous variety of ways

of living. No one who dwells in a modern city can escape the impact of this spectrum of different views on work and play, on family life and education, on what constitutes personal happiness, and on what is right and wrong.

(2) When we add to these facts of cultural and historical variability the recent psychological findings about how the individual's values reflect those of his own social group and his own time, we may begin to question the universal validity of our own values. For it is now a well-established fact that no moral values or beliefs are inborn. All our moral attitudes and judgments are learned from the social environment. Even our deepest convictions about justice and the rights of man are originally nothing but the "introjected" or "internalized" views of our culture, transmitted to us through our parents and teachers. Our very conscience itself is formed by the internalizing of the sanctions used by our society to support its moral norms. When we were told in childhood what we ought and ought not to do, and when our parents expressed their approval and disapproval of us for what we did, we were being taught the standards and rules of conduct accepted in our society. The result of this learning process (sometimes called "acculturation") was to ingrain in us a set of attitudes about our own conduct, so that even when our parents were no longer around to guide us or to blame us, we would guide or blame ourselves by thinking, "This is what I ought to do"; "That would be wrong to do"; and so on. If we then did something we believed was wrong we would feel guilty about it, whether or not anyone caught us at it or punished us for it.

It is this unconscious process of internalizing the norms of one's society through early childhood training that explains the origin of an individual's moral values. If we go beyond this and ask about the origin of society's values, we find a long and gradual development of traditions and customs which have given stability to the society's way of life and whose obscure beginnings lie in ritual magic, taboos, tribal ceremonies, and practices of religious worship. Whether we are dealing with the formation of an individual's conscience or the development of a society's moral code, then, the origin of a set of values seems to have little or nothing to do with rational, controlled thought. Neither individuals nor societies originally acquire their moral beliefs by means of logical reasoning or through the use of an objective method for gaining knowledge.

(3) Finally, the descriptive relativist points out another fact about people and their moralities that must be acknowledged. This is the fact that most people are ethnocentric (group centered). They think not only that there is but one true morality for all mankind, but that the one true morality is their

own. They are convinced that the moral code under which they grew up and which formed their deepest feelings about right and wrong—namely, the moral code of their own society—is the only code for anyone to live by. Indeed, they often refuse even to entertain the possibility that their own values might be false or that another society's code might be more correct, more enlightened, or more advanced than their own. Thus ethnocentrism often leads to intolerance and dogmatism. It causes people to be extremely narrow-minded in their ethical outlook, afraid to admit any doubt about a moral issue, and unable to take a detached, objective stance regarding their own moral beliefs. Being absolutely certain that their beliefs are true, they can think only that those who disagree with them are in total error and ignorance on moral matters. Their attitude is: We are advanced, they are backward. We are civilized, they are savages.

It is but a short step from dogmatism to intolerance. Intolerance is simply dogmatism in action. Because the moral values of people directly affect their conduct, those who have divergent moral convictions will often come into active conflict with one another in the area of practical life. Each will believe he alone has the true morality and the other is living in the darkness of sin. Each will see the other as practicing moral abominations. Each will then try to force the other to accept the truth, or at least will not allow the other to live by his own values. The self-righteous person will not tolerate the presence of "shocking" acts which he views with outraged indignation. Thus it comes about that no differences of opinion on moral matters will be permitted within a society. The ethnocentric society will tend to be a closed society, as far as moral belief and practice are concerned.

The argument for descriptive relativism, then, may be summarized as follows. Since every culture varies with respect to its moral rules and standards, and since each individual's moral beliefs—including his inner conviction of their absolute truth—have been learned within the framework of his own culture's moral code, it follows that there are no universal moral norms. If a person believes there are such norms, this is to be explained by his ethnocentrism, which leads him to project his own culture's norms upon everyone else and to consider those who disagree with him either as innocent but "morally blind" people or as sinners who do not want to face the truth about their own evil ways.

In order to assess the soundness of this argument it is necessary to make a distinction between (a) specific moral standards and rules, and (b) ultimate moral principles. Both (a) and (b) can be called "norms," and it is because the descriptive relativist often overlooks this distinction that his argument is open to doubt. A specific moral standard (such as personal courage or trustworthiness) functions as a criterion for judging whether and to what degree a person's character is morally good or bad. A specific rule of conduct (such as "Help others in time of need" or "Do not tell lies for one's own advantage") is a prescription of how people ought or ought not to act. It functions as a criterion for judging whether an action is right or wrong. In contrast with specific standards and rules, an ultimate moral principle is a universal proposition or statement about the conditions that must hold if a standard or rule is to be used as a criterion for judging *any* person or action. Such a principle will be of the form: Standard S or rule R applies to a person or action if and only if condition C is fulfilled. An example of an ultimate moral principle is that of utility, which we shall be examining in detail in Chapter 4. The principle of utility may be expressed thus: A standard or rule applies to a person or action if, and only if, the use of the standard or rule in the actual guidance of people's conduct will result in an increase in everyone's happiness or a decrease in everyone's unhappiness.

Now it is perfectly possible for an ultimate moral principle to be consistent with a variety of specific standards and rules as found in the moral codes of different societies. For if we take into account the traditions of a culture, the beliefs about reality and the attitudes toward life that are part of each culture's world-outlook, and if we also take into account the physical or geographical setting of each culture, we will find that a standard or rule which increases people's happiness in one culture will not increase, but rather decrease, people's happiness in another. In one society, for example, letting elderly people die when they can no longer contribute to economic production will be necessary for the survival of everyone else. But another society may have an abundant economy that can easily support people in their old age. Thus the principle of utility would require that in the first society the rule "Do not keep a person alive when he can no longer produce" be part of its moral code, and in the second society it would require a contrary rule. In this case the very same kind of action that is wrong in one society will be right in another. Yet there is a single principle that makes an action of that kind wrong (in one set of circumstances) and another action of that kind right (in a different set of circumstances). In other words, the reason why one action is wrong and the other right is based on one and the same principle, namely utility.

Having in mind this distinction between specific standards and rules on the one hand and ultimate moral principles on the other, what can we say about the argument for descriptive relativism given above? It will immediately be seen that the facts pointed out by the relativist as evidence in support of his theory do not show that ultimate moral principles are relative or culture-bound. They show only that specific standards and rules are relative or culture-bound. The fact that different societies accept different norms of good and bad, right and wrong, is a fact about the standards and rules that make up the various moral codes of those societies. Such a fact does not provide evidence that there is no single ultimate principle which, explicitly or implicitly, every society appeals to as the final justifying ground for its moral code. For if there were such a common ultimate principle, the actual variation in moral codes could be explained in terms of the different world-outlooks, traditions, and physical circumstances of the different societies.

Similarly, facts about ethnocentrism and the causal dependence of an individual's moral beliefs upon his society's moral code do not count as evidence against the view that there is a universal ultimate principle which everyone would refer to in giving a final justification for his society's standards and rules, if he were challenged to do so. Whether there is such a principle and if there is, what sort of conditions it specifies for the validity of specific standards and rules, are questions still to be explored. (In later chapters of this book we shall be considering some of the answers that philosophers have given to these questions.) But the facts cited by the descriptive relativist leave these questions open. We may accept those facts and still be consistent in affirming a single universal ultimate moral principle.

NORMATIVE ETHICAL RELATIVISM

The statement, "What is right in one society may be wrong in another," is a popular way of explaining what is meant by the "relativity of morals." It is usually constrasted with "ethical universalism," taken as the view that "right and wrong do not vary from society to society." These statements are ambiguous, however, and it is important for us to be mindful of their ambiguity. For they may be understood either as factual claims or as normative claims, and it makes a great deal of difference which way they are understood. (They may also be taken as metaethical claims, but we shall postpone this way of considering them until later.)

When it is said that what is right in one society may be wrong in another, this may be understood to mean that what is *believed* to be right in one society is *believed* to be wrong in another. And when it is said that moral right and wrong vary from society to society, this may be understood to mean that different moral norms are adopted by different societies, so that an act which fulfills the norms of one society may violate the norms of another. If this is what is meant, then we are here being told merely of the cultural variability of specific standards and rules, which we have already considered in connection with descriptive relativism.

But the statement, "What is right in one society may be wrong in another," may be interpreted in quite a different way. It may be taken as a normative claim rather than as a factual assertion. Instead of asserting the unsurprising fact that what is believed to be right in one society is believed to be wrong in another, it expresses the far more radical and seemingly paradoxical claim that what *actually is* right in one society may *actually be* wrong in another. According to this view, moral norms are to be considered valid only within the society which has adopted them as part of its way of life. Such norms are not to be considered valid outside that society. The conclusion is then drawn that is is not legitimate to judge people in other societies by applying the norms of one's own society to their conduct. This is the view we shall designate "normative ethical relativism." In order to be perfectly clear about what it claims, we shall examine two ways in which it can be stated, one focusing our attention upon moral judgments, the other on moral norms.

With regard to moral judgments, normative ethical relativism holds that two *apparently* contradictory statements can both be true. The argument runs as follows. Consider the two statements:

(1) It is wrong for unmarried women to have their faces unveiled in front of strangers.

(2) It is not wrong for . . .(as above).

Here it seems as if there is a flat contradiction between two moral judgments, so that if one is true the other must be false. But the normative ethical relativist holds that they are both true, because the statements as given in (1) and (2) are incomplete. They should read as follows:

(3) It is wrong for unmarried women *who are members of society S* to have their faces unveiled in front of strangers.

(4) It is not wrong for unmarried women *outside of society S* to have their faces unveiled in front of strangers.

Statements (3) and (4) are not contradictories. To assert one is not to deny the other. The normative ethical relativist simply translates all moral judgments of the form "Doing act X is right" into statements of the form "Doing X is right when the agent is a member of society S." The latter statement can then be seen to be consistent with statements of the form "Doing X is wrong when the agent is not a member of society S."

The normative ethical relativist's view of moral norms accounts for the foregoing theory of moral judgments. A moral norm, we have seen, is either a standard used in a judgment of good and bad character or a rule used in a judgment of right and wrong conduct. Thus a person is judged to be good insofar as he fulfills the standard, and an action is judged to be right or wrong according to whether it conforms to or violates the rule. Now when a normative ethical relativist says that moral norms vary from society to society, he does not intend merely to assert the fact that different societies have adopted different norms. He is going beyong descriptive relativism and is making a normative claim. He is denying any universal validity to moral norms. He is saying that a moral standard or rule is correctly applicable only to the members of the particular society which has adopted the standard or rule as part of its actual moral code. He therefore thinks it is illegitimate to judge the character or conduct of those outside the society by such a standard or rule. Anyone who uses the norms of one society as the basis for judging the character or conduct of persons in another society is consequently in error.

It is not that a normative ethical relativist necessarily believes in *tolerance* of other people's norms. Nor does his position imply that he grants others the *right* to live by their own norms, for he would hold a relativist view even about tolerance itself. A society whose code included a rule of tolerance would be right in tolerating others, while one that denied tolerance would be right (relative to its own norm of intolerance) in prohibiting others from living by different norms. The normative ethical relativist would simply say that *we* should not judge the tolerant society to be any better than the intolerant one, for this would be applying our own norm of tolerance to other societies. Tolerance, like any other norm, is culture-bound. Anyone who claims that every society has a *right* to live by its own norms, provided that it respects a similar right in other societies, is an ethical universalist, since he holds at least one norm valid for all societies, namely, the right to practice a way of life without interference from others. And he deems this universal norm a valid one, whether or not every society does in fact accept it.

If the normative ethical relativist is challenged to prove his position, he may do either of two things. On the one hand, he may try to argue that his position follows from, or is based on, the very same facts that are cited by the descriptive relativist as evidence for *his* position. Or, on the other hand, he may turn for support to metaethical condiderations. Putting aside the second move for the moment, let us look more closely at the first.

The most frequent argument given in defense of normative ethical relativism is that, if the facts pointed out by the descriptive relativist are indeed true, then we must accept normative ethical relativism as the only position consistent with those facts. For it seems that if each person's moral judgments are formed within the framework of the norms of his own culture and historical epoch, and if such norms vary among cultures and epochs, it would follow necessarily that it is unwarranted for anyone to apply his own norms to conduct in other societies and times. To do so would be ethnocentrism, which is, as the descriptive relativist shows, a kind of blind, narrow-minded dogmatism. To escape the irrationality of being ethnocentric, we need but realize that the only norms one may legitimately apply to any given group are the ones accepted by that group. Since different peoples accept different norms, there are no universal norms applicable to everyone throughout the world. Now, to say that there are no universal norms applicable worldwide is to commit oneself to normative ethical relativism. Thus, the argument concludes, normative ethical relativism follows from the facts of descriptive relativism.

Is this a valid argument? Suppose one accepts the facts pointed out by the descriptive relativist. Must he then also accept normative ethical relativism? Let us examine some of the objections that have been raised to this argument. In the first place, it is claimed that the facts of cultural variability do not, *by themselves*, entail normative ethical relativism. The reason is that it is perfectly possible for someone to accept those facts and deny normative ethical relativism without contradicting himself. No matter how great may be the differences in the moral beliefs of different cultures and in the moral norms they accept, it is still possible to hold that some of these beliefs are true and others false, or that some of the norms are more correct, justified, or enlightened than others. The fact that societies differ about what is right and wrong does not mean that one society may not have better reasons for holding its views than does another. After all, just because two people (or two groups of people) disagree about whether a disease is caused by bacteria or by evil spirits does not lead to the conclusion that there is no correct or enlightened view about the cause of the disease. So it does not follow from the fact that two societies differ about whether genocide is right that there is no correct or enlightened view about this moral matter.

A similar argument can be used with regard to the second set of facts asserted by the descriptive relativist. No contradiction is involved in affirming that all moral beliefs come from the social environment and denying normative ethical relativism. The fact that a belief is learned from one's society does not mean that it is neither true nor false, or that if it is true, its truth is "relative" to the society in which it was learned. All of our beliefs, empirical ones no less than moral ones, are learned from our society. We are not born with any innate beliefs about chemistry or physics; we learn these only in our schools. Yet this does not make us skeptical about the universal validity of these sciences. So the fact that our moral beliefs come from our society and are learned in our homes and schools has no bearing on their universal validity. The origin or cause of a person's *acquiring* a belief does not determine whether the *content* of the belief is true or false, or even whether there are good grounds for his accepting that content to be true or false.

If it is claimed that our moral beliefs are based on attitudes or feelings culturally conditioned in us from childhood, the same point can still be made. Suppose, for example, that a person who believes slavery is wrong feels disapproval, dislike, or even abhorrence towards the institution of slavery. His negative attitude, which has undoubtedly been influenced by the value system of his culture, may be contrasted with a positive stance (approval, liking, admiring) of someone brought up in an environment where slave owning was accepted. Here are positive and negative attitudes toward slavery, each being causally conditioned by the given cultural environment. It does not follow from this that the two are equally justified, or that neither can be justified. The question of whether a certain attitude toward slavery is justified or unjustified depends on whether good reasons can be given *for* anyone taking the one attitude and *against* anyone taking the other. This question requires the exercise of our reasoning powers. Exactly how we can justify attitudes, or show them to be unjustified, is a complex problem that will be dealt with in later chapters of this book. But the mere fact that the attitudes which underlie moral beliefs are all learned from the social environment leaves open the question of what attitudes an intelligent, rational, and well-informed person would take toward a given action or social practice.

The same kind of argument also holds with respect to the third fact of descriptive relativism: ethnocentrism. People who are ethnocentric *believe* that the one true moral code is that of their own society. But this leaves open the question, Is their belief true or false? Two people of different cultures, both ethnocentric but with opposite moral beliefs, may each think his particular moral norms are valid for everyone; however, this has no bearing on whether either one — or neither one — is correct. We must inquire independently into the possibility of establishing the universal validity of a set of moral norms, regardless of who might or might not believe them to be universally true.

It should be noted that these various objections to the first argument for normative ethical relativism, even if sound, are not sufficient to show that normative ethical relativism is false. They only provide reasons for rejecting one argument in support of that position. To show that the position is false, it would be necessary to give a sound argument in defense of ethical universalism. The sorts of arguments set forth by philosophers to establish universalism will be disclosed in later chapters. It is only if one or more of these arguments proves acceptable that normative ethical relativism is refuted.

A second argument by which the normative ethical relativist defends his position was mentioned earlier. This argument is based on metaethical considerations, so it is appropriate now to examine the bearing of metaethics on the relativism-universalism controversy.

METAETHICAL RELATIVISM

It will be convenient to distinguish between two forms of metaethical relativism, called "conceptual relativism" and "methodological relativism." Conceptual relativism is the view that moral concepts vary from culture to culture and therefore the moral judgments of one society are meaningless or unintelligible to the members of another. For example, the idea in our own society of individual freedom as a basic human right may not be understandable to a society lacking the concept of human rights or with a view of individual freedom different from ours. The conceptual relativist holds that the meaning of a moral idea can be understood only within the context of a given culture's ethical system as a whole. The conclusion drawn from this is that intercultural comparisons of moral judgments cannot be made. There is no standpoint outside of all cultures from which to decide whether the moral judgments of one society are more enlightened or correct than those of another. Such a comparison would require that both sets of judgments by intelligible to the same individual and this, the conceptual relativist claims, is impossible.

One logical consequence of this view is the following. Suppose a person from culture X utters the judgment "Polygamy is wrong," and a person from culture Y replies, "No, polygamy is not wrong." It would appear that the person from Y is contradicting the person from X. But according to the conceptual relativist this appearance is false; there is actually no contradiction at all between them. For the word "wrong" stands for a different idea — that is, has a different meaning — in each statement. The two persons are not talking about the same thing when they use the word "wrong" (even if they are talking about the same thing when they say "polygamy" — a point also open to doubt in the conceptual relativist's view). Thus in culture X "wrong" might mean "what is detrimental to the common good" while in culture Y it might mean "prohibited by the gods." It may be that polygamy is detrimental to the common good in culture X and is permitted by the gods of culture Y. In these circumstances both statements are true, and thus there can be no contradiction between them.

A further point is now made by the conceptual relativist. Not only do the *meanings* of words like "right" and "wrong," "good" and "bad" vary from culture to culture, but there is also great variation in what the words *refer to*. In one culture, for instance, the term "a good man" will refer to anyone who is meek and forgiving. In another culture the same term will refer to one who is quick to avenge himself on others and is ruthless with his enemies. Similarly, in one society the statement "That act is right" will be applied to every case in which it is believed that the given act is necessary to uphold the honor of one's family. In another society the same statement will apply to all situations where the given act involves treating everyone concerned — friends and strangers alike — fairly and impartially.

On the basis of considerations like these, the conceptual relativist argues that what a particular word means and what it refers to in moral discourse depend on the specific system of moral norms accepted by the society in which the discourse takes place. He concludes that it makes no sense to talk, as the ethical universalist does, about a *true* view of right action or a *correct* conception of the good man. Such talk assumes that intercultural comparisons of moral concepts are possible. But, he asserts, this assumption is false, since the meaning and application of every moral concept must be relativized to a particular culture.

Is the conceptual relativist right? Can his theory stand up to critical scrutiny when it is examined with care? The answer depends on what analysis is made of the meaning and reference of words and statements used in moral discourse, a matter which will be of concern throughout the rest of this book. So the question must be left open at this juncture.

The second form of metaethical relativism, methodological relativism, maintains that different cultures use different methods of reasoning to justify moral judgments. The conclusion drawn is that the same judgment may be justified in one culture but not in another. Each method provides its own criteria for determining whether a reason given in a moral argument is a good or valid one. If such criteria vary from culture to culture, it may be possible to establish the truth of a moral belief in one social environment and to show it to be false in another. Moral knowledge, being based on different verification procedures, would then be culturally relative. Unless there were some uniform, cross-cultural method for gaining moral knowledge or a uniform, cross-cultural set of rules of reasoning that could tell us whether a person in *any* culture is thinking correctly, no claim could be made for the universal validity of moral norms. And the methodological relativist argues that there is no such method or set of rules of reasoning. Whether his argument is to be accepted is a question that must be considered in the light of those ways that have been proposed by moral philosophers for obtaining genuine moral knowledge. A number of such ways will be found in later chapters of this book.

It has been claimed that one serious implication of methodological relativism is ethical skepticism, or the complete denial of moral knowledge. The reasoning behind this claim is as follows. When the methodological relativist asserts that all moral knowledge is "relative" to a given culture, he is ruling out the very conditions that make it possible for such a thing as genuine moral knowledge to exist at all. In effect he is saying that, if we investigate the assumptions underlying the alleged universal methods adopted by different cultures, we find that in every case one procedure will define "valid" or "good" reasons in one way and another will define them differently. It follows that the question of which, if any, of these given procedures really does lead to moral knowledge is *logically undecidable*. For to choose between any two methods, a neutral third method must be used—one that would enable us to give reasons for accepting one method and rejecting the other. But any such third way will itself merely postulate its own criteria of "valid" reasons, and we would then have to justify our choice of *these* criteria. This however, would in turn also require our giving reasons for our choice, presupposing still another procedure. Since we cannot go to infinity in seeking methods for justifying other methods, we are left at some point with an arbitrary decision. But no claim to genuine moral knowledge can rest on an arbitrary decision, since a different decision — as unjustified as the first — might lead to opposite conclusions regarding a moral issue. This is precisely the kind of situation that the word "knowledge" precludes, if that word is to be understood in its ordinary sense. Therefore genuine moral knowledge is impossible.

Moral philosophers reply to this argument simply by constructing, clearly and systematically, a method of moral reasoning whose logical principles can be shown to be in fact presupposed by anyone, in any culture, who intends to think rationally about moral matters. By considering how any reasonable being would carry on his thinking when he understands clearly the meaning of moral concepts, the uses of moral language, and the function of moral norms in the guidance of conduct, the philosopher attempts to show that there *is* a valid way of determining whether any moral judgment is true or false and, hence, that there is a warranted method for obtaining genuine moral knowledge. In this book we shall become acquainted with some of the most important of these attempts.

ETHICAL ABSOLUTISM

When someone asks, "Are moral norms relative or absolute?" there is often an ambiguity in his question, not only with respect to the word "relative" but also with respect to the word "absolute." We have seen that "relative" can mean, among other things, "causally dependent on variable factors in different cultures" (descriptive relativism); *or* "validly applicable only within the culture which accepts the norm" (normative ethical relativism); *or* "impossible to justify on cross-cultural grounds" (methodological relativism). Let us now examine an important ambiguity in the term "absolute" as it is applied to moral norms. For unless this ambiguity is cleared up, we cannot give a straightforward answer to the question of whether moral norms are relative or absolute.

That moral norms (that is, specific moral rules and standards) are "absolute" can mean either of two things. It can mean that at least some moral norms are justifiable on grounds that can be established by a cross-cultural method of reasoning and that, consequently, these norms correctly apply to the conduct of all human beings. This, we have seen, is ethical universalism. It entails the denial of normative ethical relativism and also the denial of metaethical relativism. Hence, in this first sense of the term "absolute," ethical absolutism may simply be equated with ethical universalism.

The second meaning of the term "absolute" is entirely different from the first. According to the second meaning, to say that moral norms are "absolute" is to say that they *have no exceptions.* Thus, if the rule "It is wrong to break a promise" is an absolute moral norm in this second sense, then one must never break a promise no matter what the circumstances. It follows that it is our duty to keep a promise, even if doing so brings suffering to innocent people. It means, for example, that a hired gunman who promises his boss to murder someone should commit the murder. It signifies that, if we have promised a friend to go to a movie with him on Saturday night, we must do so even if our parents are injured in an automobile accident Saturday afternoon and desperately need our help. Extreme cases like these show that, at least in our ordinary unreflective moral judgments, the rule "Do not break promises" has exceptions and that, consequently, ethical absolutism in the second sense of the term is not true of that particular moral rule.

Are there *any* rules of conduct that are "absolute" in the second sense? The reader should try to work out his own answer to this question for himself. What is important for present purposes is to notice the *logical independence* of the two meanings of "ethical absolutism."

According to the first meaning, an ethical absolutist holds that there are moral norms that apply to everyone, no matter what norms are actually accepted in a given society. According to the second meaning, an ethical absolutist is one who claims that at least some moral norms allow for no legitimate or justifiable exceptions. It is clear that the first meaning of ethical absolutism does not necessarily entail the second. In other words, it is possible to be an ethical absolutist in the first sense but not in the second. For it may be that all moral norms valid for everyone in any society are norms that allow for legitimate exceptions in special circumstances, *whenever* those circumstances occur. Let us consider an example.

Suppose we think that in almost all situations of life it is wrong for one person to take the life of another. Suppose, further, that we hold the rule "Thou shalt not kill" to be a universal moral norm, believing that it applies to all persons in all societies (even if a certain group of people in a given society do not accept the rule). Thus, with respect to this rule we are ethical universalists. Now suppose that we also think that there are very unusual conditions which, when they occur, make it permissible for one person to kill another. For instance, we might think that if a person's only means of defending his life or the lives of his children against the attack of a madman is to kill him, then it is not wrong to kill him. Or we might think that killing is permissible when such an act is necessary to overthrow a totalitarian government carrying out a policy of systematic genocide. If we hold these cases to be legitimate exceptions to the rule "Thou shalt not kill," are we contradicting our position of ethical universalism with regard to that rule? The answer is no, since we may be willing to consider these exceptions universally legitimate whenever they occur, no matter whether a given society accepts them as legitimate exceptions or not. In this case the *full* statement of our rule against killing would be expressed thus: It is wrong for anyone, in any society, to take the life of another, except when such an act is necessary for self-defense or the prevention of systematic genocide.

When a moral rule is stated in this manner, it encompasses its own exceptions. In other words, the complete rule stipulates all the kinds of situations in which an action of the sort *generally* forbidden by the rule is right. If we then accept the rule in its complete form, *including the list of exceptions,* as validly applicable to all human beings, we are ethical universalists (and hence ethical absolutists in the first sense of the term) with respect to this rule. However, we are not ethical absolutists in the second sense of the term, since we hold that the simple rule "Thou shalt not kill" does have legitimate exceptions.

It is true that in this case we may not be willing to allow for exceptions to the whole rule in its *complete* form, since we may think our statement of the rule includes all the possible exceptions it could have. With regard to the rule in its complete form, we would then be ethical absolutists in both senses of the term. On the other hand, if we are not sure we have included all the exceptions that could possibly be legitimate, then with regard to such an *incomplete* rule we would not be ethical absolutists in the second sense. The rule as we have formulated it may still have legitimate exceptions which we have overlooked, but we can nevertheless be ethical universalists about such an incomplete rule. For we might believe that, even in its incomplete form, it correctly applies to all mankind.

The main point of this discussion may now be indicated. When an ethical universalist says that there are moral norms applicable to everyone everywhere, he does not mean that the application of these norms to particular circumstances must determine that one kind of action is always right (or that it is always wrong). He means only that, whenever the norms do apply, they apply regardless of whether a given society may have accepted them in its actual moral code and another society may have excluded them from *its* moral code. The (normative) ethical relativist, on the other hand, claims that what makes an act right is precisely its conformity to the accepted norms of the society in which it occurs, while its violation of such accepted norms makes it wrong. Consider, then, two acts of the very same kind done in the very same sort of circumstances, but each occurring in a different society. One can be right and the other wrong, according to the relativist, since the moral norms of the two societies may disagree concerning the behavior in question. The ethical universalist (or "absolutist" in the first sense), however, would say that if one act is right the other is too and if one is wrong so is the other. For both are acts of an identical kind performed in identical circumstances. Therefore a rule which required or prohibited the one would also require or prohibit the other, and only one rule validly applies to such actions performed in circumstances of that sort. Thus the universalist holds that the rightness and wrongness of actions do not change according to variations in the norms accepted by different societies, even though (contrary to what the "absolutist" in the second sense says) the rightness and wrongness of actions do vary with differences in the sorts of circumstances in which they are performed.

If we keep this distinction between the two meanings of ethical absolutism clearly in mind, we can then see that it is possible to be an absolutist in one sense and not in the other. Whether either sense of absolutism is a correct view is a matter that cannot be settled without further study of normative and analytic ethics. Perhaps the reader will be able to decide these questions for himself as he pursues his own ethical inquiry.

Suggested Reading

A good collection of essays on ethical relativism, both pro and con:

Ladd, John, ed., *Ethical Relativism*. Belmont, California: Wadsworth Publishing Co., Inc., 1973.*

A classic defense of normative ethical relativism:

Westermarck, Edward, *Ethical Relativity*. New York: Humanities Press, Inc., 1960; and Paterson, N. J.: Littlefield, Adams and Co., 1960.*

*Available in paperback

A systematic criticism of conceptual and methodological relativism in the philosophy of religion and the philosophy of science, as well as in ethics:

Trigg, Roger, *Reason and Commitment.* Cambridge: Cambridge University Press, 1973.*

A general study of the relation between the social sciences and ethics, centering on the concept of ethical relativity:

Edel, Abraham, *Ethical Judgment: The Use of Science in Ethics.* Glencoe, Ill.: The Free Press, 1955.*

A refutation of ethical relativism derived from a psychological theory showing how the development of any person's moral reasoning follows a logical pattern that is common to all cultures:

Kohlberg, Lawrence, "From Is to Ought: How to Commit the Naturalistic Fallacy and Get Away with It in the Study of Moral Development," in T. Mischel, ed., *Cognitive Development and Epistemology.* New York: Academic Press, 1971.

An interesting interpretation of the history of ethics on the basis of a form of conceptual and methodological relativism:

MacIntyre, Alasdair, *A Short History of Ethics.* New York: The Macmillan Company, 1966.*

Other recent studies of ethical relativism:

Baier, Kurt, *The Moral Point of View: A Rational Basis of Ethics.* Chapters 5-12. Ithaca, N. Y.: Cornell University Press, 1958. For a shorter presentation of the argument, see the *Abridged Edition,* Chapters 4-7. New York: Random House, Inc., 1965.*

Brandt, Richard B., *Ethical Theory: The Problems of Normative and Critical Ethics,* Chapter 11. Englewood Cliffs, N. J.: Prentice-Hall, Inc., 1959.

Norman, Richard, *Reasons for Actions: A Critique of Utilitarian Rationality,* Chapters 3-6. Oxford: Basil Blackwell, 1971.

Phillips, D. Z. and H. O. Mounce, *Moral Practices.* London: Routledge and Kegan Paul, 1969.

Taylor, Richard, *Good and Evil: A New Direction,* Chapters 1-3, 9-13. New York: The Macmillan Company, 1970.*

Wellman, Carl, "The Ethical Implications of Cultural Relativity," *Journal of Philosophy,* LX, No. 7 (1963), pp. 169-184. Reprinted in the Bobbs-Merrill Reprint Series in Philosophy. Indianapolis: The Bobbs-Merrill Co., Inc.*

*Available in paperback

III

Psychological Egoism and Ethical Egoism

Among the normative ethical systems that have been advanced by philosophers as valid for all mankind (ethical universalism), there is one which, if true, would make morality entirely a matter of *self-interest*. According to this normative ethical system, a person's only duty is to promote his own good as much as possible. It would follow that being moral (or living a morally upright life) never requires a sacrifice of one's own long-range interests. This ethical system, which is known as "ethical egoism," should not be confused with the theory, known as "psychological egoism," that everyone always and necessarily acts selfishly. As far as some ethical egoists are concerned, it is perfectly *possible* for a person to act unselfishly or altruistically. But, they hold, it is never a person's *duty* to act so.

There are other ethical egoists, however, who are also psychological egoists. They claim that no one *can* behave unselfishly. They believe that ethical egoism is the only normative system of morality consistent with human motivation. Since everyone is always and necessarily motivated by self-interest, they argue, no other system besides ethical egoism provides a moral norm that human beings are psychologically able to follow. The theory of motivation being asserted by these ethical egoists—that every human action is motivated by some form of self-interest—is psychological egoism. In order not to confuse it with ethical egoism, it is necessary to look more closely at the differences between them.

THE DISTINCTION BETWEEN PSYCHOLOGICAL EGOISM
AND ETHICAL EGOISM

Psychological egoism is a factual theory about human motivation and behavior; it offers an explanation of why people act the way they do. Ethical egoism, on the other hand, is a normative theory; it sets forth a standard or

31

principle for determining how people *ought* to act. The psychological egoist tells us what ends everyone does in fact seek; the ethical egoist tells us what ends everyone ought to seek.

The basic idea of psychological egoism may be stated in various ways, of which the following are typical:

(1) Every person always acts so as to promote his own self-interest.
(2) The sole end of every act is the agent's own good.
(3) All acts are really selfish, even if some of them appear to be unselfish.
(4) Everyone always does what he most wants to do, or what he least dislikes doing.
(5) Concern for one's own welfare always outweighs, in motivational strength, concern for anyone else's welfare.

Each of these statements says something slightly different from the others, but certain features are common to them all. First, they are factual claims about human beings; they make no value judgments. Second, they are universal claims about all human beings. And third, they are universal claims about all the actions (or all the motives) of every human being. Consequently, to falsify them it is sufficient to show that at least one exception to what they state about human behavior has in fact occurred. Cases that have been cited as exceptions and attempted refutations of them by psychological egoists will be considered later.

Ethical egoism is a normative theory. Its basic tenet is that self-interest is the sole valid standard of right conduct. This standard may be explained as follows. To know in any given case which of the alternatives open to a person is the one he morally ought to do, we proceed thus. We calculate, first, the probable consequences that would result if the person were to follow one alternative; next, the probable consequences that would result if he were to choose a second alternative; and so on for every alternative open to him. We then ask ourselves, Which of the acts possible will result in furthering the self-interest of the person to a greater extent than any of the others? In other words, which of the alternatives will bring about more things that the person would like and fewer that he would dislike over his life span as a whole than any other alternative? When we have answered this question, we know what the person ought to do. For we know which act is the best alternative, as judged by the standard of his self-interest.

It should be noted at this point, however, that there are three types of ethical egoism and that the foregoing account describes only one of them. The three may be designated "universal ethical egoism," "individual ethical egoism," and "personal ethical egoism." Here is what differentiates them. Does the ethical egoist say, *"Every* person ought to do what will most further *his own* self-interest"; or does he say, *"Every* person ought to do what will most further *my* self-interest"; or does he say only, *"I* ought to do what will most further *my* self-interest"? In the first case we have universal egoism: the standard of right action is the agent's or doer's self-interest, no matter who the agent is. This is the version of ethical egoism given in the preceding paragraph. According to the individual ethical egoist, on the other hand, the standard of right action is not the agent's self-interest, but that of the ethical egoist himself. Thus if the population of the world consisted of four people, A, B, C, and D, universal ethical egoism would hold that A ought to further A's self-interest, B ought to further B's, and C and D each ought to further his own. From the point of view of individual ethical egoism, however, we would have to know which of the four people was the individual ethical egoist before we could know what any of them ought to do. Suppose he were A. Then the theory states that A ought to further A's self-interest, B ought to further A's self-interest, and so should C and D. Finally, the theory of personal ethical egoism is simply the view that the egoist alone ought to further his self-interest. It does not say anything about what other people ought to do. Thus if the personal egoist were A, then according to his theory A ought to further A's self-interest, but his theory would not tell B, C, and D what they ought or ought not to do.

This chapter will be concerned mainly with universal ethical egoism, since it is this form of the theory that has seriously been advocated by both ancient and modern philosophers. Its classic statement is found in the ethical system of Epicurus (a Greek philosopher of the fourth century B.C.), according to whom the sole valid standard of right action is the avoidance of painful or unpleasant experiences to the agent. Its most important proponent in modern philosophy is Thomas Hobbes (1588-1679), whose ethical views are set forth in his famous work, *Leviathan* (1651). Hobbes's version of ethical egoism will be discussed later in this chapter. The other two forms of ethical egoism, individual and personal, will be briefly dealt with toward the end of the chapter.

Let us now examine the relation between universal ethical egoism and psychological egoism. As was pointed out at the beginning of this chapter, some ethical egoists hold the view that ethical egoism is the only normative system of morality compatible with human motivation because all people are motivated by self-interest in everything they do. These ethical egoists are claiming, in effect, that since psychological egoism is true, we have no choice but to accept ethical egoism. Their argument may be set forth in the following way.

Suppose it is indeed true that, in all their actions, people always seek to promote their self-interest and can do nothing else. It follows that it would be foolish or illogical to say they *ought* to do something else. According to a traditional maxim of ethics, "ought" implies "can." To say that someone ought to do a certain act implies that he is able to, for it he were unable to, there would be no point in telling him that he ought to do it. Now psychological egoism holds that it is impossible for anyone to do a genuinely altruistic or unselfish act. There is always the motive of self-interest behind any act that appears to arise from the desire to further the happiness of another. Therefore, we are never justified in telling a person that he ought to forget his own happiness and act out of concern for the happiness of others, since he never will and never can do such a thing. Ethical egoism, then, the argument concludes, is the only normative ethical system consistent with human motivation.

There are two ways in which this argument might be attacked. One way is to challenge the truth of psychological egoism. (The next section of this chapter will show how such a challenge might be presented.) The other way is to question the alleged relation between ethical egoism and psychological egoism. That there at first appears to be a serious difficulty about this relation can be seen if the following facts are considered. The purpose of a normative ethical system is to have people perform, or at least try to perform, those actions the system judges to be right, and to have people refrain from those actions deemed wrong. To accomplish this, the system must tell people what it is they ought or ought not to do. Now there seems something strange in telling a person that he ought to do what he cannot help doing. If someone has no choice but to do a certain act, it is unavoidable. If it is unavoidable, why prescribe to him that he ought to do it? To say that he ought to do an act is to try to get him to do it *rather than something else,* or at least it is to hope that he will do it *instead of some alternative act.* But when we know he is going to behave that way anyway and that he cannot choose to refrain from doing it, our "ought" statement is pointless. This seems to be what is happening if we accept both psychological egoism and ethical egoism. Psychological egoism tells us that everyone always acts so as to further his self-interest — there is no choice in the matter. A person simply cannot do otherwise; he *must* act from self-interest. Yet the ethical egoist prescribes that we *ought* to further our self-interest. Why say we ought to, when we already must? Why tell us that we ought to do something when we cannot avoid doing it? A further paradox now arises. If we cannot avoid doing what we ought to do, *then we are always doing what we ought.* So all of us, at every moment, are acting in a morally perfect way. No one ever does, or can ever do, what is wrong. An ethical theory with such a consequence is simply absurd.

To this objection the ethical egoist can make the following reply. People may be intelligent or unintelligent in the pursuit of their self-interest. All persons seek their own good, but do not always use the most effective means to realize it. This is partly the result of their lack of knowledge about what the consequences of their acts will be. Thus, contrary to the conclusion drawn above, people *can* do wrong acts. These are acts that frustrate their long-range interests, or that do not promote their ends as much as some alternative conduct would have done if they had chosen it. But when people do wrong acts, they believe (mistakenly) that these ways of behaving will further their interest more than any alternative ways. Notice that this view requires a change in our statement of psychological egoism. Instead of saying, "Everyone always does what will most further his self-interest," we must now say, "Everyone always does what he *thinks* will most further his self-interest." This allows for the possibility that what a person thinks will most further his self-interest may not in fact further it as much as some other conduct, or will not further it at all.

A second reply to the above objection concerning the relation between psychological and ethical egoism is this. People sometimes let themselves be swayed by immediate pleasures, or by the attractiveness of short-range goals, and so do acts which in the long run work against their own welfare and happiness. To see a doctor and undergo treatment for a chronic ailment is unpleasant and costly. We might want to avoid the inconvenience, discomfort, and expenses involved. Yet if we do not get medical treatment, our condition might become worse and eventually prove fatal. Thus our long-range self-interest sometimes requires us to face unpleasant facts, go through unpleasant experiences, and sacrifice some of our goals. (We might have been saving the thousand dollars which the treatment finally cost us for a vacation trip to Europe.) So there is an important function served by the ethical egoist's prescription. In telling us that we ought to promote our self-interest, he is advising us to withstand the temptation to enjoy immediate pleasures or to avoid immediate pains, if such discipline is necessary to achieve our more distant. goals. And he is saying that, whenever we are faced with a choice between accomplishing a short-range purpose (such as going on a vacation trip) which involves the endangering of our long-range welfare or happiness, and on the other hand giving up the short-range goal in order to have a better chance to be happy in the long run, we ought to make the second choice. Thus the whole point of ethical egoism becomes clear. It is to advocate a certain ideal of moral character, which could be called "enlightened prudence." To become the kind of person we ought to be requires self-discipline and the development of inner strength of character. Many of us might fail to reach this ideal, or we might reject it as a false ideal. In either case ethical egoism does hold up a goal that we can choose to seek or not to seek. Its "ought" does imply a "can." Furthermore, we should notice that the egoist claims that this goal is the one true ideal of the moral life of man. Accordingly, ethical egoism is a form of normative ethical universalism, since it proposes a moral norm to be valid for all mankind.

These, then, are arguments an ethical egoist might give to defend his theory against the criticism that psychological egoism would render ethical egoism nonsensical. Let us now turn to a consideration of psychological egoism itself. What, precisely, does it mean? Is it true or is it false? How can it be shown to be true or false?

ARGUMENTS FOR AND AGAINST PSYCHOLOGICAL EGOISM

The arguments for psychological egoism are intended to point out certain facts of human life, these facts being claimed as evidence in support of the theory. The theory itself is taken to be an empirical generalization about the motives behind all human conduct. The first set of facts appealed to are simply the facts that show how selfish most people are most of the time. The second set are facts about the deceptive appearance of allegedly unselfish acts. Here the psychological egoist claims that there are always self-interested motives behind every altruistic-seeming act. Thus he tries to show that a person who gives a great deal of time, effort, and money to further a social welfare project, or who performs difficult and unpleasant tasks to alleviate human misery, or who risks his life to correct an injustice, or who even voluntarily gives up his life to prevent a disaster, is not really an unselfish person. A third set of facts given in support of psychological egoism are facts about unconscious motivation. Let us briefly look at each set of facts.

Concerning the first point — how widespread selfishness is in human life — we should notice that no *normative* ethical theory denies this. The purpose of normative ethics is to state how men ought to live, and all moral philosophers, no matter what their ethical system, have been quite aware that men do not live as they ought to. So even if it is true that most men are selfish most of the time, the facts which are cited to substantiate this claim are completely neutral between ethical egoism and those ethical theories that set up a norm other than self-interest as the supreme standard of morality. It is only if no one ever does or ever can act unselfishly that nonegoistic theories are confronted with a serious difficulty. For in that case it would be pointless to prescribe that men *ought* to be unselfish.

But is it true that *all* men are *always* selfish, that *all* the acts of *every* person are motivated by self-interest, as psychological egoism maintains? Such an absolutely universal generalization can be shown to be true only by showing that there never has been and never could be a single action with a disinterested or altruistic motive. All that is necessary to falsify this thesis once and for all is to point out one act not done to promote the agent's self-interest. This brings us to the second set of facts, since nonegoists usually cite what appear to be unselfish acts to refute the egoist's position. Here we must look carefully at what the egoist says about such cases.

First it is necessary to distinguish selfish and unselfish acts from selfish and unselfish motives. Let us define selfish and unselfish acts in terms of their expected consequences. When a person is about to perform an act, he believes that certain consequences will result from it. We shall call these expected consequences. Other consequences may occur which, at the time of the act, were not anticipated by the person. Considering only their expected consequences, all acts fall into one or another of the following rough categories:

(1) They are expected to promote the interests of others and to involve some frustration of the agent's own interests.
(2) They are expected to promote the interests of the agent and to involve some frustration of the interests of others.
(3) They are expected to promote the interests of both the agent and others and are not expected to involve the frustration of anyone's interests.
(4) They are expected to frustrate the interests of both the agent and others and are not expected to promote anyone's interests.

We may then label these various sorts of acts: (1) unselfish; (2) selfish; (3) felicitous; and (4) irrational. Most psychological egoists admit that in fact each of these types of acts does occur, but go on to say that they never meant to deny that "unselfish" acts, defined as acts of type (1), take place. People can and do choose to perform deeds which they expect will bring happiness to others and involve some unpleasantness, discomfort, or inconvenience to themselves. But, they hasten to add, all such acts are *motivated* by self-interest and hence ought not to be regarded as genuinely unselfish. Now in claiming this, the egoist wants to contrast self-interest with other kinds of motives — motives which, in his view, have been mistakenly believed sometimes to be the actual motives behind an act. So we must understand what it means to talk about these other kinds of motives (which the egoist says never motivate human conduct) if we are to understand what the egoist is saying about all actual human motives.

Let us then divide possible motives of human acts into the following categories, leaving open the queston whether instances of each possibility actually occur:

(a) The desire to promote the interests of the agent, combined with the willingness to frustrate others' interests only if this is necessary to promoting the agent's interests. (Self-interest without malice.)

(b) The desire to frustrate the interests of others as an end in itself. (Pure malice.)

(c) The desire to promote the interests of others as a means to promoting the agent's interests. (Self-interested use of others.)

(d) The desire to promote the interests of others as an end in itself. (Pure benevolence or altruism.)

(e) Performing an act because one believes it is one's duty, or acting from a sense of obligation, or doing something as a matter of principle. (Disinterestedness.)

The position of psychological egoism now under consideration may be formulated in two statements: First, all acts of type (1) arise from motives of types (a) and (c). Second, no human acts ever, in fact, originate in motives of types (d) and (e). Suppose, then, that a psychological egoist is confronted with an act of type (1) and the person who does the act claims to be motivated by a desire of type (d) or (e). What will the egoist say about this? He will say that the person is either deceiving himself, deceiving others, or both. In the first case his self-deception is explained as a psychological rationalization. The person cannot admit to himself that his motive is one of self-interest, because this would weaken his ego-image and he cannot tolerate this. In the second case, the person is deliberately lying about something he is well aware of — namely, the results he consciously desires to achieve by the act. In neither case can we say that his conduct is genuinely unselfish or disinterested, since his self-interest lies not only behind the act itself, but also behind his rationalization (a defense mechanism of his ego) and behind his deceiving others.

Consider the following example. A wealthy man who loves art decides to set up a nonprofit foundation to support medical research instead of using the money to buy works of art for his own enjoyment. When asked why he is doing this, he says that he thinks he should do what he can to alleviate the suffering of others. Let us suppose that he does not expect to benefit personally from the foundation's work, and that this expectation is in fact borne out. Here, then, is an instance of a type (1) action — the agent expects to promote the interests of others and to frustrate at least one of his interests (namely, his love of art). It would also appear to be an action having a type (d) or type (e) motive, since the agent's avowed reason for his decision can be considered to be either a benevolent concern for people's well-being or a sense of duty to help others in need. The egoist argues that in such a case the real motive behind the act is not recognized by the man himself. His conduct is indeed of type (1), but his motive is neither (d) nor (e). The man deceives himself into thinking that he acts out of concern for others or from a sense of duty. What is really important to him, the egoist claims, is the fact that the foundation he is establishing is to be named after him. His real motive is a desire for status or social prestige, and his selecting medical research as the foundation's purpose is itself the choice of a prestigious means to self-glorification. As an alternative explanation, the egoist might argue that the man is quite aware of his true motive and is simply concealing it from others. In that case his saying that he thinks he should do what he can to alleviate the suffering of others is an intentional deception, and is motivated by the same desire that leads him to set up the foundation in the first place. He knows he could not achieve status in the eyes of others if it were disclosed to them that he acted from this very desire for prestige!

By means of arguments like these the egoist explains away all apparent instances of self-sacrifice. In every case a self-regarding desire is attributed to the agent as his real motive, whether he is aware of it or not. A variety of such self-regarding desires figure in egoistic explanations. Perhaps the most frequently cited are the following:

(i) The agent believes in God and the act is done either out of fear of God's punishment or to obtain the rewards of Heaven.

(ii) The action is taken to avoid the disapproval of others or to achieve and maintain a good reputation among others (the case of the wealthy man discussed above).

(iii) If the act occurs without the knowledge of others (as in the case of giving a large sum *anonymously* to a charitable foundation), the agent acts from a sense of pride understood as ego-inflation. He wants to enjoy the feeling of self-congratulation at having done a good deed.

(iv) From past experience the agent knows that if he does *not* do the act he will feel ashamed of himself and will suffer the pangs of a guilty conscience. His motive is to avoid these unpleasant feelings.

(v) If none of the above motives is at work, the agent is satisfying unconscious desires and wishes. He is really either "acting out" a wish fulfillment, trying to escape from anxieties, protecting his ego from threats, or punishing himself in a masochistic act, and is unaware that he is doing any of these things.

Before we turn to the first four accounts of the self-interested motives behind seemingly unselfish action, a special point must be made with regard to the fifth. This account, which explains action in terms of unconscious motives, can be objected to as simply irrelevant to any ethical system — egoistic or nonegoistic. For ethics deals only with men's voluntary conduct and their conscious aims and purposes. Whatever might be happening in their "unconscious" when they experience conscious desires and make deliberate choices is a matter for the psychologist to study and for the psychotherapist to treat. The whole point of psychiatric treatment is to help a person become sufficiently aware of his real emotions and his inner conflicts to be able to make free choices — choices based on his own values and on his own thinking. The task of ethics, on the other hand, is to enlighten and guide the deliberations of the free agent as he makes his decisions in practical life. It can perform this task only on the level of conscious thought. If such thought has no influence over a person's motivation and conduct, then the person lacks the capacities of a moral agent and no ethical system, not even ethical egoism, can guide his choices. From the point of view of ethics, such a person is a "patient" who needs treatment, not an "agent" who has reasons for acting and can act for those reasons.

As far as psychological egoism is concerned, unconscious motivation no more proves that all action is selfish or self-interested than that it is all unselfish or altruistic. The words "selfish," "self-interested," "unselfish," and "altrusitic," in their ordinary meanings, are applied only to acts that are freely chosen and to motives that people are aware of. The real point of psychological egoism (namely, that people cannot act unselfishly) would be missed if all it turned out to mean was that human beings are motivated by desires and wishes of which they are not conscious, and that they act to fulfill certain psychological needs of their personalities.

Let us turn, then, to the other four kinds of explanation offered by the egoist for apparently unselfish action. Whatever conscious motive or reason is given for such an act, the egoist will insist that there is always present some element of desiring to further his own self-interest on the part of the agent, and that it is this desire that motivates him. The reader must decide for himself how objective and fair the egoist is in making this claim. In particular, he should try to think of acts which we would ordinarily suppose arise from simple kindness or affection toward others (for example, making a child happy on his birthday), or acts that we would normally believe were done because the person felt obligated to do them (for example, telling the truth when admitting responsibility for a past act), and then ask himself whether the egoist's view of the motivation behind such conduct is an unbiased, undistorted, and true description of the facts.

There is one argument given by the psychological egoist, however, which rests on a semantic confusion and not on factual claims about human motivation. Suppose an egoist is presented with a case in which a person is honest with himself and others and, as far as he is consciously aware of his own feelings and desires, he acts so as to help another person in need simply out of concern for that person at that time. He expects no praise or reward for his action, and gets none. He does not think about his action with any feelings of pride afterwards, since he forgets about it as soon as it is done. Nor would he feel guilty if he had not done it, since he did not believe he was obligated to do it. Finally, he did not do it with the conscious intention to further his own short-range or long-range interests, since he acted quite spontaneously and made no calculation of possible benefits to himself that might result from his doing the act. The egoist might then say the following about such a case: "Granted that in doing this act the person did not have what most people would call a selfish motive, or even a motive of self-interest. Still the act was a voluntary one, and all voluntary acts have some motive behind them. By doing the act the person was satisfying this motive. Hence he did gain satisfaction from doing the act. He would not have done it if no satisfaction of any of his motives would result from his doing it. Consequently the act served his self-interest after all, since it was done to satisfy whatever motive he did have in doing it."

Here the egoist has made a basic change in his position. For he is now claiming that the satisfaction of *any* motive is to be taken as self-interest, whereas what he had been saying before was that all action is motivated by a certain *kind* of motive, namely, the kind we would all classify under the general category of selfishness or self-interest. In ordinary life, we make a distinction between selfish and unselfish motives. By "unselfish motives" we mean motives of types (d) and (e) listed above. If the egoist now grants that *some* human acts, however few and far between, are motivated by motives of types (d) and (e), and yet are still to be considered as done from self-interest since these motives are being satisfied by the person when he does the act, then the egoist has changed completely the meaning of "self-interest." Indeed, his egoism is ethically harmless. For nonegoistic ethics demands that people do unselfish acts unselfishly (either out of genuine love for others or out of a sense of duty) and the egoist is now admitting that people sometimes do such acts from such motives. The psychological egoist who uses this argument, in other words, can have nothing to say against an altruist who prescribes that men ought to be unselfish in the ordinary meaning of "unselfish." It is merely an abuse of language on the part of the egoist to call all acts "selfish" or to say that they are all done from "self-interest" if his reason for using these terms is that all acts are motivated. If the egoist insists on using "selfish" and "self-interest" in this uncommon way, the altruist can simply say to him, "Call these acts what you please. What counts is that there are two different kinds of acts, one we ought to do and the other we ought to refrain from doing. That acts of the first kind are motivated takes nothing away from their moral goodness, since all acts, good and bad alike, are motivated. To call them 'selfish' simply because they are motivated is not to deny the real difference between what we ordinarily call selfish acts or motives and unselfish ones. The first are bad and the second are good. If both are to be classed as instances of self-interest, then self-interest is morally neutral. Only a certain kind of 'self-interest' would then be bad. It would be the kind which in ordinary life we call 'self-interest.' "

It is worthwhile to notice at this point that in ordinary life the terms "selfish" and "self-interest" as applied to motives do not have the same meaning. We normally say that a person acts from selfishness under such conditions as the following: He seeks to gain an advantage for himself at another's expense by deceiving or cheating the other person in some way. Or, he aims at acquiring more than his own rightful share of something which both he and others want, thereby depriving others of what is due them. Or, he relentlessly pursues his personal goals, indifferent to the fact (which he acknowledges) that others will be harmed or injured or otherwise made to suffer by his actions. In contrast to this, acting from self-interest does not *necessarily* involve benefiting at another's expense, being unfair, or causing harm. Thus a sick person who goes to a doctor is acting from self-interest, but if his doing so does not cause harm to another, he is not acting selfishly. Psychological egoism does not always distinguish between these two types of motivation. And it is important in our own ethical thinking to realize that, while it may always be wrong to act selfishly, it may be morally neutral, and sometimes even right, to act from self-interest. For example, we might consider it morally right for a person to develop his aesthetic or intellectual talents (assuming he will not use them for morally evil purposes) even if his motive in developing them is to increase only his own overall happiness in life.

Another argument in support of psychological egoism may now be examined. This states that psychological egoism is true because it follows from the principle of psychological *hedonism*. Psychological hedonism claims that the sole motive behind every action is the desire for pleasure, always understood as the pleasure of the person who does the action, not of someone else. The argument for this principle runs as follows. How can anyone desire anything but his own pleasure, since every action that is motivated is done to satisfy the desire which motivates it? But to satisfy a desire is to bring about a pleasure, namely, the pleasure felt when the desire is satisfied. Thus every action resulting in the satisfaction of a desire will bring pleasure to the person who does the action. For satisfying a desire is nothing but the obtaining of a pleasure, just as displeasure is felt whenever a desire is frustrated. Now since every act is aimed at the bringing about of a pleasure for the agent, every act is motivated by self-interest. Therefore, psychological egoism is true.

This argument has been criticized on the following ground. Suppose a man is motivated by the desire to have and to exercise power over others. That is, his desire for power is the reason why he acts in certain ways. And let us further suppose that his having and exercising power over others gives him great pleasure. Given these assumptions, it follows that the man's desire for power cannot itself be a desire for the pleasure he experiences in having and exercising that power. For the man's experiencing pleasure *presupposes* his desire for power. Unless he wanted power, he would not be gratified upon obtaining it. But this means that what he desires is the power, not the pleasure he gets from having and exercising it. In other words, we must be careful to distinguish the *object* of a desire (the thing aimed at) from the *effects* of satisfying the desire. The fact that a person's satisfying his desire for something has the effect of giving him a pleasant experience does not mean that the something he desires is the pleasure experienced. Indeed, the pleasure itself *cannot* be what he desires (that is, cannot be the object of his desire), since it is experienced by him only as a result of his wanting something else.

Now take the case of a person who does an action with the *conscious aim* of helping someone who is in trouble. If the person who performs such an act gets pleasure as a result of achieving his aim, are we to say that he is therefore really behaving from self-interest, since he obtains the pleasure of satisfying a desire (namely, fulfilling his aim) by doing the action? The answer is no, because the motive of an action is determined by the goal being sought (the person's "project" or "end in view," the realization of which is his reason for acting), not by the effects of achieving that goal. In fact, a person who gets pleasure or satisfaction as a result of his achieving the goal of helping someone in trouble is *by definition* an unselfish person. The pleasure he gets is the *sign* that what he desired was to assist the other person, since he would feel frustrated and unhappy if he were unable by his action to fulfill his goal. In other words, one who acts to alleviate the suffering of another and *experiences satisfaction just because and insofar as he successfully accomplishes that purpose* is precisely the person who would be described as having acted unselfishly!

This raises a final question for our reflection. It concerns what exactly it is that psychological egoism is asserting. Is not the principle of psychological egoism actually an empty tautology (a redundancy) which tells us nothing about human conduct and motivation? One asks this when one hears the following kind of argument, often propounded by the egoist. In support of his claim that everyone always does what he most wants to do—see statement (4), page 32—the egoist argues thus: Suppose a person were confronted with two alternative acts, A and B. Suppose, further, that act A would ordinarily be called an unselfish act and B, selfish. Now if the person chooses to do A rather than B, this shows:

(a) That his motives for doing A are stronger than his motives for doing B;
(b) That he prefers doing A to doing B;
(c) That he would not like doing B as much as A;
(d) That he really wants to do A.

Therefore, the egoist concludes, everyone always does what he really wants to do. And since the person really wants to do the so-called "unselfish" act A, he is not truly unselfish in doing it. He is doing what he, in the given situation, prefers, likes, or really wants to do.

Two replies can be made to this argument. The first resembles the reply to an argument considered earlier. It is that the egoist is choosing to use the phrase "doing what one really wants to do" in a way entirely different from its ordinary meaning. For it can be seen from the egoist's argument that he will describe *every* act in this way, since the evidence that the act is the person's real preference is simply the fact that he chooses to do it. Thus there can be no distinction between two kinds of acts, those that a person really wants to do and those he believes he must or ought to do, but does not really want to do. In ordinary life, however, when we recognize our duties toward others and feel obligated to do something we do not enjoy doing (something we would not choose to do if we were not under such obligation), we say of the act that "we do not really want to do it." Usually such acts require us to go to some trouble or to spend time, effort, and money on something when we would clearly prefer not to be so inconvenienced and when we would very much prefer to spend the time, effort, and money on something we find enjoyable to do. Our moral obligations are sometimes burdensome (though not always so) and these are precisely the situations in which we say that we "must" or "have to" do something even though we would really like to do something else. It is with regard to such situations as these that we make the distinction between two kinds of acts, those we really want to do and those we are obliged to do, whether we want to or not. The psychological egoist, on the other hand, makes the phrase "doing what we really want to do" apply to every act. He thereby takes away its meaning, since the phrase is not being used to contrast one kind of act with another.

The second reply goes deeper into the confusions involved in the way the egoist uses language. We saw in the argument given above that when the egoist claims that a person always does what he really wants to do, the only evidence in support of this claim is the fact that the person chooses to do the act. In order to know what someone really wants to do, all we have to do is to wait until he chooses one act rather than another in a situation of choice. Then the fact that he chooses one of the alternatives is sufficient to show us that this is what he really wants to do. Now it follows from such an argument that to say "Person P really wants to do act A" is equivalent to saying "Person P chooses to do act A in a situation of choice." But then the egoist's important sounding statement "Everyone always does what he really wants to do" becomes nothing but the statement "Everyone always chooses to do what he chooses to do," which is a tautology. Such a statement asserts nothing; it gives us no information about human conduct. Yet the egoist intends to tell us something he considers important about human conduct, something empirically true about every action. Therefore, if he still wishes to make a factual claim, he cannot use the argument examined above.

Whether psychological egoism, despite the foregoing objections, can still be maintained as a correct theory of human motivation is left for the reader's further thought and study. It is now time to give some consideration to ethical egoism.

ETHICAL EGOISM

At the beginning of this chapter, the distinction between psychological egoism and ethical egoism was made as follows. Psychological egoism is intended to be a factual, explanatory account of human motivation, stating a universal empirical truth about man's nature. Ethical egoism, on the other hand, is intended as a normative theory which sets up an ultimate standard or principle for determining right and wrong conduct. Psychological egoism means to tell us why people act the way they do, while ethical egoism attempts to tell us how people ought to act. The question now is, What reasons are there for accepting, or rejecting, the principle of ethical egoism as a guide to conduct?

One proposed argument for accepting the principle has already been examined. This states (1) that psychological egoism is true, and (2) that ethical egoism provides the only normative principle which it is psychologically possible for people to comply with. Since the purpose of accepting a normative principle is to guide people's conduct, once psychological egoism is accepted, ethical egoism must be accepted, too. For if psychological egoism is true, each person's actions can only be motivated by what he believes will promote his self-interest. What actually *will* promote his self-interest must then become the sole basis for judging conduct. No other principle could function as a norm for human conduct because every individual, being egoistically motivated, would be unable to use a nonegoistic principle in deciding how to act.

Some reasons for questioning the truth of psychological egoism have been brought out in the preceding section of this chapter, and its final acceptance or rejection is left open. Whatever one's views on psychological egoism might be, however, the normative principle of ethical egoism must still be considered on its own merits. For some ethical egoists do not believe that their theory presupposes the acceptance of psychological egoism. Furthermore, they do not appeal to psychological egoism in support of their theory since they think psychological egoism actually gives a false account of human motivation. These ethical egoists hold that a person *can* be altruistically motivated to perform actions which he himself correctly believes to be contrary to his own self-interest. Nevertheless, these ethical egoists continue, no action is *right* unless it does further the individual's well-being. So let us now inquire into the grounds for accepting—or rejecting—ethical egoism independently of any stand we might take regarding the truth or falsity of psychological egoism.

When the ethical egoist is asked why everyone ought to act so as to promote his own self-interest, there are two sorts of reply he might make. First, he can simply assert that this is an ultimate principle of normative ethics. Or secondly, he might argue that this principle, if consistently followed by everyone, would have better results than some other guiding norm. Putting aside the first reply for the moment, let us look at the second.

The claim that everyone's following one principle would have *better* results than everyone's following another principle presupposes a standard of goodness or value by which some results are judged superior to others. If this standard were anything but the fulfillment of everyone's self-interest to the greatest possible extent, it would seem that the position is not (universal) ethical egoism. Yet the fulfillment of everyone's self-interest in this argument constitutes an *end* to which the practice of each person following the rule "Do what will most promote my own interests" is taken as a *means*. Now suppose there were another, more effective means for bringing about this same end. For example, suppose that everyone's following the rule "Do what will most promote the interests of all people affected by my action" would actually tend to result in the fulfillment of everyone's self-interest to a greater extent than would result form everyone's complying with "Do what will most promote my own interests." In that case, the egoist would have to admit that it is our duty to follow the first rule. But that rule, as we shall see in the next chapter, is a principle of utilitarianism, not of egoism. To justify his own theory, the egoist would have to show that the universal following of the rule of self-interest will in fact more effectively promote everyone's self-interest than will the universal practice of utilitarianism. Whether this can indeed be shown is left to the reader's judgment, after consideration of utilitarianism in the next chapter.

However, most ethical egoists have supported their theory in the first way mentioned above. They have held each person's promotion of his own self-interest to be the supreme norm or ultimate principle of ethics, not merely a means to some further end. A famous example of this position is to be found in the philosophy of Thomas Hobbes. In his work, *Leviathan* (1651) Hobbes begins by distinguishing between two conditions of human life, which he calls "the state of nature" and "the Commonwealth." The state of nature is the human condition (as we may imagine it to be, even if it never occurred in actual history or in prehistorical times) where there is no legal or political system governing the relations among men. People in the state of nature do not recognize anyone as having authority over them. Their conduct is not regulated by laws, nor are they organized into a civil community with an established government to make and enforce laws and set policies binding on everyone. In such a social condition, it is impossible to break the law since there is none to break. We might then inquire, What about moral laws? Even if a group of people have no legal system or form of government, they might still have a set of moral rules which they acknowledge as binding upon them and which they back up by sanctions. But Hobbes denies this. The state of nature, in his view, is neither a legal nor a moral community. It is impossible in the state of nature to do anything morally wrong, since a "wrong" act means one that violates a moral rule, and no such precepts are binding upon men in that state.

Nevertheless, in the state of nature there is a standard of value. Meaning can be given to the words "good" and "bad," and the meaning Hobbes gives to them may be considered a form of ethical (or valuational) egoism. *"Good* and *evil,"* Hobbes says, "are names that signify our appetites and aversions." That is, good is what we like or desire; evil is what we dislike or wish to avoid. "In the condition of mere nature," he asserts, "private appetite is the measure of good and evil." Thus a person's only directive for right conduct is what will bring about the things *he* wants and prevent those he does not want. Furthermore, a person can do no wrong or injustice to others in the pursuit of his self-interest, because in the state of nature, Hobbes says, "the notions of right and wrong, justice and injustice, have there no place." Therefore Hobbes's position can be considered a form of ethical egoism.

It is true that Hobbes speaks of "laws of nature" as guiding men's conduct in the state of nature. One such law, for example, is *"to seek peace, and follow it."* Another is *"by all means we can, to defend ourselves."* But these laws of nature, as Hobbes views them, are not moral rules. They are simply maxims of prudence and carry with them no moral obligations toward others. That is, they are rules which an intelligent man will see he ought to follow if he is to pursue his self-interest successfully, but the interests of others can make no claim on him. The only reason he has to consider the welfare of others is to avoid their hostility, since this might lead them to try to frustrate his own interests. Thus the clever man in the state of nature will see that it is to his benefit to protect himself from others. This might require that he join with someone else, if necessary, for mutual protection from the hostile action of a third person. But joining with others and cooperating with them is never an end in itself; nor is there a moral duty on one person's part to protect or further the interests of others.

Once a civil society is formed, however, a new condition of human life arises, one in which persons are members of a Commonwealth. It is only in this condition of life, according to Hobbes, that the concept of obligation is applicable. But even here the obligation is not other-regarding or altruistic (that is, an obligation grounded on the claims which the interests of others make upon us). It is and remains a self-regarding obligation. The obligation, binding upon everyone in the Commonwealth, is simply to obey the law set up by the Sovereign, who is given the authority to punish violators. The purpose of the law is to maintain the security of each person by protecting him from the harm others might do him. Hence the obligation to obey the law is grounded on self-interest and is binding only so long as the Sovereign makes sure that others will obey. For unless the ruler does so, one individual's obedience will not be a means for the protection of his own interests. Thus each person has good reason to obey the law only when others do likewise. Furthermore, each person is motivated to comply with the law by fear of punishment and not by a sense of duty toward others nor by a desire to further the common good. These considerations make clear that Hobbes's view of man in civil society is essentially as egoistic as his view of man in the state of nature. Indeed, an element of psychological egoism is introduced in this account of the basis of moral obligation. At one point Hobbes says, "Of the voluntary acts of every man, the object is some *good to himself*," — a clear statement of the principle of psychological egoism. Hobbes makes this statement in explaining why a person would voluntarily renounce the condition of having no obligation to obey law and accept such an obligation (thereby creating the necessary conditions for the social contract or covenant and, with it, the Commonwealth). Hobbes thus gives self-interest as the motive for a person's deciding to join a moral and legal community where his conduct can be judged to be right or wrong. Whether or not his psychological egoism is accepted, Hobbes's ethical egoism does provide a systematic account of how the principle of self-interest can function as the ultimate ground of right conduct, not only in a "state of nature" where there are no moral rules, but also in a rule-governed community of moral agents.

What objections might be raised against the theory of universal ethical egoism, and what replies might be given to those objections? The most frequent criticism of universal ethical egoism is that it must be false because it contains an *internal inconsistency*. The argument goes as follows. The universal ethical egoist says that each person should promote his own self-interest. There will be many situations, however, in which a conflict of interest occurs between the egoist and others. In such situations, if others pursue their ends the egoist himself will be hindered or prevented from pursuing his own, and vice versa. Yet according to his theory, an action ought to be done whenever it furthers the interests of the agent, *whoever that agent may be*. It follows that in all cases of conflict of interest between the egoist himself and others, the principle of universal ethical egoism entails contradictory ought-statements. For it entails that another person ought to do a certain action (because it would promote his interests) and at the same time it entails that he ought not to, since his doing it would interfere with the egoist's pursuit of his own interests. Similarly, if the egoist's action would benefit him, then according to his theory he ought to do it. However, in a situation where his action conflicts with another's self-interest, that other would *correctly* judge that the action ought not to be done. Thus the two contradictory judgments: "The egoist ought to do the act" and "The egoist ought not to do the act" would both be true of the same action. It follows, therefore, that universal ethical egoism is internally inconsistent.

The egoist's reply to this argument is that, according to his theory, he need not *assert* that others ought to pursue their interests when doing so conflicts with the promotion of his own. He can simply keep quiet about the matter. Indeed, if he is to further his interests in the most effective way possible he should publicly urge others to be altruistic, since by following his counsel they will not interfere with him but, on the contrary, will help him attain his goals. If, then, he is true to the egoist principle that he ought to do everything that will most effectively further his own ends, he will not advocate publicly that everyone be an ethical egoist. Instead, he will declare that all persons should be altruists — at least with regard to the way they treat him!

It has seemed to the critics of egoism, however, that this reply does not get rid of the inconsistency. They point out that it follows from the theory of universal egoism that *each and every person* ought to think in the way described above. Thus everyone ought to urge others to be altruistic as a means to promoting his self-interest. And since each person's pursuit of self-interest requires that he not become altruistic himself, the theory implies that no one should be an altruist. Hence, every individual ought to do something (namely, promote his own self-interest by getting others to be altruistic) and at the same time ought to prevent another from doing what that other ought to do (namely, getting others to be altruistic without becoming altruistic himself).

The logical consequence of universal ethical egoism thus appears to be that everyone should do a certain sort of thing while actually it is impossible that everyone do it successfully. If one person succeeds in doing it (that is, succeeds in getting another to be altruistic while remaining egoistic himself), someone else must fail to do it (if he happens to be the person whom the other has successfully made altruistic). Ethical egoism need not be *advocated* universally for this internal inconsistency to arise. It is an inconsistency that arises from everyone's *practicing* ethical egoism by *not* advocating that everyone become an ethical egoist.

It should be noted that these considerations apply to what we have called "universal ethical egoism." The other two forms of ethical egoism, which were designated by the terms "individual" and "personal," can escape the foregoing difficulties, since neither claims that every person should promote his own self-interest. The "individual" ethical egoist holds that *he* should promote his self-interest and that all others should also promote his, the ethical egoist's, self-interest. There is nothing internally inconsistent with everyone's putting this principle into practice. The "personal" ethical egoist, on the other hand, asserts that *he* should promote his own self-interest and simply has nothing to say, one way or the other, concerning what anyone else ought to do. Here also, no contradiction is involved in what the personal ethical egoist claims ought to be done.

Can we accept, then, either of these forms of ethical egoism as a justifiable normative system? That there remain certain problems which each of them has to face becomes clear from the following reflections.

Consider, first, the position of the individual ethical egoist. He says that his interests ought to be furthered not only by his own actions but also by those of everyone else. One implication of his view is that his wishes, desires, and needs have a right to be fulfilled even at the cost of frustrating the wants of others. His ultimate principle, in other words, entails an inequality of rights among persons. We can then formulate a challenge which will reasonably be addressed to the egoist by all others: "Why should your self-interest count more than anyone else's? On what grounds do your wants and needs make a higher claim to fulfillment than those of anyone else? Unless you can show that you merit special consideration, there is no reason why others owe you a duty (namely, to further your interests) which you do not owe to them. And your theory itself offers no basis for your claim to special consideration, since anyone else can propose the same ultimate principle on his own behalf and thus endow his interests with a higher claim to fulfillment than yours. Your theory provides no *reasons* why you should be given unique treatment." It is difficult to see how the egoist could reply to this challenge. As long as others knew that it was contrary to their interests to accept his principle, they would need to be shown why they should accept it before they could have a reason to do the actions it required of them. But the only way the individual egoist could justify others' accepting his principle would be by pointing out some *characteristic* of himself that made him deserving of special consideration. If he were to do this, however, the possession of the given characteristic would be the supreme principle of his system, not the principle of egoism itself. He would then have to admit that if anyone else were found to have the attribute in question, that person's interest would have a claim to fulfillment equal to his own. And this would be giving up individual ethical egoism.

Let us look, next, at the position of personal ethical egoism. The personal egoist escapes the foregoing criticism since he does not claim that others ought to promote his self-interest. He simply says that he ought to do those actions that will most benefit him, and makes no ought-statements about anyone else's actions (not even the statement that they ought not to interfere with or frustrate him in the pursuit of his interests). It is important to realize that the principle of personal ethical egoism does not provide any basis for judging the rightness or wrongness of the conduct of any individual other than the egoist himself. Once we see clearly that personal ethical egoism has this implication, we see how it is possible to raise the following objection to it. (It is an objection, be it noted, which cannot be raised against the theories of universal or individual ethical egoism.)

How can personal ethical egoism be considered a normative ethical system at all? Since it tells only one person in the world what *he* ought and ought not to do but remains completely silent about the actions of everyone else, it turns out to be nothing more than a private policy of action adopted by one person with regard to himself alone. It is a policy by which he can guide his own conduct, but it cannot serve to guide anyone else's. Consequently it does not qualify as a moral principle. Even if everyone were to accept the principle, it would leave all but one person completely in the dark about what they morally ought or ought not to do. It may indeed be *consistent* for someone to adopt the principle for himself and use it as a policy governing his own actions. But such a personal policy cannot provide others with moral reasons for or against doing anything they please.

This argument assumes that an ethical system must give an account of *moral* reasons for action and that a *moral* reason for action cannot be merely a personal policy adopted by one individual as a guide to his own conduct alone. If a statement about the properties or consequences of an action constitutes a moral reason for (or against) the action, then it must be a reason for *anyone's* performing (or refraining from) that kind of conduct, whenever *anyone* is in a situation in which doing and refraining from an action of the given kind are alternatives open to him. Whether this view of a moral reason for action is itself acceptable is an issue that requires further inquiry into normative ethical systems. In the following two chapters, two ethical systems that provide alternatives to ethical egoism will be considered in detail, each being advocated by its proponents as a valid system of ethics for *all* moral agents, that is, for all beings capable of acting for moral reasons.

Suggested Reading

Two good collections of writings on psychological egoism and ethical egoism:

Gauthier, David P., ed., *Morality and Rational Self-Interest.* Englewood Cliffs, N. J.: Prentice-Hall, Inc., 1970.*

Milo, Ronald D., ed., *Egoism and Altruism.* Belmont, California: Wadsworth Publishing Co., Inc., 1973.*

Classic works:

Epicurus, *Writings.*

————, Russell Geer, trans., *Letters, Principal Doctrines, and Vatican Sayings.* Indianapolis: The Bobbs-Merrill Co., Inc., 1955.*

Hobbes, Thomas, *Elements of Law.* 1640.

————, *De Cive, or Philosophical Rudiments Concerning Government and Society.* 1642.

————, *Leviathan, or the Matter, Form and Power of a Commonwealth, Ecclesiastical and Civil.* 1651.

Selections from these works are included in:

————, *Leviathan, Parts I and II.* Edited by Herbert W. Schneider. Indianapolis: The Bobbs-Merrill Co., Inc., 1958.*

————, *Man and Citizen.* Edited by Bernard Gert. New York: Anchor Books, Doubleday and Co., 1972.*

*Available in paperback

An excellent collection of essays on the argument of Hobbes's *Leviathan* (including discussions of his psychological egoism and his ethical egoism):

Baumrin, Bernard H., ed., *Hobbes's* Leviathan: *Interpretation and Criticism.* Belmont, California: Wadsworth Publishing Co., Inc., 1969.*

A classic criticism of psychological egoism:

Butler, Joseph, *Sermons Preached at the Rolls Chapel.* 1726. Selections from this work are included in Baumrin and Milo, cited above.
————, *Five Sermons.* Edited by Stuart M. Brown, Jr. Indianapolis: The Bobbs-Merrill Co., Inc., 1950.* The most important of Butler's sermons.

An interesting contemporary version of ethical egoism:

Olson, Robert G., *The Morality of Self-Interst.* New York: Harcourt Brace Jovanovich, Inc., 1965.*

*Available in paperback

IV

Utilitarianism

TWO KINDS OF ETHICAL SYSTEMS

A normative ethical system is an ordered set of moral standards and rules of conduct by reference to which, with the addition of factual knowledge, one can determine in any situation of choice what a person ought or ought not to do. In this chapter and the one following are set forth the two normative ethical systems that are most widely discussed and defended in contemporary moral philosophy. The first system, utilitarianism, received its classical formulation in the writings of the British philosophers, Jeremy Bentham(1748-1832) and John Stuart Mill (1806-1873). The second system, which may be designated "ethical formalism," was originally propounded by the great German philosopher, Immanuel Kant (1724-1804). There is some disagreement among philosophers at present whether the two sets of doctrines are necessarily inconsistent with each other, although their earlier proponents thought that they were. The purpose of these two chapters is to present each system and examine critically the arguments supporting it. Whether there is a wider framework of moral principles within which both systems can be consistently integrated is a question to be left open here.

Utilitarianism and formalism are often contrasted with one another on the basis of the general type of ethical system each exemplifies. Utilitarianism is a *teleological* ethical system (from the Greek word *telos*, meaning end or purpose); formalism is a *deontological* ethical system (from the Greek word *deon*, meaning duty). The distinction between the two kinds of system may be conveniently summarized as follows. A teleological theory holds that an action is morally right either if a person's doing it brings about good consequences, or if the action is of a kind which, if everyone did it, would have good consequences. In either case, ultimately it is the goodness or badness of the consequences of actions that make them right or wrong. A deontological theory holds that an action is right if it accords with a moral rule, wrong if it violates such a rule. Moral rules are based on an ultimate principle of duty which, in contrast to teleological ethics, does not specify an end or purpose whose furtherance makes actions right. What the ultimate principle does specify is a set of conditions that are necessary and sufficient for any rule of moral obligation to apply to a kind of action. Let us take a closer look at this distinction.

In a teleological ethical system, the test of right and wrong actions consists in applying a standard of value to the consequences of the actions. If the consequences of someone's doing a particular action or of everyone's doing a type of action fulfill the standard of value, the consequences are good and the action or action-type is therefore right. If the consequences are bad (because they fail to meet the standard), the action or action-type is wrong. In this kind of ethical system the "consequences" of an action are understood to comprise *all* the effects which the action has in the future of the world. They include everything that happens *because* the action is done, that is, everything which would have been different in the future if the action had not occurred. Thus, suppose the assassination of Abraham Lincoln in 1865 by John Wilkes Booth caused a difference in United States history during the period of Reconstruction following the Civil War. Then that difference is to be considered one of the consequences of Booth's action. If what occurred as a result of Lincoln's murder is neither good nor bad (when judged by a certain standard of value), then even though it is a consequence of Booth's action, it has no bearing on the rightness or wrongness of that deed. If it is good or bad (to however slight a degree), it does have such a bearing.

On this point deontological ethics disagrees with teleological ethics. Deontologists hold that it is not the goodness or badness of the consequences of an action that make it right or wrong, but the *kind* of action it is. An action is right in their view if it is of a kind that all moral agents have an obligation to perform; it is wrong if it is one that all moral agents are obligated to avoid. The statement that all moral agents are obligated to do or to refrain from doing a certain kind of action is a *moral rule of conduct,* and deontologists believe that the ground of such obligation lies in the fact that the moral rule in question satisfies the requirements of an *ultimate norm* or *supreme principle* of duty, which is often designated as "the Moral

Law." We shall see in the next chapter what sort of requirements are stipulated in such an ultimate ground of moral obligation. For the present it is enough to point out that, in a deontological ethical system, the supreme principle of morality does not lay down, as either a necessary or a sufficient condition of a right action, that it bring about good consequences. It should be noted, however, that consequences may be relevant to *identifying the kind of action* required or prohibited by a deontological moral rule (and hence the kind of action we have a duty to perform or avoid). For example, the rule "Do not kill" tells us that we are obligated to refrain from intentionally taking the life of another. The rule forbids conduct of a certain type (killing). Now consider Booth's action of aiming and firing a loaded pistol at Lincoln. The fact that it caused Lincoln's death is relevant to its wrongness. For this consequence of the action—namely, Lincoln's dying—makes the action not merely one of aiming and firing a loaded pistol at a person, but one of intentionally *killing* someone. As such, the action is seen to fall under the rule of "Do not kill." Assuming that this rule is entailed by the ultimate principle of morality, the deontologist would conclude that Booth's conduct was morally wrong. Its wrongness, he would say, depends on its being of the type, killing. It is wrong, in other words, because it is a kind of act that includes someone's death among its consequences. It is not wrong because acts of killing have *further* consequences (occurring *after* someone's death) which, when judged by some standard of value, are bad.

Some moral philosophers hold that the grounds of right conduct are both teleological and deontological, and that there is no single supreme principle from which, ultimately, the moral rightness or wrongness of every action can be derived. According to this view, which is generally known as "ethical pluralism," the moral reasons for (or against) some actions lie in the consequences of those actions, while the moral reasons governing other actions arise from their being of a kind required (or prohibited) by a rule of duty or obligation. Ethical pluralists argue that both sorts of reasons, in fact, can apply to one and the same action. A person may therefore find himself in circumstances where he has moral reasons of the first sort *for* doing a particular action and moral reasons of the second sort *against* doing it, or vice versa. Consider the situation in which a policeman's carrying out his duty to apprehend a criminal might lead to a riot. If he does his duty, bad consequences are likely to result. If he avoids the consequences, he fails to do his duty. A contrasting case, where the reasons *for* an action are teleological and the reasons *against* deontological, occurs when a person can save someone's life only by stealing. An instance would be a poor man stealing medicine for his sick child.

In such situations, how is one to decide what the agent ought to do? The answer given by the ethical pluralist is that one must weigh the comparative importance of these various reasons to see which reasons outweigh or override any others applicable to the given action. Sometimes the consequences of an action will be so bad that it ought not to be done, despite a prima facie obligation to do it (that is, an obligation that would make the deed one's duty *if* there were no moral reasons against it). In other cases the prima facie obligation will be sufficiently heavy or stringent to outweigh the badness of the consequences. Only the development of a capacity for sensitive moral discrimination will enable one to decide how the weighing should go. Even among equally competent and sensitive moral thinkers, there will at times be disagreements about the relative importance of the various reasons for action. All that can fairly be demanded of anyone in such circumstances, say the ethical pluralists, is that the individual in question be thoroughly conscientious and impartial, weighing *all* the considerations morally relevant to *every* alternative course of action open to him. He must include in his deliberations, when applicable, both teleological and deontological factors, and he must not allow his self-interest, or the interests of his friends, relatives, class, nation, religion, or race to distort the importance he places on any given consideration (unless, of course, the furthering of one of these specified interests is itself a morally relevant factor that ought to be taken into account by *any* impartial and conscientious thinker in *any* situation of the given kind).

For purposes of this book, only "monistic" systems of ethics shall be examined—systems which have a single supreme principle, whether teleological or deontological, as the ultimate ground of morality. This will lead to a clear understanding of the fundamental differences between the two types of ethical systems. The reader will then have a firm grasp of the two sorts of moral reasons for (or against) an action: those based on the goodness or badness of the consequences of the action, and those based on the rules of obligation or duty under which the action falls. This will, in turn, enable the reader to consider on his own the possibility of constructing a form of ethical pluralism that would combine both sorts of reasons in one coherent system. Chapter Five of this book will be concerned with the monistic deontological theory of ethical formalism, while the remainder of this chapter will consider the most important type of monistic teleological ethics: utilitarianism.

UTILITY AS THE TEST OF RIGHT AND WRONG

The basic concept of utilitarian ethics is, as its name indicates, the idea of utility: an act is right if it is useful. As soon as this is said the question arises, Useful for what end? For unless we know the end to which something is to be judged as a means, we do not know how to decide whether it is useful or not.

The answer given by utilitarianism is that an act is right when it is useful in bringing about a *desirable* or *good* end, an end that has *intrinsic value*. The concept of intrinsic value will be studied in detail in Chapter Six. A preliminary account, however, must be given if we are to understand utilitarian ethics. By "intrinsic value" is meant the value something has as an end in itself, and not as a means to some further end. This may be explained as follows. There are certain things we value because of their consequences or effects, but we do not value them in themselves. Thus we think it is a good thing to go to the dentist because we want healthy teeth and we have reason to believe that the dentist is a person who can help bring about this end. But few people find visiting the dentist good in itself. In other words, the act of visiting the dentist is done not for its own sake but for the sake of something else. This something else may in turn be valued not as an end in itself but as a means to other ends. Eventually, however, we arrive at certain experiences or conditions of life that we want to have and enjoy just for their own sake. These are ends that we judge to be intrinsically good; they have for us intrinsic value. The experience of undergoing dental treatment, on the other hand, has only instrumental value for us. We consider it good only because we think it is a means to some further end. If we did not value the end, the means would lose its value. Thus suppose we did not mind losing our teeth or having toothaches. We would not then think going to the dentist was worthwhile. So the value of some things is entirely *derivative*. They derive all their value from the value of something else. Other things—things that are sought for their own sake—have *nonderivative* value. Their value is not derived from the value of something else and hence is intrinsic to them. Derivative value, in short, is instrumental value; nonderivative value is intrinsic value. Of course it is possible for one and the same thing to have both kinds of value. For example, if a person enjoys playing tennis and also does it for the exercise, the game of tennis has both intrinsic and instrumental value for him. In this case playing tennis is both intrinsically good and instrumentally good. In contrast to this, going to the dentist is intrinsically bad but instrumentally good. Two other com-

binations are also possible. Something can be instrinsically good but instrumentally bad (for example, eating too much of our favorite dessert), and
something can be both instrinsically and instrumentally bad (for example,
having a painful illness involving heavy medical expenses).

Now the basic principle of utilitarian ethics is that *the right depends on
the good.* This means that we can know whether an act is morally right only
by finding out what its consequences are and then determining the intrinsic
goodness (or badness) of those consequences. The moral rightness of an act is
not itself an intrinsic value. On the contrary, an act is right only when it is
instrumentally good and its rightness consists in its instrumental goodness.
Our next question is, What is the standard of intrinsic value by which
utilitarians judge the goodness of the consequences of a right act? Classical
utilitarians have proposed two different answers to this. Some, like Jeremy
Bentham, have said "pleasure"; others, like John Stuart Mill, have said
"happiness," and have added that happiness is not merely a sum total of
pleasures. A third answer has been suggested by a twentieth century
utilitarian, G.E. Moore (1873-1958), who has claimed that intrinsic goodness cannot be defined in terms of either pleasure or happiness, but is a
unique and indefinable property of things. Thus we have three types of
utilitarianism, categorized according to these three views of the end to which
morally right conduct is a means. They are called "hedonistic utilitarianism"
(from the Greek word *hedone,* meaning pleasure); "eudaimonistic utilitarianism" (from the Greek word *eudaimonia,* meaning happiness or
well-being); and "ideal utilitarianism" or "agathistic utilitarianism" (from the
Greek word *agathos,* meaning good). Some of the differences between
pleasure and happiness, and their relation to the concept of intrinsic value,
will be discussed in Chapter Six.

The fundamental norm of hedonistic utilitarianism may be stated thus:
An act is right if it brings about pleasure (or prevents the bringing about of
pain); an act is wrong if it brings about pain (or prevents the bringing about
of pleasure). The fundamental norm of eudaimonistic utilitarianism may be
stated in a corresponding way, merely by substituting "happiness" for
"pleasure" and "unhappiness" for "pain." Similarly, ideal or agathistic
utilitarianism may be formulated by substituting "intrinsic good" for "pleasure" and "intrinsic evil" for "pain." As soon as the norm of utilitarian ethics
is stated in any of these ways, another question immediately arises: Pleasure
or happiness or intrinsic good *for whom,* pain or unhappiness or intrinsic
evil *for whom?*

Many alternative answers are possible. One can say, pleasure, happiness, or intrinsic good for the agent himself, that is, for the person doing the act. The resulting ethical system would then be a form of ethical egoism. (Refer to Chapter Three for a discussion of ethical egoism.) Another possible answer is, pleasure, happiness, or intrinsic good for the agent's family and friends, or for the members of his class or caste, his tribe or nation, his race, religion, or sex. This would yield an ethical system in which the interests of some people are understood to have a greater claim to fulfillment than the interests of others. Still another possibility is, pleasure, happiness, or intrinsic good for everyone *but* the agent. This answer would entail an ethics of pure altruism or brotherly love, in which the moral ideal for each agent is to devote himself to the welfare of others at whatever cost to his own interests. Finally, the answer to our question which utilitarians give is, *everyone's* pleasure, happiness, or intrinsic good.

According to utilitarianism, whether it be hedonistic, eudaimonistic, or agathistic, the standard of value for judging the consequences of actions must be completely impartial and universal in its application. In calculating the positive or negative value of consequences, one person's pleasure (or happiness or intrinsic good) is to count exactly as much as another's. The agent's own interests are to be considered along with everyone else's, but no greater (and no lesser) weight is to be given to his interests than to those of any other individual. Between his own pleasure (happiness, intrinsic good) and that of someone else, the agent must be strictly impartial, never allowing himself to be prejudiced in his own favor or in favor of those whom he happens to like. All human beings, for the utilitarian, have an equal right to the fulfillment of their interests.

Given this principle of impartiality, how does the utilitarian apply it in determining the rightness or wrongness of a particular action? For the sake of simplicity in answering this question, the differences among hedonistic, eudaimonistic, and agathistic forms of utilitarianism will be disregarded. (Their differences will be fully considered, however, in Chapter Six.) To find out what one morally ought to do in any situation of choice, utilitarianism prescribes the following decision-making procedure. First we specify all the alternatives that comprise the possible courses of action open to our choice. We then calculate to the best of our ability the probable consequences that would ensue if we were to choose each alternative. In this calculation we ask ourselves, How much pleasure (or happiness) and how much pain (or unhappiness) will result in my own life and in the lives of all people who will be affected by my doing this act? When we have done this for all the alternatives open to us, we then compare those consequences in order to find out which one leads to a greater amount of pleasure (or happiness) and a smaller amount of pain (or unhappiness) than any other alternative. The act that in this way is found to *maximize intrinsic value and minimize intrinsic disvalue* is the act we morally ought to do. To do any other act in the given situation would be morally wrong.

In the practical affairs of everyday life, of course, we cannot stop and make such detailed calculations every-time we have alternative courses of action open to us. Indeed, if we were to do this we might cause more unhappiness or less happiness to be brought about in the world than if we were to make choices on the basis of habits we had developed from our past experience. Thus it would be wrong for us, according to the principle of utility, to try to make an accurate calculation each time. What we must do is to use our common sense and choose on the basis of similar situations in the past. After all, it does not take much thought to predict that murdering someone is going to produce more unhappiness in the world than respecting the person's life. We need not have committed a murder in the past to know this. We need only to use our reason and imagination to be able to make a reasonable prediction about what would happen if we were to do such an act.

It is important to realize that for the utilitarian no act is morally wrong in itself. Its wrongness depends entirely on its consequences. Take the act of murder, for instance. If the consequences of murdering a particular man in a particular set of circumstances (say, assassinating Hitler in 1935) were to bring about less unhappiness in the world than would be caused by the man himself were he to remain alive, it is not wrong to murder him. Indeed, it is our duty to do so, since the circumstances are such that our refraining from doing the act will result in more unhappiness (intrinsic disvalue) and less happiness (intrinsic value) than our doing it. This might at first appear to be a shocking and outrageous teaching. But the utilitarian would argue, What, after all, is wrong with the act of murder? Is it not that it causes so much pain and unhappiness both to the victim and to his kin, and prevents the victim from having the chance to enjoy his right to the pursuit of happiness? Suppose the nature of man and the world were very different from what they in fact are, so that everyone at the age of thirty suddenly deteriorated physically and mentally and became incapable of having any pleasant experiences thereafter in life. Suppose, further, that there was a way of killing people at that age which gave them great pleasure up to the final moment of death. Finally, suppose that their death at this time in their lives was celebrated by others as a happy event, in the way births are often celebrated in our own culture. In such a world why should the murder of people at thirty be condemned? Since there would be more unhappiness in the world as a result of respecting their lives, what would be wrong in ending their lives? Indeed, it is just such considerations as these that have led some people in our actual world to advocate the painless killing of human beings under certain specified circumstances. Thus it has been suggested that a doctor be permitted to administer a drug that will painlessly cause the death of a person who has an incurable disease when, first, there is no likelihood that a cure will be discovered in the period the person will remain alive; second, when his suffering is intense and cannot be alleviated by medical means; and third, when both the person himself and his relatives have asked that such a drug be administered to him.

This example brings to light another aspect of utilitarian ethics. It shows that, from the utilitarian point of view, it is sometimes right to do an act which is known to bring about unhappiness. But this is true only when the act in question will bring about *less unhappiness than any possible alternative*. In that sort of situation to do anything else — even to "do nothing," that is, to let events take their course without trying to change them — would be deliberately to cause more unhappiness to people than is necessary. Situations of this unfortunate kind may occur in time of war or when there are natural disasters such as floods and earthquakes, as well as in cases of people suffering from incurable diseases.

ACT-UTILITARIANISM AND RULE-UTILITARIANISM

What is the function of moral rules of conduct, according to utilitarianism? Two different answers are given to this question by utilitarians, and this has been used as a basis for distinguishing two types of utilitarianism, one called "act" or "unrestricted" utilitarianism, the other called "rule" or "restricted" utilitarianism. The distinction may be put this way. For all utilitarians, the principle of utility is the *ultimate* test of the rightness or wrongness of human conduct. But in applying this test, do we apply it directly to particular acts, or do we restrict its application to rules of conduct, and let those rules determine whether a particular act is right or wrong? In the first case, which is unrestricted or act-utilitarianism, we must find out what are the consequences of a *particular act* in order to know whether it is right or wrong. It is this type of utilitarianism that has been presented in the foregoing paragraphs. The principle of utility is applied directly to each alternative act in a situation of choice. The right act is then defined as the one which has greater utility than any other alternative. It would be wrong for a person to do any of these other alternatives, because if he were to do any of them he would *not* thereby maximize intrinsic value and minimize intrinsic disvalue in the world, and a person's duty is always to do that act among all those open to his choice which has such consequences.

According to restricted or rule-utilitarianism, on the other hand, an act is right if it conforms to a valid rule of conduct and wrong if it violates such a rule. And it is the test of utility that determines the validity of rules of conduct. Thus the one true normative ethical system binding upon all mankind is a set of rules such that, if people regulated their conduct by these rules, greater intrinsic value and less intrinsic disvalue would result for everyone than if they followed a different code. To "regulate one's conduct by a rule" is explained by reference to the two kinds of rules, positive rules or requirements, and negative rules or prohibitions. A positive rule specifies the properties of an action-type which is required of everyone. It states that every person is to do a certain kind of action in circumstances where he can either do or refrain from doing such an act. Thus the rule "Keep your promises" tells us that when we have promised someone to do something and then have the choice to keep or to break our promise we must keep it. The right act is to do what the rule requires, the wrong conduct is not to do what it requires. A negative rule forbids everyone to do a certain kind of act. It requires that a person refrain from a certain kind of behavior when he has the choice of doing or not doing it. Thus the rule "Thou shalt not steal" tells us what we must not do rather than what we must do. Just as acting in accordance with a positive rule means doing what it requires, so acting in accordance with a negative rule means refraining from doing what it prohibits. And just as it is wrong to omit what is required by a positive rule, so it is wrong to perform an act contrary to a negative rule. In this way "right" and "wrong" can be defined as action that conforms to, or violates, a rule of conduct which is binding upon us. But how do we know, among all the possible rules that could regulate our conduct, which ones do really bind us? The rule-utilitarian's answer is, those rules which, when generally complied with, bring about more happiness or pleasure for everyone and less unhappiness or pain than would result from general compliance with any other set of rules.

Rule-utilitarianism has been proposed as a way out of certain difficulties that seem to be entailed by act-utilitarianism. Consider, for example, our ordinary moral judgments concerning the wrongness of acts perpetrated without the knowledge of others. Suppose a man were to commit the "perfect" crime by murdering someone without leaving any clues. As a result, the murderer is never caught and punished. Now compare this case with an exactly similar act of murder, except that the killer leaves some clues, is eventually caught, and is sentenced to life imprisonment. Ordinarily we would say that the two acts of murder were equally wrong, and that whether a murderer is caught has nothing to do with the wrongness of his act. Yet according to act-utilitarianism it would seem that the first act is not as bad as the second. For the consequences of the first act do not involve as much unhappiness as is involved in the consequences of the second, since the murderer gets away with his act and does not suffer imprisonment. The fact that his act is a "perfect" crime makes it better than the same crime done by someone who is careless about leaving evidence. This seems the very opposite of our ordinary moral judgments of the two cases. If there is any moral difference between them, we would say the first is worse than the second precisely because the criminal escapes punishment.

The act-utilitarian might reply that in fact the first case is worse than the second because, although the criminal does not suffer punishment by law, he will suffer the pangs of a bad conscience and will forever live in fear of the police. Furthermore, his not getting caught may encourage him and others to commit more crimes, and so bring about worse consequences than would have happened if he had been caught and imprisoned. Still, the argument against act-utilitarianism can be revised to take at least some of these points into account. Suppose the man who commits the "perfect" crime is a hardened, amoral kind of man without a conscience, is fully confident that he will never be caught or even suspected by the police, and has no desire to commit another murder because the motive for his one crime was revenge directed at the particular person who was his victim. Again we would say that none of these facts makes the crime any the less wrong; indeed, we should say they are all completely *irrelevant* to the wrongness of his action. Yet by the theory of act-utilitarianism all of these factors *are* relevant, since they make a difference to the consequences of the action.

It should be observed that the foregoing type of argument cannot be used against the rule-utilitarian. According to his theory both acts of murder are equally wrong, since both are violations of the same rule of conduct — namely, that we ought to respect the lives of others. The consequences that follow the performance of each particular act do not determine the rightness or wrongness of the act, and therefore the crime can be judged to be wrong regardless of whether the criminal is caught, feels guilty, or will be encouraged to commit another crime. The rule that all murderers are to be punished by law is itself a valid rule for rule-utilitarians because the consequences of having such a rule regulating people's conduct are better than the consequences of not having it regulate their conduct. Hence, by the same reasoning that shows the act of murder to be wrong, the rule-utilitarian shows the act of apprehending and punishing a murderer to be right.

It is now possible to see how the two forms of utilitarianism differ with regard to the place of rules of conduct in an ethical system. For rule-utilitarianism, rules of conduct are the *criteria* of right and wrong action when those rules are utilitarian rules. By a "utilitarian rule" is meant a rule (like the one mentioned above: "All murderers are to be punished by law") the universal following of which would have greater utility than would universal compliance with any alternative rule applicable to the same action-type. To say that utilitarian rules are the criteria of right and wrong action is to say that conformity of a particular act (that is, an act which is performed at a particular time by a particular agent) to such a rule is what *makes* it right, while the fact that a particular act violates a utilitarian rule is what *makes* it wrong. In contrast, the function of rules of conduct in an act-utilitarian system is radically different. This can be made clear by the following considerations.

According to act-utilitarianism, the principle of utility itself (that is, productivity of maximum intrinsic value and minimum intrinsic disvalue) is applied directly to particular acts in order to determine their rightness or wrongness. What *makes* a particular act right is not its conformity with a valid rule (as is the case with rule-utilitarianism), but the actual consequences of its being performed at a specific time and place. If its performance results in more intrinsic value and less intrinsic disvalue than would result from any alternative in the given circumstances, it is the act that ought to be done. However, the act-utilitarian does say that there is a place for moral rules in practical life, even though they do not determine what acts are right or wrong.

For act-utilitarianism, rules of conduct are useful as practical guides in situations where it is difficult or impossible to predict the consequences of alternative ways of acting. Theoretically, the ideal decision-making proce-dure for an act-utilitarian would not need any reference to rules, since the consequences of each alternative would be calculated on the basis of complete and perfect empirical knowledge of causes and effects. But in the world as it is, human beings lack such knowledge. The complexities of the effects of our conduct often make it practically impossible to know whether we will in fact produce more good and less evil in the world by doing one thing rather than another. (Let the reader ask himself, Right now, is my reading this book more likely to lead to the greatest good for the greatest number of persons when compared with my doing anything else that it is within my power to do at this time?) Given this inescapable fact of human ignorance and people's tendency to let self-interest influence their predictions of the effects of their actions, it becomes clear that utility itself is enhanced if human beings guide their actions, not by their own calculations of consequences, but by certain general rules of conduct.

Which rules? The act-utilitarian would answer, those rules that have proven in past experience to serve the principle of utility effectively in the vast majority of cases. Just as we find it practical to follow certain rules of thumb as guides in some complex task (such as making a bookcase, cooking a five-course dinner, or learning how to ski), so moral precepts can function as rules of thumb in helping us to conform our actions to the principle of utility. Thus moral rules are understood as inductive generalizations or statistical probabilities about the kinds of action that, in the past, have been found usually to have produced the greatest amount of utility.

This way of conceiving of moral rules has the following implications. First, a rule is a "summary" of judgments of particular acts that are right or wrong independently of the rule. Their rightness or wrongness lies in their utility or disutility, which depends on the consequences they have when done in specific circumstances. Secondly, it is never legitimate for a person to follow a rule, even one with well-established utilitarian consequences in the past, if in his particular case breaking it will probably have greater utility than abiding by it. Thus deceiving a person, betraying a trust between oneself and another, or taking any action that would normally be described as a violation of others' rights, is never in itself or by its very nature wrong. Nor is it wrong because, as rule-utilitarians hold, the rules "Do not deceive"; "Remain faithful to trusts"; "Never violate the rights of others" are valid criteria of moral conduct. For the act-utilitarian, such rules have absolutely no weight in determining the morality of conduct that conforms to or violates them. However, adherence to them by most people has generally had good consequences in the past, and in the practical affairs of everyday life, they have proven useful as rules of thumb. Therefore, moral rules should be broken only when it is clear to the one who breaks them that by doing so he is indeed maximizing utility in his given circumstances.

ARE ACT-UTILITARIANISM AND RULE-UTILITARIANISM INCOMPATIBLE?

Is it ever the case that a particular act which is right according to act-utilitarianism would be wrong according to rule-utilitarianism, or vice versa? That there seem to be such instances was shown by our example of the "perfect" crime. However, recent studies of the two types of utilitarianism have raised the question of whether they are indeed incompatible when all their implications are carefully considered. Let us look again at some situations where they at least *appear* to yield contradictory moral judgments about the same particular act. Take the following example as a case in point. We would all agree that the rule "Never lie to a person who asks you a direct question" has much greater utility than the opposite "Always lie to a person who asks you a direct question," since many of the advantages of civilized life would not exist if people were constantly trying to deceive one another. Yet we can easily imagine a set of circumstances in which following the first rule will produce much more pain and unhappiness than following the second. For example, suppose the Gestapo in Nazi Germany asked someone who was hiding a group of Jews in his home if he knew the whereabouts of any Jews; the person's act of telling the truth would result in the Jews he had been protecting being sent to a concentration camp. Given this situation, the ethical system of act-utilitarianism would clearly indicate that it would be right to lie and wrong to tell the truth. But it would seem that rule-utilitarianism implies the opposite moral judgment, since the rule "Tell the truth" has greater utility when everyone follows it than the rule "Do not tell the truth."

Consider another case. Suppose someone finds a wallet containing $500 and also a card clearly showing the owner's name and address. Suppose further that the situation is such that the person could easily remove the money, leave the wallet where he found it, and walk away without anyone's knowing what he had done. Finally, let us suppose the wallet belongs to a millionaire, whereas the finder is poor and needs the money to keep his family from starving. Here is a set of circumstances where act-utilitarianism appears to imply that it would be right for the man to take the money even though it does not belong to him. Rule-utilitarianism, it would seem, has the opposite implication, since taking the money is forbidden by the rule, "Thou shalt not steal," one that is of greater general utility than the rule, "Steal whenever it is probable you will not be caught."

Examples like these have been cited by philosophers to show that an act may be right (or wrong) according to act-utilitarianism and wrong (or right) according to rule-utilitarianism. Thus it is argued that the usefulness of a person's doing a *particular* act is quite different from the usefulness of a society's having a set of general rules requiring everyone to do or refrain from doing certain *kinds* of action. The basic point at issue between act- and rule-utilitarians concerns this distinction between judging the morality of a particular act and judging the morality of a rule-governed social system as a whole. Is utility the proper test for the rightness or wrongness of particular acts, or is it the proper test for what general social practices and institutions a society ought to have? Perhaps the point can be brought out most sharply by considering the morality of paying debts. Although it may cause more unhappiness in a particular case for a poor man to pay his debts to a wealthy man than to default, the general social practice of paying debts yields less unhappiness in the long run for everyone than not paying them. Now if (as rule-utilitarians hold) the usefulness of the rule "One must pay one's debts" determines the rightness or wrongness of every particular act that falls under the rule, it would be wrong for the poor man not to pay his debts to the rich one. The conclusion is that act-utilitarianism and rule-utilitiarianism cannot both be true, since they entail contradictory moral judgments of the same act.

This conclusion, however, has recently been disputed by some philosophers. They claim that, when the full logical consequences of act-utilitarianism and rule-utilitarianism are made explicit, they turn out to be *extensionally equivalent.* That is, if a judgment concerning the rightness or wrongness of a particular act is true according to act-utilitarianism, it must also be true according to rule-utilitarianism, and if it is false according to the one, it must be so according to the other. A closer scrutiny of our foregoing examples is in order.

In each case it was argued that a certain act would be judged right by an act-utilitarian (because it maximized utility) but wrong by a rule-utilitarian (because it violated a valid moral rule). Yet there is a way of looking at these acts which would allow a rule-utilitarian to argue that they are right, and thus agree with the act-utilitarian's view. Here is how this can be done.

Each act may be considered not as a violation of, but as a legitimate exception to, a moral rule. What makes an exception legitimate? The answer might be either that the exception is required by a higher moral rule or that its consequences are better than those of strict observance in the given circumstances. According to the first answer, whenever a conflict of rules occurs (that is, where following one rule involves breaking the other, and vice versa) we must make an exception to one of the conflicting rules. Our exception is legitimate when the rule requiring the exception imposes a heavier obligation or higher duty on us than that to which we make the exception. Thus in the example of lying to the Gestapo, the duty to obey the rule, "Prevent harm to innocent people" outweighs the rule, "Tell the truth." In this case it is right to lie. According to the second test of a legitimate exception, we must balance the duty of following the rule with the evil consequences of observing it in the given circumstances. If the badness of the consequences outweighs the duty, an exception to the rule is legitimate. Thus in the example of stealing, if the harm of having one's family starve is judged to be worse than stealing from a millionaire, it is right to steal.

Whichever of these two methods for determining legitimate exceptions to rules is used, a rule-utilitarian could fit it into his ethical system. Concerning the first method, he would say that there must be some *principle* by which the two conflicting rules are weighed against each other. This principle will be a *second-order moral rule,* according to which one first-order rule (say, to prevent harm) imposes a heavier obligation than another first-order rule (say, to tell the truth). *And the test for the validity of any second-order rule is the same as that of first-order rules, namely, its utility.* If the consequences of everyone's following a certain second-order rule, whenever two of the first order conflict, are better than everyone's following the opposite second-order rule in the same circumstances, then the former second-order rule is valid. With regard to the second method, the rule-utilitarian would say that reference to some *principle* is necessary in deciding whether the evil of the consequences in a given case is to count more heavily than the breaking of a rule. Here again the test for the validity of any such "weighing" principle is taken to be the utility of the general practice of everyone's using it whenever it is applicable. If the consequences of everyone's following it are better than the consequences of everyone's using some alternative principle, then it is a valid moral principle.

Since a rule-utilitarian could in this manner account for every case in which his position is apparently contradicted by act-utilitarianism, it would seem that the two theories are extensionally equivalent.

Nevertheless, there remain the "hard core" cases where rule-utilitarians want to deny what seem to them the erroneous views entailed by act-utilitarianism. Consider the case in which the driver of a car bribes a policeman not to give him a ticket for speeding. If this act is done in secret rather than openly, the policeman would not lose his job and the driver would not be brought into court (consequences that would occur if the act were to become known to the public). The rule-utilitarian would argue that this difference in the consequences of doing the act secretly and doing it openly does not affect the wrongness of the act, whereas an act-utilitarian would have to admit such a difference to be relevant. To take another case, if a teacher knowingly allows a student to cheat and ignores it, the rule-utilitarian would say that the student and the teacher are both doing wrong acts, and that it makes no difference whether anyone else finds out about it. The act-utilitarian, on the other hand, would have to admit that the consequences of people's finding out about the offenses in comparison with the consequences of their unawareness of them would be relevant to judging the moral wrongness of the deception.

These "hard core" cases are now a matter of controversy among utilitarians. They appear to show not only that act-and rule-utilitarianism are indeed incompatible, but also that act-utilitarianism (but not rule-utilitarianism) runs counter to most people's thoughtful, considered judgments about right and wrong actions. In response to this latter claim, some act-utilitarians have argued that such acts as bribery and cheating (when done successfully and in secret) are *not* morally permissible. They have tried to account for the *wrongness* of such acts within an act-utilitarian framework. The two most important arguments they give are the following.

(1) Such actions tend to corrupt the perpetrators, *especially* when they are done secretly so that those committing them escape social condemnation. Having "gotten away with" such an action, a person will be all the more tempted to do similar things in the future. Thus the probability will increase that he will harm someone (a harm that could have been avoided had he refrained from such actions in the past and so strengthened his moral character). In other words, the more frequently a person behaves in this way, the more vicious his character will become, *as judged by act-utilitarian standards*. When these effects on people's character are taken into account, then, it turns out that every particular act of bribery, cheating, and the like is wrong after all. When compared with the strengthening of character which results from a person's refraining from such acts (especially in situations where it is quite certain that he could "get away

with it" if he did it), the consequences of doing such actions are clearly of less utility than are the consequences of refraining from them.

(2) Such actions tend to break down people's trust in certain social institutions and practices that have great utility. Although offenses like bribery and cheating are done secretly, the more often they occur the more they weaken the social institutions and practices which they violate. Every act of bribing a law enforcement official undermines the justice of the legal system. Every act of cheating in academic matters erodes the integrity of the educational process. Thus the very foundations of law and of academic life are subverted, leading in turn to a loss of public confidence in the moral legitimacy of such institutions. Assuming that the legal and educational systems of a given society are not already working for bad ends, as judged by the principle of utility, the harmful results of the actions in question become clear. Therefore, concludes the act-utilitarian, contrary to what at first appears to be the case, these actions do have bad consequences and are accordingly wrong.

Whether these arguments are sufficient to show that act- and rule-utilitarianism are extensionally equivalent, and whether they provide a satisfactory account of what most people, on reflection, would consider to be the wrongness of such acts as bribery and cheating, are questions left for the reader to decide for himself.

UTILITY AND JUSTICE

Some contemporary philosophers claim that, whether or not act- and rule-utilitarianism are compatible with each other, *neither* theory is acceptable as a normative ethical system. In the present section the reasoning behind this rejection of both forms of utilitarianism is examined. Afterwards, in the last section of the chapter, we shall consider a philosophical defense of utilitarianism.

The objection raised against both forms of utilitarian ethics is that *the principle of utility does not provide a sufficient ground for the obligations of justice.* Since the idea of justice is a fundamental moral concept, no normative ethical system can be considered adequate that does not show the basis for our duty to be just. The argument starts with a careful examination of the ultimate norm of utilitarian ethics, the principle of utility itself. Exactly what is utility? It has been described in the words, "the maximizing of intrinsic value and the minimizing of intrinsic disvalue." What, precisely, does this mean?

It will be helpful in answering this question to think of measurable units of intrinsic value and disvalue. We shall accordingly speak of units of happiness and unhappiness, giving plus and minus signs to happiness and unhappiness, respectively. This will enable us to see the difficulty more clearly, although no particular view of what is to be taken as the measurement of a unit of happiness or unhappiness will be presupposed. We all know in general what it means to be very happy, quite happy, not especially happy, rather unhappy, and extremely unhappy. Thus the idea of degrees of happiness corresponds to something in our experience. We also know what it means to be happy for a brief moment, or for a day, and we use such phrases as "It was a happy two-week vacation," "I was not very happy during my early teens," and "He has led an unhappy life." There is some basis, therefore, in our everyday concept of happiness (and also of pleasure) for giving meaning to the idea of quantities or amounts of happiness, even though we do not ordinarily measure these quantities in arithmetical terms.

What, then does the utilitarian mean by maximizing intrinsic value and minimizing intrinsic disvalue? There are three variables or factors that must be introduced in order to make this idea clear. First, it means to bring about, in the case of *one* person, the greatest balance of value over disvalue. Thus if one act or rule yields +1000 units of happiness and −500 units of unhappiness for a given person, while another act or rule yields +700 units and −100 units for that person, then, all other factors being equal, the second alternative is better than the first, since the balance of the second (+600) is greater than the balance of the first (+500). Similarly, to "minimize disvalue" would mean that an act or rule which yielded +100 and −300 for a given person would be better than one that yielded +500 and −1000 for the same person, other things being equal (even though more happiness is produced by the second than by the first).

The second factor is that the happiness and unhappiness of *all persons* affected must be considered. Thus if four persons, A, B, C, and D, each experiences some difference of happiness or unhappiness in his life as a consequence of the act or rule but no difference occurs in the lives of anyone else, then the calculation of maximum value and minimum disvalue must include the balance of pluses and minuses occurring in the experience of every one of the four persons. Suppose in one case the balance is +300 for A, +200 for B, −300 for C, and −400 for D. And suppose the alternative yields +200 for A, +100 for B, −400 for C, and +500 for D. Then if someone were to claim that the first is better than the second because D's happiness or unhappiness does not count (D, for example, might be a slave while A, B, and C are free men), this conclusion would not be acceptable to utilitarians. For them, the second alternative is better than the first because the second yields a higher total balance than the first when *all* persons are considered.

The third factor in the utilitarian calculus has been tacitly assumed in the foregoing discussion of the second factor. This is the principle that, in calculating the units of happiness or unhappiness for different persons, the same criteria for measuring quantity are used. If totals of $+500$ and -200 represent sums of happiness and unhappiness in the experience of A and $+300$ and -400 represent sums of happiness and unhappiness in the experience of B, then one unit of plus (or minus) for A must be equal to one unit of plus (or minus) for B. No differences between A and B are to be considered as grounds for assigning a different weight to one or the other's happiness or unhappiness. When utilitarians assert that everyone's happiness is to count *equally*, they mean that, in calculating consequences, it is irrelevant *whose* happiness or unhappiness is affected by the act or rule. This may be called the principle of the equality of worth of every person as a person. (It does not mean, of course, that everyone is just as morally good or bad as everyone else!)

Now when these three factors are used in calculating utility, it is still possible for some persons to be unfairly or unjustly treated. For the greatest total balance of pluses over minuses may be brought about in a given society by actions or rules which discriminate against certain persons on irrelevant grounds. Although a greater quantity of happiness and a lesser amount of unhappiness are produced, they are distributed unjustly among the persons affected. To illustrate this possibility, consider two societies, one of which distributes different amounts of happiness to people on the basis of their race or religion, the other dispensing them on the basis of people's different needs, abilities, and merits, where "merits" are determined by contributions to the common good or general happiness. In the first society, people belonging to one race or religion are favored in educational opportunities, comfortable housing, and high-paying jobs, while people of another race or religion are disfavored. Race and religion function in that society as grounds for discrimination. In the second society, on the other hand, race or religion do not matter as far as education, housing, and jobs are concerned. All that counts are such things as, Does the individual have a need for special treatment, a need which, if overlooked, would unfairly handicap him in matters of education, housing, or jobs? (For example, a blind person might be given special schooling and a special job, so that his blindness will not mean that he has less of a chance for happiness in life than others.) Or, has the individual, through fair and open competition, proven himself qualified for a high-paying job? Or, does he have exceptional abilities — such as musical genius or mathematical brilliance — which deserve the society's recognition, so that advanced education and scholarships are made available to him? Here race and religion do not function as grounds for discrimination, since they are not considered in determining the proper distribution of happiness and unhappiness throughout the population.

The problem of utility and justice arises when it is seen that, in the two societies described above, it is possible for the first to produce a greater total net balance of happiness over unhappiness than the second. Thus suppose the first society can force the members of the disfavored race or religion to work long hours for little or no pay, so that they produce much more and use up much less of what is produced than they would without such coercion. Then, even if the calculation of utility includes the unhappiness of the disadvantaged, the total balance of happiness over unhappiness could be greater than that resulting from the second society's system of production and consumption. A utilitarian, it seems, would have to say in that case that the first society was morally better than the second, since its policies and rules yielded a higher net utility. Yet the first society, if not simply and self-evidently unjust, would at least be considered (even by utilitarians) to be less just than the second. Hence, utility and justice are incompatible when applied to certain types of societies under certain conditions.

Such conflicts between utility and justice can occur because, as far as utility alone is concerned, it is always morally right to increase one person's happiness at the expense of another's, if the total net balance of pluses over minuses is greater than would be the case were the two persons treated equally. It would seem, in contrast to this, that justice requires that no individual serve as a mere instrument or means to someone else's happiness. (If a person freely consents to sacrifice his happiness for the sake of another, he is not, of course, being used merely as a means to someone else's ends.) On this point the opposition between justice and utility appears to be fundamental.

It should be noted in this connection that utility not only permits but actually requires one individual's being made unhappy if doing so adds to a group's happiness, *however small an increase in happiness might be exper-ienced by each of its members,* as long as the total amount of happiness to the group outweighs the unhappiness of the individual in question. Thus suppose an innocent man is made a scapegoat for the guilt of others and accordingly suffers punishment. If he experiences, say, −100 units of unhappiness and if there are 101 persons who, in victimizing him, gain +1 unit of happiness each (perhaps in relief at seeing another blamed for their own wrongdoing), then the principle of utility *requires* that the scapegoat be punished. This is not because the scapegoat's unhappiness is being ignored or is being assigned less intrinsic worth than the happiness of others. Each unit of unhappiness (−1) experienced by the scapegoat is equal in "weight" to a unit of happiness (+1) of someone in the group. It just happens that in the given situation the total quantity of the group's happiness is greater than that of the scapegoat's unhappiness. Consequently the principle of utility, when applied to this situation, entails that the scapegoat be made to suffer.

It is in this way that the idea of justice seems to present a major philosophical difficulty for all forms of utilitarianism. How might utilitarians reply to this criticism? They would begin by pointing out that, when we leave abstract speculations about theoretical possibilities behind and face the actual world around us, we find that any conflict between justice and utility is highly unlikely. The apparent plausibility of the cases given above, they would say, depends on their being abstracted from the real processes of historical and social development. They hold that when these processes are fully taken into account, it becomes clear that injustice inevitably yields great disutility.

In support of this claim, utilitarians ask us to consider how the principle of utility would apply to situations of social conflict, where one person's (or group's) interests can be furthered only if another person's (or group's) interests are frustrated. For this is where the concepts of justice and injustice are applicable. Now with regard to such situations, the principle of utility requires social rules which enable people to resolve their disagreements and live in harmony with one another. To live in harmony means, not that no social conflicts occur, but that whenever they do occur, there is a set of rules everyone can appeal to as a fair way to resolve them. Such rules will (a) take everyone's interests into account, (b) give equal consideration to the interests of each person, and (c) enable all parties to a dispute to decide issues on grounds freely acceptable by all. For it is only when everyone can appeal to such a system of conflict-resolving rules that the society as a whole can achieve its maximum happiness and minimum unhappiness.

This can be seen by referring to the condition of anyone who does *not* accept a set of conflict-resolving rules as fair. Such a person will simply consider himself to be under social coercion with respect to those rules. That is, he will conform to the rules only because he is forced to by society. If his interests are frustrated by their operation, he will believe he has legitimate moral complaints against the rest of society, and will then think any action necessary to right the wrongs carried out in the name of the rules to be justified. The greater the number of such disaffected persons, the deeper will be the state of social disharmony. It is obvious that very little happiness can be realized in such a society.

At this point the following objection might be raised. To make sure that social conflict will not get out of hand, let those who accept the rules establish a power structure which will ensure their domination over those who reject them. In this way, although some (the powerless) may suffer, those in power can maximize their happiness. To this the utilitarian replies, History has shown us that no such power structure can last for long; even while it does last, the effort spent by the "ins" on maintaining domination over the "outs" makes it impossible for the "ins" to obtain much happiness in life. A social system of this kind is constantly liable to break down. The need to preserve their position of power drives the "ins" to ever greater measures of surveillance and repression. The society as a whole becomes a closed system in which the freedom of all individuals is diminished. Accompanying this curtailment of human freedom is a dwindling in the very conception of man and his creative powers. Inevitably, there develops an intolerance of diversity in thought, in speech, in styles of life. A narrow conformity of taste, ideas, and outward behavior becomes the main concern of everyone. What kind of "happiness" is this? What amount of intrinsic value does such a narrow way of life really make possible for people, even people who have the power to advance their interests at the expense of others?

The upshot of the argument is now apparent: Given a clearheaded view of the world as it is and a realistic understanding of man's nature, it becomes more and more evident that injustice will never have, in the long run, greater utility than justice. Even if the two principles of justice and utility can logically be separated in the abstract and even if they can be shown to yield contradictory results in hypothetical cases, it does not follow that the fundamental idea of utilitarianism must be given up. For it remains the case that, when we are dealing with the actual practices of people in their social and historical settings, to maximize happiness and minimize unhappiness requires an open, freely given commitment on the part of *everyone* to comply with the rules for settling conflicts among them. Anyone who is coerced into following the rules when he, in good conscience, cannot accept them as being fair to everyone (and consequently to himself) will not consider himself morally obligated to abide by them. Since he will either feel unjustly treated himself or see himself as a participant in the unfair treatment of others, society stands condemned in his judgment. From his point of view, he will have good reason to do what he can to change or abolish the rules. He will join with anyone else who rejects them as unfair, in an effort to overcome his powerlessness. Thus injustice becomes, in actual practice, a source of great social disutility. If society's reaction to the challenge of its dissidents is only a stronger attempt to impose its rules by force, this response will, sooner or later, bring about a situation in which no one really benefits. Not only is it profoundly true that "might does not make right," it is equally true that might cannot create the maximum balance of human happiness over human misery, when the lives of everyone are taken into account.

Whether this argument provides a successful rebuttal to the criticism of utilitarianism when viewed in the light of justice is a matter for the reader's own reflection. Further investigation into the concept of justice will be undertaken in the next chapter, where a deontological ethical theory is presented. As a contrast with utilitarianism, it offers a radically different way of conceiving of, and justifying, moral rules.

A DEFENSE OF UTILITARIANISM

Despite the difficulties raised in connection with the relation between justice and utility, it is appropriate to end the present chapter with a general defense of this ethical theory which a great many philosophers have found attractive. Utilitarianism is the only theory, its proponents claim, that makes good sense when we ask ourselves, What, after all, is the whole point of morality, *including* the rules of justice? Even if the rules of justice cannot be derived from utility taken strictly as a happiness maximizing principle, nevertheless there would be no point (that is, no intelligible purpose) in having moral norms guide people's conduct unless they contributed ultimately to human happiness. For the rules of morality, including those of justice, restrict individuals' actions. These limitations need to be justified, and it is only by appealing to the principle of utility that, in the last analysis, they *can* be justified. Why is this so? The utilitarians' answer to this question, which is aimed at showing the rationality of utilitarian ethics as a whole, may be summed up as follows.

The first step in their reasoning is offered in support of the proposition: No limitation on human freedom is justified unless it serves a good purpose.

This is true, they argue, because a curb on one's freedom of choice and action is never desired for its own sake (or valued as an end in itself) by the person so limited. Consequently, if society is to impose rules which require people to refrain from actions they might want to do (either as means to an end or as ends in themselves), or which prescribe that a person must do something which, independently of that prescription, he would not choose to do, there must be some consequence thereby brought about whose goodness outweighs the intrinsic badness of these restrictions themselves.

The next step is to imagine what would be missing in human life were no such bounds placed on people's freedom of action. Here the utilitarian argues that in such a situation the amenities of social existence would be impossible. All the benefits obtained from the advancement of the arts and sciences as well as from the production and maintenance of a high economic standard of living could not be achieved without some restrictions on human freedom. Thus moral rules, from this point of view, may be conceived as devices invented by men to ensure the carrying on of civilized life. They are not good as ends in themselves, but only as necessary means for realizing those conditions of social existence which make civilization possible. Their "reason for being" lies in their social function, and as long as they bring about more benefits to people than would occur in their absence, they are justified.

This argument so far appeals to the principle of utility as the rational ground of morality. If someone were to challenge this appeal, the utilitarian would reply (as the third step in his argument), "How else can we justify rules of conduct other than by showing the *purpose* for which rational beings would use them as guides to their conduct? Furthermore, if this purpose were anything other than the promotion of their happiness, could we consider such beings rational? The principle of utility, in short, is built into the very conception of a rational ground for rules of conduct."

This argument can be put even more succinctly in terms of intrinsic and instrumental value. If any restrictions on human freedom are intrinsically disvaluable (that is, unwanted in themselves), then they can only be justified by showing that they have instrumental value to something that has intrinsic value. More specifically, the restrictions placed upon human conduct by moral rules are unjustified unless they can be shown to bring about a greater amount of happiness or pleasure than would be possible without them. It would be a paradigm of irrationality for a society not to use utility as its basic moral principle, for if it used any other it would be imposing something intrinsically bad on people (restrictions on their freedom) without a compensating intrinsic good (the maximum happiness possible for everyone). Thus utilitarianism is simply that normative ethical system which satisfies, in the most rational manner possible, the need for justifying a society's moral code to those who live under it.

Suggested Reading

Basic writings of the classical utilitarians:

David Hume, *An Inquiry Concerning the Principles of Morals.* 1751.
Jeremy Bentham, *An Introduction to the Principles of Morals and Legislation.* 1789.
John Stuart Mill, *Utilitarianism.* 1863.
Henry Sidgwick, *The Methods of Ethics.* 1874.
George Edward Moore, *Principia Ethica.* 1903.
———, *Ethics.* 1912.

Each of the following volumes contains a wide selection of writings on utilitarian ethics, both pro and con:

Bayles, Michael D., ed., *Contemporary Utilitarianism.* New York: Anchor Books, Doubleday and Co., 1968.* Includes ten articles by contemporary philosophers discussing various aspects of utilitarianism from different, and sometimes opposing, points of view.
Brody, Baruch A., ed., *Moral Rules and Particular Circumstances.* Englewood Cliffs, N. J.: Prentice-Hall, Inc., 1970.* Includes antiutilitarian writings of Immanuel Kant and Sir David Ross, as well as a selection from Sidgwick's *Methods of Ethics* and four articles by contemporary writers.
Gorovitz, Samuel, ed., *Mill: Utilitarianism, Text and Critical Essays.* Indianapolis: The Bobbs-Merrill Co., Inc., 1971.* Includes the entire text of Mill's *Utilitarianism,* a selection from Mill's *System of Logic,* and twenty-eight articles. There is also an extensive bibliography on utilitarianism.
Hearn, Thomas K., Jr., ed., *Studies in Utilitarianism.* New York: Appleton-Century-Crofts, 1971. Includes a selection from Bentham's *Introduction to the Principles of Morals and Legislation,* the entire text of Mill's *Utilitarianism,* selections from Moore's *Principia Ethica,* and seven articles by contemporary writers.

*Available in paperback

Smith, James M. and Ernest Sosa, eds., *Mill's Utilitarianism: Text and Criticism.*
    Belmont, California: Wadsworth Publishing Co., Inc., 1969.* Includes a selec-
    tion from Bentham's *Introduction to the Principles of Morals and Legislation,*
    the entire text of Mill's *Utilitarianism,* a selection from his *System of Logic,* a
    selection from his *Remarks on Bentham's Moral Philosophy,* and seven articles
    by contemporary writers.

A clear, complete, and well-argued presentation of a utilitarian ethical system:

Narveson, Jan, *Morality and Utility.* Baltimore: The Johns Hopkins Press, 1967.

The first half of the following book contains a well-known defense of act-utilitarianism, by Professor J. J. C. Smart. The second half consists of arguments against
utilitarianism, by Professor Bernard Williams:

Smart, J. J. C. and Bernard Williams, *Utilitarianism: For and Against.* Cambridge:
    Cambridge University Press, 1973.*

Other recommended books which explore and critically assess utilitarian ethics:

Hodgson, D. H., *Consequences of Utilitarianism: A Study in Normative Ethics and
    Legal Theory.* London: Oxford University Press, 1967.
Lyons, David, *Forms and Limits of Utilitarianism.* London: Oxford University Press,
    1965.
Norman, Richard, *Reasons for Actions: A Critique of Utilitarian Rationality.*
    Oxford: Basil Blackwell, 1971.
Quinton, Anthony, *Utilitarian Ethics.* New York: St. Martin's Press, 1973.*
Rawls, John, *A Theory of Justice.* Cambridge, Mass.: Harvard University Press,
    1971.*
Rescher, Nicholas, *Distributive Justive: A Constructive Critique of the Utilitarian
    Theory of Distribution.* Indianapolis: The Bobbs-Merrill Co., Inc., 1966.* This
    book contains a detailed bibliography on utilitarianism.
Singer, Marcus George, *Generalization in Ethics: An Essay in the Logic of Ethics,
    with the Rudiments of a System of Moral Philosophy.* New York: Atheneum
    Press, 1971.*
Toulmin, Stephen Edelston, *An Examination of the Place of Reason in Ethics.*
    Cambridge: Cambridge University Press, 1950.*

*Available in paperback

V

Ethical Formalism

TELEOLOGICAL AND DEONTOLOGICAL ETHICS

At the beginning of Chapter Four, a distinction was made between two types of normative ethical systems: teleological and deontological. The difference between them lies in how each answers the question, What makes right actions right? If the answer is either "An action is right insofar as it has good consequences" or "An action is right if it conforms to a set of rules which, when generally followed, have good consequences," then the ethical system is teleological. The moral rightness of either a particular action or a type of action is based on its instrumental value as a means to an end, this end being judged to have value in itself. If, on the other hand, the reply is "An action is right when it conforms to a rule of conduct which meets the requirements of a supreme principle of duty, this principle of duty *not* being itself a matter of the production of good consequences," then the system is deontological. The moral rightness of an action does not consist in its being instrumental (directly or indirectly) to the realization of a good end, but in its being a kind of action which the Moral Law requires all agents to perform as a matter of principle.

Since this chapter is mainly concerned with the logical construction and defense of a deontological ethical system, it will be helpful to examine more closely how such a system differs from a teleological one. A fresh example will serve to bring out this difference.

Suppose a person tells a slanderous lie about someone he dislikes, thereby causing the one he slanders to lose his job. Here it is easily possible to distinguish between a type of action and a consequence of an action. The type of action is "telling a slanderous lie." A consequence of the action is "someone loses his job." Note that the action's consequence, in this case, is not part of the concept of the action's type, since we can identify an action as being of the type "slanderous lying" without knowing that the action brings about the loss of a job. According to a teleological ethical system, an action cannot be known to be right (or wrong) merely by understanding it as being of a certain type. It is necessary to know either what consequences result when people generally perform actions of that type, or what consequences result from a particular act of that type performed at a particular time. If the consequences are bad (as judged by a standard of intrinsic value or, secondarily, of instrumental value), the action is wrong. If the consequences are good, the action is right. When both beneficial and harmful consequences result, the action is right if its consequences are better than those any alternative action would have produced in the given situation: otherwise it is wrong.

It can be seen from these considerations that the *primary* norm of a teleological ethical system is a standard of intrinsic value which is used in judging whether, and to what degree, the consequences of actions are good or bad. It is called a standard of intrinsic value because it defines what is good "in itself," that is, something which is desirable or worthwhile as an end and not merely useful as a means to a further end. (In the next chapter the idea of intrinsic value will be examined in detail.) In a teleological system, then, unless we apply a standard of intrinsic value to the consequences either of a particular act or of an action-type, we cannot tell whether it is right or wrong.

From the standpoint of a deontological ethical system, on the other hand, once we know what moral rules to apply to action-types and also know that a particular act exemplifies an action-type that falls under a rule, we can tell whether the act in question is right or wrong, independently of our knowing whether its consequences are good or bad, or indeed, independently of our knowing *anything* about its consequences. Given a description of the act as being of a certain type (say, the telling of a slanderous lie), we determine whether that action-type conforms to or violates a moral rule which correctly applies to it. If (and only if) it conforms to the rule, the act is right; if (and only if) it violates the rule, it is wrong.

Of all the possible rules of conduct that could be applied to a given action-type, which ones are *moral* rules? The deontologist answers, those that satisfy the conditions stated in the Moral Law as the ultimate ground of all moral obligation or duty. Thus the *primary* norm of a deontological

ethical system is the Moral Law. It is this ultimate principle which determines what specific rules of conduct impose a moral duty on everyone to
comply with them. Consideration will shortly be given to what such an
ultimate principle of morality does state as the necessary and sufficient
conditions for a rule of conduct to be a valid moral rule. At this juncture we
simply note that, in contrast to a teleological system of ethics, the tendency
of an action-type to bring about good (or bad) consequences is neither
necessary nor sufficient, in deontological ethics, for an act of that type to be
morally right (or wrong).

The last chapter dealt with what has come to be considered the most
important teleological ethical system, utilitarianism. This chapter will be
concerned with the most famous system of deontological ethics, the ethical
formalism of the German philosopher, Immanuel Kant (1724-1804). Kant
has had a profound influence on contemporary moral philosophy, and some
of the current ideas in ethical theory that stem from Kantian thought will be
explored. The reason why Kant's ethical system is called "formalism" will
soon become clear, when the ultimate principle of his deontological system
is discussed.

Kant's main writings on ethics (in their translated English titles) are:

Lectures on Ethics (Kant's lectures at the University of Königsberg, given during the
years 1775-1780.)
Fundamental Principles of the Metaphysics of Morals (1785) (This book is sometimes
    titled: *Groundwork*, or *Foundations, of the Metaphysic of Morals.*)
Critique of Practical Reason (1788)
Religion within the Limits of Reason Alone (1793)
The Metaphysics of Morals (1797)
    PART I: *The Metaphysical Elements of Justice* (Also titled: *The Doctrine of
    Law,* or *The Science of Right.*)
    PART II: *The Metaphysical Principles of Virtue* (Also titled: *The Doctrine of
    Virtue.*)

The one book which offers the best introductory account of Kant's ethical
ideas is the second one on this list. Its original title is *Grundlegung zur
Metaphysik der Sitten,* and it is judged by many philosophers to be among
the half-dozen greatest works written in the history of ethics. An analysis of
the basic argument of the book will be given here. Someone wishing to read
the book may find it helpful, and it will provide a convenient way of
presenting the essential ideas of Kant's ethical theory for further investigation in this chapter.

THE ETHICS OF IMMANUEL KANT

Kant's *Fundamental Principles of the Metaphysics of Morals* is divided into a Preface and three Chapters or Sections. In the Preface, Kant states his overall purpose. This is to show that, in his own words, "the basis of obligation must not be sought in the nature of man, or in the circumstances in the world in which he is placed, but *a priori* simply in the conceptions of pure reason." Kant believes that what he calls "the metaphysics of morals," which is that branch of ethics whose task is to establish the ultimate criterion (that is, the necessary and sufficient conditions) for the validity of moral rules, must be "pure." By this he means it must show how the ultimate criterion can be established *a priori,* entirely free of empirical considerations. Once this criterion is shown to be grounded on pure reason, its application to particular rules and actions may require the use of empirical knowledge about man and his situation in the actual world.

In the First Section, Kant analyzes what he takes to be the key concept of morality, which he calls "the good will." This is the key concept because without it Kant does not think we can even understand what the terms "right conduct" and "moral duty" mean, to say nothing of knowing what specific conduct is right or what our moral duty is. Kant's analysis of the concept of the good will is to be found in his "three propositions of morality." The first proposition describes what kind of motive or reason for acting an individual must have to be properly called a morally good person, or as Kant puts it, a person of good will. The main point here is that the motive must be entirely separate from (though not necessarily antagonistic to) the individual's inclinations and self-interest. The person of good will not only acts in accordance with duty, he acts for the sake of duty. This means that his sole motive for doing what is right is his recognition of the fact that it is the right thing to do. He does what is right just because it is right, and for no other reason. If a person does what is right simply because he likes doing that kind of act (that is, because his inclinations lead him in that direction) or because doing it serves his self-interest, there is nothing morally admirable about him. Having a good will, therefore, is a necessary condition for being a good person. Kant also argues that it is a sufficient condition. Even if an individual were unable to carry out what duty required of him, he must be judged, from the moral point of view, to be a good person as long as he "summoned all the means in his power" to do his duty. This is not to say that having good intentions is enough to be a good person. One must not only have good intentions (which for Kant means that one seeks to do one's duty for duty's sake), but must also strive with all one's will-power and determination to perform the act which is one's duty.

The second proposition of morality concerns the moral worth or value of the good will. Here Kant is asking, What must be the basis of its value if its presence alone is sufficient for judging a person to be morally good? His answer is that because the good will has such unconditional worth, its value cannot depend on the bringing about of any ends or purposes. For in that case it would be judged merely as a means, and its value would be conditional upon the achievement of ends as well as upon their worth. But since its value is unconditional, it must derive its value solely from the *principle* which it exemplifies. At this point Kant does not tell us what this principle is.

The third proposition of morality describes the inner attitude that governs a person's state of mind when he is motivated by a good will. The attitude is not that of kindliness, benevolence, or love. (This, it should be noted, distinguishes Kant's concept of the good will from the popular view found in such common expressions as "men of good will.") For these have to do with a person's inclinations, not with the pure will to do one's duty. The latter is the motive to perform an action as a matter of principle, regardless of one's inclinations (that is, regardless of whether one likes, enjoys, or wants to do it). The predominant attitude of the person of good will must be appropriate to the motive to do his duty for its own sake. Such an attitude, Kant believes, can only be a deep sense of the binding obligation to obey the Moral Law, which he calls "respect for the moral law." Thus if we wish to have an explanation of why the person of good will acts as he does, the explanation will simply be that he acts out of respect for the Moral Law.

Throughout this discussion of the good will Kant has not told us what our duty actually is. He has not yet answered the question, How do we know what acts are right? This will be the main subject of the Second Section of his book. However, at the end of the First Section he makes a transition from the concept of the good will to the concept of right action, paving the way for the argument of the Second Section. It is clear from Kant's idea of the good will that, whatever may be the standard of right action, that standard cannot be the utility of the action in producing certain results (as an act-utilitarian would claim). The only other possibility is to make the standard a matter of the conformity of an action to a rule or principle. Our next question is, What conditions must be satisfied by a rule if it is to be a valid moral rule, that is, if it is to be binding upon all mankind as a moral duty? Again, we cannot appeal to the consequences of following the rule (as a rule-utilitarian would do), since this would make the ground of duty empirical, which it cannot be if duty is to be recognized as binding upon one's will regardless of ends, consequences, and inclinations. So we are left with the claim that, to be valid, a rule must pass the test of the supreme principle or ultimate criterion of morality which is, for Kant, an *a priori* Moral Law. He calls this Law "the categorical imperative." It is this principle which a person consciously or unconsciously recognizes when he acknowledges an act to be his moral duty. Kant now argues that if the Moral Law operates in this way, binding the will of an individual independently of his inclinations and purposes, it must be of a certain sort. It cannot demand that any *particular* ends be brought about, so it can only demand that the individual act on a "maxim" or principle which he, as a rational being, could prescribe as a rule for every other person to act on. Kant sums this up in the following statement, the full meaning of which he intends to explain in the Second Section: "I ought never to act except in such a way *that I can also will that my maxim should become a universal law.*"

The Second Section opens with a reiteration of the idea that the ultimate principle of morality must be grounded *a priori* if it is to have that necessity and universality which it must have for the person of good will to recognize it as the ground of his duty and so be motivated by pure respect for the Moral Law. In Kant's terms, the Moral Law must be "apodictic," that is, universal (applying to everyone without exception) and necessary (not contingent upon the nature of the world).

He then begins a careful analysis of the conditions that any rule of conduct must satisfy if it is to be considered a moral rule — a rule validly binding upon all mankind and binding upon them in the way he has described in the First Section. These conditions are as follows:

For a rule to be a moral rule, it must prescribe to us categorically, not hypothetically. Reason: A moral rule prescribes what we ought to do without reference to any purposes or consequences, as was shown in the First Section. Now a hypothetical prescription (or "imperative") only tells us what we ought to do if we want to bring about certain ends. If we did not seek those ends, it would lose its prescriptive force. But a moral rule never depends for its prescriptive force upon what ends a person seeks. Therefore it must prescribe to us independently of our ends, that is, categorically.

In this way Kant has explained what a categorical imperative is; he has given a definition of the term "categorical imperative." But he must now tell us how this ultimate test of a moral rule is to be applied, so that we can know whether a rule does or does not satisfy its conditions. Otherwise we would be left in the dark about what the categorical imperative commands us to do. So Kant proceeds to give us three formulations of the categorical imperative, which he believes are simply different ways of saying the same thing. Each formulation, however, throws a new light on morality and brings out a new aspect of its supreme principle. Although the fundamental nature of moral duty remains the same, each formulation in its own way sets forth the conditions that must be fulfilled by a rule of conduct if it is to be a moral rule.

First Formulation: For a rule to be a moral rule, it must be consistently universalizable. Reason: The ground of moral duty rests on no empirical conditions, for if it did, it could not be the object of respect by the good man and could not motivate him independently of all his inclinations and purposes. Now if the reason for acting in accordance with a rule or "maxim" was anything but the fact that the rule could become a universal law, empirical conditions would be placed upon the ultimate test for a moral rule and the rule would thereby lose its *a priori* necessity and universality. Therefore, only the one condition, that the rule can become a universal law, is sufficient as the ground of its moral validity. And this condition simply means that the rule can be prescribed as a guide to everyone's conduct (that is, it is universalizable) without involving a self-contradiction.

Second Formulation: For a rule to be a moral rule, it must be such that, if all men were to follow it, they would treat each other as ends in themselves, never as means only. Reason: A moral rule is binding upon a person as a rational being. A rational being would always treat every other rational being the same way he would treat himself, for if he did not he would be inconsistent and this is contrary to the nature of a rational being. But each rational being recognizes himself as having an absolute worth as an end, and not merely a relative worth depending on some end for which he can be used as a means. Therefore, no rule of conduct universally prescribing to all persons *as* rational beings can prescribe action by which one treats another merely as a means.

Third Formulation: For a rule to be a moral rule, it must be capable of being self-imposed by the will of each person when he is universally legislating (that is, when he is deciding to adopt rules for the guidance of his own and others' conduct). Reason: If a rule of conduct were imposed upon a person by someone else's will (for example, by the will of the State, by one's parents' will, or by God's will), it could not be a moral rule unless it was recognized by the person himself as validly binding upon him. Absence of such recognition would mean that he sees himself as being coerced or forced to obey the rule, not as being under an obligation to act in accordance with it. Now to see himself as being under an obligation to act in accordance with the rule, when he is *not* coerced to obey it, is to recognize the rule as validly binding upon him. He thus sees that it is his own will — not anyone else's — which is the source of his obligation to follow it. In other words, he sees that he is prescribing the rule to himself. Now this rule binds him as a rational being, not as an individual with a unique personality. But if it binds him as a rational being, it binds everyone else as a rational being (again disregarding their individual personalities). Thus in prescribing the rule to himself, he is prescribing it to everyone. By imposing upon himself an obligation to follow it, he imposes the same obligation upon all others. A moral rule, then, is a rule that is self-imposed by a universally legislating will.

The concept of a will that is a universal legislator and is the source of the very rules of conduct that bind a person regardless of his inclinations and ends is given the name "the autonomy of the will" by Kant. This concept becomes of central importance in the Third Section of the book, but Kant also uses it in the Second Section as the basis for his view of the moral community of mankind. This moral community, which he calls "the kingdom of ends," may be briefly explained as follows.

If all men were to prescribe rules binding upon themselves, each would be a sovereign because he would be the creator of the rules, and each would be a subject because he would be under an obligation to obey the rules. Furthermore, what would be a duty for one member of such a rule-governed community would be a duty for everyone else, since the same rules would prescribe to everyone equally. No one would be exempt from the obligation to obey, and no one would have rules imposed upon him against his (rational) will. Each would therefore have the same worth as a person. There would be no inferiors or superiors. No individual and no group would have special privileges, that is, privileges not granted to everyone alike. No one would be permitted to use another merely as a means to his own ends, since no one would be willing to set up a rule allowing others to use *him* merely as a means to *their* ends. In such a community of rational beings, the autonomy of the will is the ground of individual worth. This is Kant's vision of the community of all moral agents, a community that includes everyone whose conduct falls within the scope of the Moral Law.

It should be noted that this "kingdom of ends" is not to be identified with any existing society's system of law or with any moral code actually accepted by a given society. Nor is it merely a possible utopian ideal that may or may not be realized in some future time. It is rather a way of looking at the moral order which, in the past and in the future as well as here and now, unites all human beings together under one set of binding rules. For according to Kant, we are all members of this moral community by virtue of two facts about ourselves: first, we each *have the capacity to act for moral reasons* (that is, each of us is a moral agent); and second, we are each *the authors or legislators of the Moral Law* (that is, each of us lays down that Law as a normative principle for all moral agents to follow).

Let us now turn to the Third Section of the book. Here Kant is giving his proof that there is a Moral Law, whose nature he has been analyzing in the First and Second Sections. Up to this point he has explained what kinds of rules must be binding upon men, and in what manner they must be binding, if there is such a thing as morality at all. He now sets himself the task of showing that morality is a fact, that the categorical imperative does impose a valid obligation upon all rational beings, including all men. There are three basic steps in his argument. The first is given in the opening subsection, titled "The Concept of Freedom Is the Key That Explains the Autonomy of the Will." Here Kant argues that *if* men have freedom of the will *then* they must be obligated to obey the categorical imperative. The argument consists in showing that freedom of the will is nothing but the autonomy of the will ("the property of the will to be a law to itself"), and that the autonomy of the will, as has been shown in the Second Section, is another way of expressing the principle of the categorical imperative. Therefore, Kant concludes, "a free will and a will subject to moral laws are one and the same." So, *if* men are free, they are bound by moral rules. He must next show that men are in fact free.

In the second step of the argument, contained in the subsection titled "Freedom Must Be Presupposed as a Property of the Will of all Rational Beings," he argues that anyone is really free who can act only under "the idea of freedom," that is, who must *conceive of himself* as being free when he is using his practical reason in deliberating about what he ought to do. Now all rational beings are like this, because in reasoning about what they ought to do they identify whatever reasons or "judgments" they have for or against doing one thing rather than another as *reasons of their own,* not as coming from others. This is what Kant means by saying that the practical reason "must regard itself as the author of its principles independent of foreign influences." Consequently, all rational beings, and hence all men, must think of themselves as being free when they deliberate about actions open to their choice, and if they must think of themselves as free, they are free (as far as moral choice is concerned).

This two-step argument may be summed up as follows, placing the second step first:

(1) All rational beings must conceive of themselves as free.
(2) If any being must conceive of himself as free, he is free, from the practical point of view.

(3) Therefore, all rational beings (and hence all men) are free, from the practical point of view.

Next comes the first step of Kant's argument, consisting of statements (4), (5), and (6):

(4) To be free is to have autonomy of the will.
(5) The autonomy of the will is one way of expressing the principle of the categorical imperative.

(6) Therefore, to be free is to be subject to the categorical imperative.

Using these two steps, Kant derives his conclusion in the following way:

(7) All men are free, from the practical point of view. [By (3).]

(8) Therefore, all men are, from the practical point of view, subject to the categorical imperative. [By (6).]

It should be noted that Kant always qualifies his assertion that men are free by the phrase "from the practical point of view." He does this for the following reasons. Although men *may* be mistaken in conceiving of themselves as free, nevertheless they must think of themselves in this way in their practical life. Moreover, our reason cannot *show* that we are mistaken in believing ourselves to be free. It is true that we are unable to give either an empirical or an *a priori* argument to guarantee our freedom, but neither can it be established by argument that we are not free. We are therefore justified in regarding ourselves as free agents because in the conduct of our lives we cannot help conceiving of ourselves this way and we have no reason to deny our freedom.

Kant then proceeds to show how the nature of man must be understood if he is to be seen as free "from the practical point of view." This is the third step of the argument. It is Kant's attempt to account for the freedom of the will in a world which can be known in terms of cause and effect. (In Chapter Seven we shall consider this problem in greater detail.) The solution Kant offers is that we can take two standpoints in viewing human conduct and human reasoning. We can take the scientific or psychological point of view, or we can take the moral or practical point of view. From the first standpoint, we try to understand the causes of behavior and of thought. We are interested in explaining why a person does what he does and thinks as he thinks. We see how his action and thought fit into the order of the empirical world of nature. In Kant's terms, we understand man as a member of the phenomenal world, the world we come to know through our senses. From the other standpoint, however, we see human conduct and thought in a different light. When we take this standpoint we are not interested in causal explanation. Instead, we are asking, What ought a person to do, and why? We shift from facts to values, from "is" to "ought." We adopt this second point of view whenever we carry on moral discourse by making moral judgments, justifying them, and prescribing conduct to ourselves and others. It is within this framework that man is conceived to be a free moral agent. As such, he can deliberate about alternatives open to his choice and can act according to his deliberation. When we take this point of view toward a person, whether it is ourself or another, we think of the person as being subject to obligations and duties. In Kant's terms, we understand man as a member of the intelligible world, that is, as a rational being confronted with choices and at the same time bound by moral rules. Only in this double light can we fully comprehend the nature of man and his place in the universe. And it is just because we take these two standpoints that the categorical imperative can apply to us when we have the freedom to decide to conform to it or to violate it. Not being perfect, we do not always do what we ought. The person of good will is not forced to do his duty, and that is why he can be admired as a good person when he does his duty for its own sake.

So much for the actual structure of Kant's argument. We can now ask the question, Why is his theory called "ethical formalism"? There are three reasons for this designation. The first is that the concept of universalizability (given in the First Formulation of the categorical imperative) is taken to be a sufficient condition for moral duty. Kant thought of it as a purely formal test or criterion, since the statement of it (as distinct from its *a priori* ground) is abstracted from any empirical description of actions or their consequences in the actual world. The statement of it reads, "Act only on that maxim through which you can at the same time will that it should become a universal law." No reference is made to specific properties of actions or of agents.

The second reason concerns the *a priori* basis or derivation of the Moral Law, as distinct from its formulation. Kant derives the Moral Law solely from considerations regarding its *a priori* universality and necessity, rather than from any content or subject matter it might have. For Kant the Moral Law applies to all moral agents without exception, and independently of any contingent facts (that is, facts that could have been other than they are) about their nature or circumstances. Thus, it would have been possible for Kant to set forth and defend all the steps in his argument without ever appealing to empirical knowledge of matters of fact. At least, this is how he conceived of the argument.

The third reason for classifying Kant's theory as "formalistic" is that, according to it, morality is basically a certain *relation* that holds among beings having practical reason. It is the relation of equality under law. All beings who have practical reason (that is, who have the capacity to use their reason in the guidance of conduct) are equal in that they have the same duties and the same rights in their double roles of subjects and legislators in the "kingdom of ends." This concept of morality is formalistic because it defines the relations among the members of a moral community without reference to their personal characteristics and without reference to their varying interests and goals in life. Morality sets a formal framework within which people pursue their interests and goals. It is not itself one of their personal goals.

In the remainder of this chapter the basic ideas of Kant's ethical system will be examined in detail, including the developments, modifications, and reformulations they have undergone in recent moral philosophy. They will be considered under five general headings: The Concept of a Moral Agent; Universalizability; Man as End in Himself; The Autonomy of the Will; and The Principles of Justice. The purpose of the last of these sections is to show how the idea of justice can be conceived in terms of a formalistic ethical theory. In the last chapter the special problem that justice raises for utilitarianism was seen. Whether the problem can be successfully overcome by a nonutilitarian theory is considered below.

THE CONCEPT OF A MORAL AGENT

A moral agent may be defined as a being who can act morally or immorally. This definition does not restrict the class of moral agents to *human* beings, although one might hold that, as far as our present day knowledge of the universe goes, we know of no beings other than humans who are moral agents. The definition also leaves open the question of whether lunatics, imbeciles, and other humans lacking certain basic capacities are to be excluded from the class of moral agents. Finally, it leaves open the question of how old a human being must be before he is to be considered, by himself or by others, a moral agent.

To say that a being can act morally or immorally is to say something quite complex. It is to say, first, that the being is one who can perform *actions,* as distinct from merely being able to make bodily movements in response to internal or external stimuli. Being able to perform actions means being able to do things intentionally. And this requires the capacity to recognize and describe what one is doing or intends to do. A person acts intentionally when he has certain reasons for acting and acts accordingly. Thus animals like dogs and cats do not, in *this* sense, perform actions. They cannot recognize themselves as acting for certain reasons, or describe (to others or even to themselves) what they are doing in terms of their intentions.

Secondly, to say that a being can act morally or immorally is to say that the actions performed by the being can appropriately be judged (evaluated, criticized, appraised) on the basis of moral rules of conduct. Another way to put this is to say that the actions of such a being can properly be included in the range of application of moral rules.

Thirdly, to say that a being can act morally or immorally is to say that he possesses what Kant called "practical reason" or a "rational will." This is the capacity to do an action (or to refrain from an action) on moral grounds. It is being able to act from moral considerations, that is, to have moral reasons for action and to act *because* one has those reasons for action.

A formalistic ethical system makes a fourth stipulation regarding the nature of a moral agent. This is the ability *to act on principle*, that is, to do an action regardless of one's inclinations, wants, or interests. Kant expressed this, as we have seen, by saying that a person of good will acts from duty or for the sake of duty. Such a person does an action just because it is right, disregarding whether he likes doing it, and disregarding any facts about the effects of the action in fulfilling his wants or achieving his goals.

It is important to keep in mind that a moral agent conceived in the above way is not a being who always acts morally (that is, who always does what is right because it is right). It is, instead, a being who has the *capacity* to act in that way and for that reason. Thus one who acts immorally by breaking a moral rule is still a moral agent as long as he can think of his action as falling under it and hence think of himself as having a duty which is transgressed when he violates the rule. He understands himself to be bound by a rule — in the sense of being under an obligation to comply with it — even when he fails to obey it. A moral agent is, therefore, a being who has a conscience, a sense of duty, and is thus *capable* of a "good will" in Kant's sense. Such a being holds himself accountable and can think of himself as being at fault when he does not do what he acknowledges he ought to do.

We shall see below that the idea of a moral agent is central to Kant's view of moral rules as being universal in scope. For he held that a rule of conduct is a moral rule only if it validly applies to the actions of *all moral agents*. Unlike the laws of a nation, which pertain to its own citizens but not to the citizens of another nation, moral rules apply *universally*. A closer analysis of the complex set of concepts involved in the idea of universalizability is now in order.

UNIVERSALIZABILITY

"Universalizability" means "the possibility of being universalized." To clarify this, three different meanings of the term "universalizable" will be distinguished. Each meaning specifies a way in which something can be universalized. Kant's ethical theory includes all three meanings, though he did not explicitly distinguish them from one another. And it appears that he did not notice a very important point, namely, that a moral judgment or rule can be universalizable in one sense of the term without necessarily being so in the other senses. However, all three meanings contribute something essential to our understanding of a formalistic ethical system. Indeed, as was shown above, one of the very things that makes an ethical system formalistic is the idea that universalizability provides a sufficient condition for right conduct.

(1) Logical Universalizability

The first meaning of "universalizable" applies to all evaluative and prescriptive judgments of actions, that is, judgments of the form "This action is right (or wrong)"; "One ought to do that action in those circumstances"; "It is your duty to do such-and-such"; et cetera. Now take any particular judgment of the form, Person A ought to do action X in circumstances C. This judgment is universalizable in the sense that it entails the universal judgment that *anyone* in circumstances C ought to do an

X-action. For there must always be some property or set of properties belonging to action X that make it the kind of action that ought to be done in the given circumstances. In other words there must be something *about* X by virtue of which it is the right action for person A to do in circumstances C. We would contradict ourselves if we said that A ought to do X but that someone else in the same circumstances should not do an action having the same "right-making" properties that X has. For example, suppose it is asserted that someone who has made a promise ought to keep it, unless there are more important reasons to the contrary that outweigh fulfilling it. This assertion implies that *everyone* who has made a promise ought to honor it (unless there are more important contrary reasons that outweigh keeping it).

Logical universalizability can be used as a basis of *moral reasoning* about whether a given action is to be judged right or wrong. To see how this is so, consider an action in which one person A treats another person B in a certain way. Examples might be: A inflicts pain on B; A interferes with B's freedom; or A makes a promise to B which he, A, does not intend to keep. Now suppose A wishes to claim that it is right for him to treat B in the given way. As soon as he does this, we have seen, he makes a judgment that is universalizable. From his *particular* judgment:

(i) It is right for me, A, to do X to B,

we derive the corresponding *universal* judgment by the principle of logical universalizability:

(ii) It is right for anyone in A's position to do an X-action to anyone in B's position.

It can then be pointed out that this universal judgment has, as one of its instances, the following *particular* judgment:

(iii) If the positions of A and B were reversed, it would be right for B to do an X-action to A.

Now (iii) is entailed by (ii), which is entailed by (i). So if A sincerely makes judgment (i), he is committed to accepting the truth of judgment (iii). But in the kind of case mentioned above, where the X-action is one of inflicting pain on a person, or interfering with his freedom, or making a deceitful promise to him, A would not sincerely give his assent to a judgment of form (iii). Therefore, by the rules of logic, he must give up his orginial judgment (i).

There is, however, one way for A to avoid this result. He might claim that there is a relevant difference between himself and B, so that it is right for him to do X to B but not right for B to do X to him. Suppose, for example, that A is a traffic policeman and B is a driver parking his car in front of a fire hydrant. Then the action of A's interfering with B's freedom could be considered right, but an otherwise similar action in which B interferes with A's freedom might not be considered right, on the ground that A has authority over B in the given situation but B lacks such authority over A. So A can be perfectly consistent in holding that it is right for him to treat B in a way that is not right for B to treat him.

Nevertheless, the original argument still retains considerable force. In the first place, A must claim that there is a *relevant* difference between himself and B. He cannot merely refer to the difference as being that he, A, wants to do X to B, while B does not want X to be done to him. For, when their positions are reversed, B may well want to do an X-action to A and A may not want it done to him. So if wanting to do X were a relevant difference, A would again have to give his assent to the judgment that, the positions having been reversed, it would be right for B to do an X-action to him.

Furthermore, if A does claim sincerely that there is a relevant difference between himself and B, then this relevant difference itself must be universalizable. To take another example, suppose property P, which A has but which B lacks, is considered by A to be a relevant difference between himself and B. A, a Caucasian, is a White Supremacist and B is a Black. Now if A claims it is right for him to do X to B (say, prevent B from getting a certain job) but wrong for B to do the same kind of action to A, because A has property P but B lacks P, then by logical universalizability it follows that, if B were to have the property P and A were to lack it, it would be right, when their positions were reversed, for B to do an X-action to A. That is, if property P is a relevant difference in one case of doing X, it must be a relevant difference in all cases of doing X-actions, no matter who may be the particular persons occupying the positions or roles of the one who does the action and of the one to whom it is done.

The limitations of arguments based on logical universalizability should now be mentioned. First, all that these arguments come to is that one must be *consistent* in one's value judgments about actions. As long as a person is willing to accept all the propositions or judgments entailed by one of his assertions, no flaw in his reasoning can be uncovered by means of the principle of logical universalizability alone. So if the White Supremacist in our example were willing to give his sincere assent to the judgment that, if he were a Black and someone else were a Caucasian, it would be right for the other person to prevent him from getting a certain job, then no error in his judgment can be revealed by logical universalizability. Secondly, it is worth noticing that, since *all* value judgments of actions are logically universalizable, logical universalizability does not serve to distinguish moral from nonmoral value judgments. "You ought not to eat so much ice cream" is just as universalizable as "You ought not to cheat on your income tax." In the third place, logical universalizability does not set any restrictions on what kinds of actions are right. The judgment "It is right for A to break his promise to B" is just as universalizable (given the judge's willingness to be consistent) as the judgment "It is right for A to keep his promise to B." This point has an important implication. It means that logical universalizability cannot, by itself, serve as a *sufficient* condition for moral duty. It is not enough to be able consistently to universalize one's judgment, since a contrary judgment can also be consistently universalized. Finally, logical universalizability does not lend support to a deontological ethical system any more than to a teleological system. "It is right in situation S to do what will bring most pleasure to people" is just as universalizable as "In situation S one's duty is to be honest, even if honesty in that situation brings somewhat less pleasure to people than dishonesty."

Logical universalizability, then, cannot be, in and of itself, the ground of all moral obligation in a deontological ethical system. It must, however, be accepted as a *necessary* condition for such obligation, since it is needed to guarantee the internal consistency of the system as a whole.

(II) The Universal Applicability of a Rule

The second meaning of "universalizability" has to do with the scope of rules of conduct. The scope of a rule is its range of application, as defined by the class of persons who are bound by the rule and the kinds of actions of such persons that it specifically requires, permits, or forbids. Some rules, for instance, apply only to people in certain social roles or positions. Thus the institutional or organizational rules of a bank might state that tellers have such-and-such duties; that they are allowed to make certain decisions regarding their transactions with customers but must refer other decisions to the bank manager; that they have a right to a yearly vacation and to a certain level of pay; and so on. All these rules apply to persons solely and specifically in their role as bank tellers. They do not apply to individuals in other positions in the same bank nor, of course, do they apply to anyone who is not a member of that organization. Furthermore, they do not apply to the actions of those very bank tellers when they are off duty, that is, when they are eating lunch, returning home from work, or otherwise going about their personal business.

Similarly, the rules of etiquette that tell us what is the "correct" or "proper" thing to do at a formal wedding include in their scope only the conduct of those who are guests at or participants in a formal wedding ceremony. What is the correct thing to do in such a situation is not necessarily proper at a wedding ceremony of Amazonian Indians or at an American formal wedding held in 1820. Customs and mores not only vary from society to society and from age to age, but the customary rules are "relativized" to the particular group which accepts them. No one outside the group is considered to be bound by such rules. The same sort of limitation in the scope of rules is true of the positive law of a society. Within the legal system of a sovereign political body, a valid law applies only to those who are legally defined as citizens (and perhaps to noncitizens who reside within the area of jurisdiction of the sovereign state).

Two other types of rules of conduct that are restrictive in scope are the rules of a game, which apply only to those who choose to play, and the "how-to" rules specifying the most effective way to achieve an end, which apply only to people who seek the end in question.

Are there any rules of conduct that are unlimited or universal in their range of application? If there are, they would apply to a person regardless of his social position, his role in a particular organization or his citizenship in a certain nation, his choosing to participate in rule-governed practices like games, and regardless of whatever ends he is pursuing. What we are interested in examining here is the claim that there are, indeed, such universally applicable rules of conduct, and that they are, by definition, the rules of morality.

There is a *prima facie* case (that is, an apparently well-grounded case) for this claim. Think of how we might distinguish between, say, the *special* duties of a quarterback in football and the *general* duty of a quarterback not to gain an advantage over an opponent by cheating. We think of the second duty as one that applies not only to the quarterback but to all football players, and indeed to all players in all games. And even in the case of people who are not playing a game, we consider the duty not to cheat (and thereby gain some unfair advantage over another person) as *a duty owed to everyone by everyone,* whether or not the relations between two individuals happen to be governed by a system of restricted rules. Again, think of the virtues (valued qualities) that make a bank teller a good bank teller or those that make a quarterback a good quarterback, and then consider those that make a man or woman virtuous. The former vary from role to role, while the latter are the same for everyone, no matter what his or her role may be.

Reflections like these have led some philosophers to the conclusion that a rule of conduct is a *moral* rule only if it satisfies the principle of universal applicability. The rule must be universal in scope, applying to all moral agents. This is not meant to deny the obvious fact that the actually accepted ruli̇s of a given society's conventional moral code may differ from those of another society's (where "moral" refers to the kind of sanctions, such as guilt and blame, supporting the code). But if we think that any moral rule is *ideal* in the sense that it ought to be accepted as a guide to human conduct, then, according to the principle of universal applicability, it must apply to *all* human conduct, whenever and wherever a particular act of the type it specifies occurs. It is, in other words, a rule of conduct *that is binding upon all moral agents as such.* And this means that it is a rule by which one can correctly judge the rightness or wrongness of actions done by any being who—as we saw in our earlier account of moral agency—is capable of understanding the rule and conforming to it as a guide to his conduct.

It follows from this view of moral rules that if it is morally right (or wrong) for one moral agent to do a certain kind of action in certain circumstances, it must be morally right (or wrong) for every other moral agent to do the same kind of act in similar circumstances. For what is morally right or wrong is what a moral rule requires or prohibits, and these rules are the same for all moral agents. Thus it is possible to derive from the principle of universal applicability what has been called "the Generalization Principle" in ethics: What is right (or wrong) for one person is right (or wrong) for everyone.

The Generalization Principle entails what might be described as a *moral equality* holding among all persons with the capacities that define a moral agent. Since everyone is bound by the same rules, whatever rights are ascribed to one must also be ascribed to another. There can be no special privileges or favors granted to some but not to others (as, in accordance with nonmoral rules, there can be differences in salaries, special benefits, et cetera, attached to various positions in an organization). As with rights, so with duties. There can be no special moral duties or obligations imposed upon some but not upon others, who are in the same circumstances. Thus it is possible to construct a conception of a moral community whose membership includes all moral agents, human and superhuman (if there be any). It will be a rule-governed group of beings who conceive of one another as moral agents, owing to each other voluntary obedience to the same rules. We shall see below that this conception of a moral community corresponds in important respects to Kant's view of "the kingdom of ends."

Is the principle of universal applicability—with its corollary, the Gen-

eralization Principle—a purely formal principle? Is it like logical universalizability in placing absolutely no restrictions on the *kinds* or *descriptions* of
actions that are morally right? The answer is no, because there is one
restriction it does place on such actions: They must be of such a kind *that it
is possible for everyone to perform them.* As Kant himself argued, although
it may be possible for one person or a few people to make promises without
intending to keep them, if everyone were to try to do this, no promises
would be accepted by anyone and hence the very act of making a promise
without intending to keep it would become impossible. It follows that a
deceitful promise cannot be morally right, since a universally applicable rule
that prescribed or even permitted the making of such a vow when it was to
one's advantage would be impossible. And unless a rule is universally
applicable, it cannot be a moral rule.

The principle of universal applicability nevertheless expresses a *formal*
condition for moral conduct in that it allows any kind of action to be moral
as long as people's performing such actions is a universal possibility. To put
it in another, perhaps clearer, way: As long as we can, without contradicting ourselves, describe a world where everyone can perform a kind of action,
then that kind of action is a possible candidate for being either permitted or
required by a moral rule.

Kant has sometimes been criticized on the ground that this criterion of
the possibility of everyone's doing a certain kind of action does not rule out
as immoral many actions which Kant himself, as well as most of the rest of
us, would consider to be morally wrong. Thus it is argued that Kant did not
realize, for example, that although it is not possible for everyone always to
make false promises, it would be possible for a certain percentage of them to
be made falsely. As long as the general trust in promising was maintained in
the group, a certain number of deceitful promises would be possible. Yet
Kant surely held, as most of us do, that every dishonest pledge is wrong. Or
else, to be more accurate, it is held that making such a vow could be
justified by a very special overriding reason, but that the reason could never
be the mere fact that not many deceitful promises were being attempted by
people.

It would appear, however, that Kant could reply to this objection,
basing his reply on the principle of universal applicability itself. If a certain
percentage of deceitful promises were *morally* permissible, it would have to
be because there was a moral rule permitting such action. But a moral rule
must be universally applicable. If it permits one moral agent to make a
deceitful promise, it must permit every moral agent to do so. And this would

entail a universal practice of deceitful promising, which was shown above to
be impossible. Now it may be the case that a moral rule *would* permit, in
extremely unusual circumstances, the making of a deceitful promise. For
example, if an unjust and cruel tyrant can be overthrown only by making
such a pledge to him, it may be permissible to do so. This would be an
instance of a special overriding reason that justifies an action which, in
normal circumstances, is morally wrong. But then *every* moral agent would
be permitted to do likewise whenever the same (or a relevantly similar)
situation occurs. Since such situations are exceptional, the universal practice
of deceitful promising *in those circumstances* is possible. In this way Kant
could still maintain that a moral rule must be universally applicable to all
moral agents, even though the kinds of actions done by such agents include
making exceptions to general rules like promise-keeping. As long as such exceptions are possible when done by everyone (in the appropriate circumstances), there is no violation of the principle of universal applicability.

We now have one further problem to face. The possibility of everyone's
doing an action-type cannot serve, by itself, to distinguish legitimate
(morally acceptable) exceptions to general rules from illegitimate (morally
unacceptable) ones. Thus both of the following practices *could* be universally followed:

(A) Tell the truth except when lying will save someone's life.
(B) Tell the truth except when lying will successfully enable one to exploit
someone weaker than oneself.

Since either (A) or (B) is logically consistent and is practically possible when
universalized, the two principles of logical universalizability and the universal applicability of a rule do not, by themselves, give us a way to determine
what exceptions to general rules are morally right. Thus the first two
meanings of "universalizability" do not provide a sufficient condition for the
moral rightness of every action. Something more is needed.

Kant did, in fact, include something more. This additional condition is
found in the third meaning of "universalizability," examined below.

(III) The Universal Acceptability of a Rule

So far we have seen that, according to Kant, if a rule is to be a moral
rule it must be possible (logically possible and practically possible) for
everyone to act in accordance with it. To this twofold condition Kant adds
another: It must be possible for everyone to *will* the rule as a universal law.
By this he means that the rule must be such that each person whose conduct

falls within its scope can freely and knowingly subscribe to it as a principle of duty for himself and for all other moral agents. The rule, in short, must be not only universally applicable; it must also be universally acceptable (will-able).

We may define the universal acceptability of a rule as follows: A rule is universally acceptable when and only when (a) a freely given commitment to comply with it (b) as a normative principle of conduct (c) can be made on the part of every moral agent. In order to understand fully what a moral rule is, and in what way it imposes an obligation on everyone whose conduct comes within its range of application, it is necessary to analyze the three elements — designated (a), (b), and (c) — that define the idea of universal acceptability.

(a) For a rule to be a moral rule, it must at least be one that a person can voluntarily decide to use as an action guide in his own life. It must be such that the person can freely subscribe to it as providing him with a moral reason for acting. Suppose a rule were imposed upon a person against his will; he would then correctly consider it a form of social pressure or coercion. He would see himself as being manipulated by others and forced to obey their will, but he would not think of himself as under a moral obligation to obey them. The rule would not constitute, for him, a ground of duty, since he would only conform to it out of self-interest, as a way of avoiding the unpleasant consequences of disobedience. (Think of those children who obey their parents only from fear of punishment.) The rule itself would not, in his judgment, give him a moral reason for acting.

For a precept to qualify as a rule of morality, therefore, it must be capable of functioning as the basis for a moral reason fo. acting. And it can take on this function only when it is freely accepted by every agent whose actions come within its scope. In Kantian terms, each moral agent must be able to "will" the rule as a law for his own being. This is why morality is never a matter of what a person is forced to do, but of what he recognizes as a duty even when he is not forced to do it.

(b) Let us now suppose that a person does freely choose to follow a certain rule as an action guide in his own life. This rule will still not be a moral rule unless it is adopted by the person in a specific way. He must adopt it (subscribe to it, commit himself to it) *as a normative principle of conduct.* This means the person acknowledges his obligation to comply with the rule, irrespective of his desires, inclinations, and ends. As we saw in connection with the definition of a moral agent, action in accordance with a moral rule must be done as a matter of principle, not as a matter of self-interest. A rule of morality thus sets a standard of conduct that places a normative requirement upon a person regardless of his wishes and preferences in any particular situation. To accept a rule in this manner is to make a deep commitment of one's whole self with respect to all future actions that might fall under the rule.

On the basis of the considerations given so far under (a) and (b) we may now draw an important conclusion: It is only when a person conceives of himself as having moral obligations *because* he has accepted a set of rules in the way indicated in (a) and (b) that the rules can operate as moral principles in his life. In other words, the person must understand what it means to make a free commitment to follow a rule as a matter of principle if he is to be a moral agent with respect to that rule. If, on the contrary, he understands himself to be following a rule out of fear of punishment, to avoid feeling guilty, to gain moral "status" in the eyes of others, or simply out of unquestioned habit—in all such cases his actions may indeed conform outwardly with moral rules, but he will not, in the true sense of the term, be *acting morally.* For he will not be one who, by his own commitment, places his conduct under the requirements of normative principles.

(c) All of the foregoing propositions concerning the acceptance of moral rules must be true, not only of this or that particular individual, but of the entire class of moral agents. The reason for this is that, insofar as anyone is a member of that class, his actions by definition are subject to moral dicta and he is morally bound to comply with them. A moral rule has universal applicability (by the second meaning of universalizability) and therefore defines the moral duty of *every* being capable of acting for moral reasons. Thus all moral agents, precisely because they are moral agents, must be able freely to commit themselves to a rule as a normative principle if that rule is to qualify as moral. This, then, is the third sense in which a moral rule must be universalizable: It must be universally acceptable within the class of all beings having the capacities of moral agents.

Let us now consider the question: Having defined moral rules as those that satisfy all three conditions of universalizability, what sort of rules will these be? We may infer at once that they cannot be biased in favor of any particular person or group, for they must be rules that *every* person can freely and knowingly accept as guides to his own conduct. Hence, if the rules allow for certain discriminations among persons, they can do so only on grounds acceptable to all. Whatever criteria of relevant differences among persons are embodied in the rules must be criteria which each person can approve of, when he considers the specific differences of treatment that such criteria entail. Therefore no one will be discriminated against on grounds he himself does not accept as legitimate.

We may note, next, that since the first condition of logical universalizability will be adhered to, all moral rules will be consistently applied. No exceptions in anyone's favor will be made. There may indeed be exceptions to rules, as we saw above, but we can now see that such exceptions will not favor any particular person or group, since the exceptions themselves must be universally acceptable. Each person can agree that they are justifiable exceptions, whether or not that person himself will gain an advantage from the recognition of such exceptions. Since they are made whenever *anyone* is in the circumstances specified as justifying an exception, no exception is being made in favor of one person as opposed to others. This means that the Generalization Principle still holds true: What is right (or wrong) for one person is right (or wrong) for everyone.

The three criteria of universalizability may be considered as formalistic in the sense that they do not tell us the *content* of the moral rules that satisfy their conditions. By themselves, they simply give us certain abstract tests to apply to any rule to see if it qualifies as moral, without mentioning the kind of action that it requires, permits, or forbids. Moreover, since they do not stipulate any end or purpose with reference to which actions are to be judged as means, such rules comprise an ethical system which is deontological, not teleological.

It is this formalistic conception of a community of moral agents which lies behind Kant's idea of a "kingdom of ends." In order to round out our picture of this "kingdom" and to show in what way it constitutes a realm of justice, we shall now consider two further concepts of Kantian ethics: the idea of humanity as an end in itself and the idea of the autonomy of the will.

MAN AS END IN HIMSELF

Kant's second formulation of the categorical imperative states that we must never treat humanity, in ourselves or in others, merely as a means, but always as an end. Careful analysis of the meaning of this rather obscure statement reveals why Kant should have thought that it is basically another way of saying that one ought only to perform actions of a kind that are universalizable.

Kant gives an interesting argument as to why humanity (that is, each human being as such) should always be treated as an end and never only as a means. His argument begins with a distinction between that which has merely conditional worth and that which has unconditional or absolute worth, a distinction based on the following considerations. If we judge any object to have value, whether because it is a means to some end we judge to be valuable or because it is itself an end we consider worth seeking, the *value* of that object depends on our *valuing* it. Were no one to place value on the object for either of the two reasons mentioned, it would lack all value. It would literally be worthless. Thus anything which has value only because and insofar as it is valued by someone has *conditional* worth. Whatever worth it has is completely dependent upon the condition that someone values it. (If diamonds were not valued by anyone either as means to an end, e.g., social prestige, or as ends in themselves, e.g., as beautiful things to look at, diamonds would be worthless.)

In contrast with this, the person who values an object and accordingly is the ultimate source of the object's value belongs to an entirely different category of entities. Since persons are beings who bestow value on objects, they are themselves creators of conditional worth. As such, they must regard themselves as having unconditional worth. This becomes clear when we try to see what it would be like to view ourselves as things rather than as persons. We can quite easily conceive of our *bodies* as things, which have value because they are necessary for our lives, our thought, and our valuing activity itself. But we cannot conceive of our *personhood* as merely a thing. For to do so, we would have to judge it to be without any worth unless it happened to be valued by some other person. But then *that* individual would be the source of value, and there is no reason why one person should be such a source and not another, namely, oneself. So each person, as a person, necessarily thinks of himself as having a worth that does not wholly depend on someone else's considering him to be valuable, as a thing's worth does. Therefore a person is not a thing. A person has unconditional worth; a thing has only conditional worth.

It follows that if anyone treats a human being as if he were a thing, a mere instrument having value only because and insofar as he is valued by someone else, he is making a fundamental mistake. He who treats another only as a means is making what philosophers have called a "category-mistake." He is confusing a person with a thing, and thereby denying the fundamental fact that a person has absolute worth, while a thing has only conditional worth.

It is possible that one person can serve the ends of another and yet not be treated as a *mere* means (that is, as a thing) by that other person. Thus we go to a doctor because we believe he will be instrumental in our regaining health. In one sense, we use him as a means to our ends. But this is not what Kant means by treating a person like a thing, or *merely* as a means to our ends. To do that, we must disregard his being a person. We would do this in our dealings with a doctor if we *exploited* him (by refusing to pay him for his services, or by making him a slave who has no claims upon us, but must serve us or be killed). We treat a person like a thing whenever we *manipulate* him in order to get him to do what we want, without respecting his own wants as an independent person.

We are now in a position to see that treating a person as if he were a thing is precisely what is ruled out by the third principle of universalizability analyzed above. There cannot be a rule permitting one person to use another merely as a means if all rules governing the treatment of persons by others satisfy the condition of universal acceptability. For no individual who understood what he was doing would freely commit himself to a dictate that allowed others to use him only as a means to their ends. Even a person who wished to sacrifice himself for someone else (giving up his life to save that of someone he loves, for example) would want to be respected as one who chose his action of his own accord and in full awareness of what he was doing. Such a person would not be letting others use him *without his consent* or *against his will*. Indeed, the absolute, unconditional worth of his person-hood or humanity would be recognized and respected in others' allowing him the freedom to make his own self-sacrificial choice.

It is to be noted in this connection that the first two conditions of universalizability (logical universalizability and universal applicability) do *not* rule out the treatment of persons like things. With regard to the first condition, there is nothing inconsistent about judging it right, for example, that one portion of a population enslave another and use the slaves as mere instruments to their ends. Logical universalizability, by itself, is not suffi-cient to show that the institution of slavery is wrong. Nor can the principle of the universal applicability of rules be used to prove that one must never treat a person as a mere means. For we have seen that universal applicability allows for making exceptions to such rules as keeping promises and telling the truth. If such exceptions involved using a person as a mere means, the second principle of universalizability would still be satisfied as long as those exceptions could be practiced (in the appropriate circumstances) by everyone. Thus we saw that the rule "Tell the truth except when lying will successfully enable one to exploit someone weaker than oneself" is just as universalizable in the second sense as the rule "Tell the truth except when lying will save someone's life." So the fact that a set of rules of conduct includes the actions of all moral agents in its scope does not exclude the use of some persons as mere means to the ends of others. In order to rule out that kind of practice, appeal must be made to the third condition, universal acceptability.

THE AUTONOMY OF THE WILL

In the "kingdom of ends," Kant says, each person has a dual role: He is a sovereign or legislator, and he is also a subject, obligated to obey the very rule he lays down as sovereign. Thus Kant envisages a moral community as a group of autonomous persons who prescribe for themselves the rules that they shall live by. The reasoning that underlies this conception of a moral community has already been set forth. We saw that all moral rules must be freely accepted by each person. For otherwise they would be external constraints, forcing people to act without, in their view, providing reasons why such actions *ought* to be done. But a moral rule is not simply a coercive pressure imposed by society to get people to behave in a certain way. It is a guide to self-directed conduct, and for this very reason makes a claim upon our conscience.

This difference between being under a coercive power and being under a moral obligation is central to Kant's doctrine of the autonomy of the will. When we believe we have a moral duty to do a certain action, we think that an action of that kind is right, that is, that there are moral reasons for doing it. Because we accept these reasons as our own, we believe it our duty to comply with a rule, even when we are not forced to do so and could, unknown to others, avoid doing so. To acknowledge that we are under a moral obligation is therefore to think that we ourselves have good moral reasons to do what a rule requires. The rule is, indeed, nothing but the expression, in normative terms, of *our own* moral reasons for action. We consider it to be a moral rule binding upon us only to the extent that it expresses what we accept as valid moral reasons for doing what it tells us to do. For if we did not accept such reasons, we would not think of ourselves as morally obligated to comply with the rule.

Now the autonomy of the will, according to Kant, is the capacity of a rational agent to prescribe to himself what he must do. An autonomous will is a self-directive will. In light of the foregoing remarks, this capacity may be viewed as an individual's power to give or withhold his assent concerning the reasons that are proposed for doing a certain kind of action. Whatever reasons of a moral sort are suggested (by oneself or by others) as reasons for acting with respect to a given situation, one's autonomous will must make the final decision to accept or reject those reason as one's own. If one accepts them, one thereby *commits oneself* to act in accordance with them (even if one fails so to act when the time comes). And this is simply another way of saying that one prescribes to oneself a moral rule and adopts it as a guide to one's own conduct.

Worth noticing here is the close connection between the autonomy of the will and the doctrine of man as an end in himself. To treat a person as an end, we recall, is to recognize him as a being who has absolute or unconditional worth. Such recognition means, among other things, that one acts toward that being in such a way as always to respect his autonomy as a self-directed agent, thinker, and valuer. It is this very autonomy that is violated when a person is treated as if he were a thing having only conditional worth. For he is then being used for purposes that he has not chosen for himself or willingly accepted as purposes of his own. In exploiting or manipulating a person, one is not only getting him to do what one wants him to do; one is also refusing to take into consideration the person's own thoughts and feelings about the matter.

Now a *moral* relationship among persons, according to a formalistic ethical system, is one in which each person's autonomy is respected. Thus it necessarily precludes the use of any person as a mere means to another's ends.

THE PRINCIPLES OF JUSTICE

The final task in presenting the main concepts of a formalistic ethical system is to show how the principles of justice can be accounted for within the framework of such a system. The problem that justice raises for utilitarian ethics was scrutinized in the last chapter. If the principle of utility is taken as the sufficient condition for morally right action, it would appear that the use of individuals as means to a good social end (the greatest happiness of the greatest number) could be morally justified, even if those individuals did not consent to their being so used. As long as any treatment of persons would have, as its consequences, the producing of a greater net balance of intrinsic value over disvalue in the long run, it is the right thing to do. There is nothing in the principle of utility itself that rules out the treatment of persons as means only. In the formalistic ethical system we have been examining, on the other hand, such treatment of persons violates one of the basic principles of the system. Regardless of how good the consequences might be of a rule that involved the denial of someone's autonomy of the will, it would be directly contrary to the universal acceptability of that rule. Hence, no such rule could be part of a valid formalistic ethical system.

Justice is a distributive concept, not an aggregative one. That is to say, it concerns the distribution among people of all the things they value. It is not concerned with producing a maximum total aggregate or sum of valued things, disregarding how they are distributed. Utility, on the contrary, is an aggregative concept, and it is precisely for that reason that it cannot adequately account for the importance most people place on the justice (or fairness) of a distribution of goods among the members of a given population. The only relevance that justice has to utility is a contingent one, not a necessary one. It is the contingency that, for a given group of persons, an unjust method of distribution will cause a decrease in the total amount of value resulting from it when compared with the total amount that would result from a just distribution. Only under those contingent circumstances will utility require justice (requiring it as a means to an end).

In the formalistic system stemming from Kant's ethical theory, on the other hand, justice is fundamental to the relations among persons in a moral community. A mode of distribution of valued things is just if, and only if, *it is considered to be fair by every person as an autonomous being.* The rules of justice will specify criteria of relevant differences among persons, and as shown earlier in the discussion of universalizability, these criteria must be such that *everyone* can accept them as justifiable grounds for differences of treatment. For if one person, using his own reason, concludes that he is being discriminated against on irrelevant grounds, then to claim he must nonetheless conform to the rule of distribution is to transform that rule from a moral rule into a social constraint. The rule, being unacceptable to that person, cannot *morally* obligate him, since his autonomous will does not adopt it as a guide to his own conduct and his autonomous reason does not recognize a duty to comply with it. He can, of course, be forced to comply outwardly with the rule. But we have seen that this involves his being treated merely as a means to someone's (the group's) ends, thus violating a basic ethical principle.

Anyone in the position just described would consider the rule unfair because, in his judgment, it discriminates among persons on irrelevant grounds. To generalize from this case, we can say that a rule is just if, and only if, it is not considered unfair by any agent whose conduct falls within its range of application. And justice is simply the manner of distribution of valued things that accords with just rules so defined. It follows from this that the concept of a moral community which has been developed in this chapter necessarily includes rules of distributive justice. For all the rules of a moral community must be such that they can be freely and knowingly accepted by each moral agent as an autonomous being. Since a rule of distribution is just if it is acceptable to all whose actions fall under it, the total set of rules of a moral community will include rules of distributive justice as a subset.

This concludes the account of a formalistic system of ethics and the place of justice in it. Whether it is possible to work out a wider conceptual framework in which both justice and utility can function as moral principles (perhaps with one taking priority over the other in cases of conflict) is a task beyond the scope of this chapter.

Suggested Reading

Some of Kant's ethical writings available in English translation:

Kant, Immanuel, *Lectures on Ethics,* Louis Infield, trans. New York: Harper Torchbooks, Harper and Row, Publishers, 1963.*

——— , *Foundations of the Metaphysics of Morals,* Lewis White Beck, trans. Indianapolis: The Bobbs-Merrill Co., Inc., 1959.* This translation is also to be found in the volume edited by Robert Paul Wolff, cited below. Another excellent translation of the same work, which contains an analysis of the argument of the book, is:

——— , *Groundwork of the Metaphysic of Morals,* H.J. Paton, trans. New York: Harper Torchbooks, Harper and Row, Publishers, 1964.*

——— , *Critique of Practical Reason,* Lewis White Beck, trans. Indianapolis: The Bobbs-Merrill Co., Inc., 1956.*

——— , *Religion within the Limits of Reason Alone,* T. M. Greene and H. H. Hudson, trans. New York: Harper Torchbooks, Harper and Row, Publishers, 1960.*

*Available in paperback

————, *The Metaphysical Elements of Justice: Part I of The Metaphysics of Morals,* John Ladd, trans. Indianapolis: The Bobbs-Merrill Co., Inc., 1965.*

————, *The Metaphysical Principles of Virtue: Part II of The Metaphysics of Morals,* James Ellington, trans. Indianapolis: The Bobbs-Merrill Co., Inc., 1963.*

An excellent collection of writings on Kant's ethics:

Wolff, Robert Paul, ed., *Kant: Foundations of the Metaphysics of Morals, with Critical Essays.* Indianapolis: The Bobbs-Merrill Co., Inc., 1969.* This volume includes the entire Lewis White Beck translation of Kant's *Grundlegung zur Metaphysik der Sitten,* along with nine critical essays.

Some recent studies of Kant's ethical theory:

Beck, Lewis White, *A Commentary on Kant's Critique of Practical Reason.* Chicago: Phoenix Books, University of Chicago Press, 1960.*

Paton, H. J., *The Categorical Imperative: A Study in Kant's Moral Philosophy.* New York: Harper Torchbooks, Harper and Row, Publishers, 1967.*

Ross, William David, *Kant's Ethical Theory: A Commentary on the Grundlegung zur Metaphysik der Sitten.* London: Oxford University Press, 1954.*

The most important contemporary theory of deontological ethics, greatly influenced by Kant:

Rawls, John, *A Theory of Justice.* Cambridge, Mass.; Harvard University Press, 1971.*

An interesting system of ethics based on Rawls's theory of justice:

Richards, David A. J., *A Theory of Reasons for Action.* London: Oxford University Press, 1971.

A theory that purports to show why ethical formalism defines the highest stage in the development of a person's moral reasoning:

Kohlberg, Lawrence, *Moralization: The Cognitive-Developmental Approach.* New York: Holt, Rinehart & Winston, 1974.

Theories of ethics combining both teleological and deontological elements without a single ultimate moral principle (ethical pluralism):

Gert, Bernard, *The Moral Rules: A New Rational Foundation for Morality.* New York: Harper Torchbooks, Harper and Row, Publishers, 1973.*

Hare, R. M., *Freedom and Reason.* London: Oxford University Press, 1963.*

Ross, William David, *Foundations of Ethics.* London: Oxford University Press, 1939.

*Available in paperback

———, *The Right and the Good.* London: Oxford University Press, 1930.
Warnock, G. J., *The Object of Morality.* London: Methuen and Co., Ltd., 1971.*

Studies of the principle of universalizability:

Baier, Kurt, *The Moral Point of View,* Chapter 8. Ithaca: Cornell University Press, 1958. *Abridged Edition,* Chapters 5 and 6. New York: Random House, Inc., 1965.*
Gert, Bernard, *The Moral Rules: A New Rational Foundation for Morality.* New York: Harper Torchbooks, Harper and Row, 1973.* Gert's concept of "publicly advocating" corresponds to Kant's principle: "to will that the maxim of an action become a universal law."
Hare, R. M., *Freedom and Reason.* London: Oxford University Press, 1963.*
Singer, Marcus George, *Generalization in Ethics: An Essay in the Logic of Ethics, with the Rudiments of a System of Moral Philosophy.* New York: Atheneum Press, 1971.*
Wolff, Robert Paul, ed., *Kant: Foundations of the Metaphysics of Morals, with Critical Essays.* Indianapolis: The Bobbs-Merrill Co., Inc., 1969.* This volume contains several essays on the principle of universalizability as it occurs in Kant's ethical theory.

Studies of the concepts of justice, equality, human rights, and man-as-end-in-himself:

Bedau, Hugo A., ed., *Justice and Equality.* Englewood Cliffs, N. J.: Prentice-Hall, Inc., 1971.*
Frankena, William K., "The Concept of Social Justice," in *Social Justice.* Edited by Richard B. Brandt. Englewood Cliffs, N. J.: Prentice-Hall, Inc., 1962.*
Grice, Geoffrey Russell, *The Grounds of Moral Judgement.* Cambridge: Cambridge University Press, 1967.
Haezrahi, Pepita, "The Concept of Man as End-in-Himself," in *Kant: Foundations of the Metaphysics of Morals, with Critical Essays.* Edited by Robert Paul Wolff. Indianapolis: The Bobbs-Merrill Co., Inc., 1969.*
Melden, Abraham I., ed., *Human Rights.* Belmont, California: Wadsworth Publishing Co., Inc., 1970.*
Vlastos, Gregory, "Justice and Equality," in *Social Justice,* ed. Richard B. Brandt. Englewood Cliffs, N. J.: Prentice-Hall, Inc., 1962.* Parts of this essay are reprinted in Melden, A. I., ed., *Human Rights,* cited above, and in Feinberg, J., ed., *Moral Concepts.* London: Oxford University Press, 1969.*

A brilliant interpretation and defense of an existentialist ethical theory, in which the concept of individual moral autonomy holds a central place:

Olafson, Frederick A., *Principles and Persons: An Ethical Interpretation of Existentialism.* Baltimore: The Johns Hopkins Press, 1967.*

*Available in paperback

VI

Intrinsic Value

In the preceding two chapters we have been exploring one of the central issues in ethics, the relation between the right and the good. Does morally right conduct ultimately depend on what is nonmorally good, or is it logically independent of the nonmorally good? A teleological ethical system such as utilitarianism holds the first position; a deontological system such as ethical formalism holds the second. According to act-utilitarianism, for example, the test for right action is whether its consequences are good, or better than those of any alternative action in the given circumstances. Here there is presupposed some standard of "good" by which the consequences of actions are being judged. Similarly, in the case of rule-utilitarianism a right action is determined by a valid moral rule, and a moral rule is valid when the consequences of everyone's following the rule are good, or better than those resulting from everyone's following an alternative rule. Again, some standard of goodness is presupposed by which to judge the results of everyone's following a rule. For any such teleological ethical system, the relation between the right and the good is understood to be a relation of logical dependence of *moral* value (rightness and wrongness of action; goodness and badness of character) upon *nonmoral* value (the *intrinsic* goodness of what results from right action and good character). According to this view, one cannot know what is right unless one first knows what is intrinsically good. Knowing what is intrinsically good, however, does not depend on knowing what is morally right.

In a deontological ethical system (such as that set forth in the last chapter) there is no such relation of logical dependence between moral and nonmoral value. An action (either particular act or action-type) is morally right or wrong independently of its having intrinsically good or bad conse-

114

quences. The deontologist would say that the moral rightness of an action is a value that attaches to the kind of action it is, that value being defined by some principle of morality (such as universalizability in its various senses) which does not appeal to any standard of nonmoral value. The principle itself is understood as providing an ultimate moral ground of right conduct. To know what our moral duty is, we need only know whether our action satisfies the conditions specified in the principle. We do not need to make any judgment of nonmoral or intrinsic value concerning the consequences of actions of that kind.

THE CONCEPT OF INTRINSIC VALUE

Clear thinking about this issue regarding the relation between the (morally) right and the (nonmorally) good requires careful examination of the idea of intrinsic, nonmoral value. What is intrinsic value and how can it be known? As a first step in answering these questions, four ideas in terms of which the concept of intrinsic value has been understood by philosophers need to be distinguished:

(i) To say that something has intrinsic value is to say that it is *sought for its own sake,* or is *desired as an end in itself.*

(ii) To say that something has intrinsic value means that its value is due to its *nature* rather than to its consequences or its relation to other things.

(iii) To say that something has intrinsic value is to say that its value is a *non-natural, objective property* belonging to it.

(iv) To say that something has intrinsic value means that its value is *nonde-rivative.*

A critical analysis of these four ideas and their interrelations follows.

(i) The Greek philosopher Plato (427-347 B.C.) was among the first to point out that all the things people desire fall into three classes: things they desire as ends in themselves, things they desire as means to ends, and things they desire both as ends in themselves and as means to further ends. Sometimes, for example, a person will want to attain an end because he expects to find it satisfying or enjoyable in itself, regardless of any further purposes it might serve. He wants it for its own sake. Other things he will desire because without them he cannot attain his ends. They are objects he would never want to have if he were able to achieve his ends without them. Such things are sought not for their own sake but for the sake of something else. Another way to put it is that they are *valued* not as ends in themselves but merely as means to ends.

This way of thinking leads to the distinction between what is "good as an end" and what is "good as a means," which in turn serves as the basis for the distinction between intrinsic and extrinsic value. Intrinsic value thus becomes identified with "being sought for its own sake." In order to discover what things have intrinsic value, we only need to see what things people desire as ends in themselves or, in other words, what they seek for its own sake and not for the sake of something else. A clear example of this procedure is given in John Stuart Mill's book, *Utilitarianism* (published in 1863). Mill tried to prove that happiness is the only thing intrinsically *desirable* by showing that the only thing people *desire*, other than as a means to happiness or as a part of happiness, is happiness itself. (See the later subsection of this chapter, "Pleasure and Happiness.")

The difficulty with this approach is that it overlooks the difference between fact and value. The statement "So-and-so desires X for its own sake" is a factual assertion, verifiable in ordinary empirical ways. The statement "X is intrinsically good (or desirable)" is a value judgment. That the two assertions do not mean the same thing can quite easily be seen when we consider what happens if we affirm one and deny the other. Take the following two statements:

(1) Having absolute power over others is desired by person P as an end in itself.
(2) It is undesirable for anyone to have absolute power over others.

If both statements are asserted by someone, he is claiming that what is *desired* by a person is *undesirable*. This is not a self-contradiction, which it would be if "undesirable" meant either "not desired" or "not capable of being desired." When something is said to be *desired* by a person, a fact is being expressed. No value judgment is being made as to whether the thing desired is good, bad, or indifferent. But when it is said that something is *undesirable,* a negative evaluation is being expressed. To deem it undesirable is not merely to claim that, in fact, no one does or can desire it. Something is called "undesirable" when it is judged to be bad, as something that *ought not* to be desired. So it is perfectly possible for people to desire what is undesirable. The reverse is also possible. A person might not actually desire something that is desirable for him. (A hard-working person may not want to take a vacation even though, were he to do so, he would find it desirable.)

The conclusion to be drawn from these considerations is that we do not show that something is desirable as an end in itself, or that it has intrinsic value, merely by pointing out that someone desires it solely for itself. For something a person desires for its own sake may be (in the judgment of others *or even in his own judgment*) undesirable. One does not contradict oneself in sincerely asserting, I would like to have this as an end in itself, but it would be undesirable for me to have it. (A more detailed examination of the differences between factual statements and value judgments will be given in Chapter Eight.)

(ii) With regard to the second definition of intrinsic value, (as grounded on the nature of an object) it is necessary to distinguish two ways of judging the value of something: judging it to be good because of its nature, and judging it to be good because of its consequences or its relation to other things. Suppose that someone finds great satisfaction in playing tennis. He does not play the game to make money, as a means to keep physically fit, as a matter of social prestige, or for any reason other than that he simply enjoys it. Since he does it not as a means to some further end but entirely for its own sake, we can say that he finds tennis playing to be a *worthwhile* pursuit or a *good* thing to do as an end in itself. Now this means that the consequences resulting from his playing tennis are *not* reasons for his considering it to be good, nor is any relation between the game and other things (such as the social life at his tennis club, or his reputation as a good player among his friends). The sole reason he thinks it good to play the game is that it is the kind of game it is. The reason for his valuing tennis, the one he would give if asked why he found it so desirable as a game, would be simply that it is tennis. Or else he might indicate certain aspects of tennis which are not found in other games and which he finds especially interesting, exciting, challenging, or fulfilling to him. In neither case, be it noted, is he citing any effects or consequences that come after his playing a game. It would distort the ordinary meanings of words to say that, after all, he does not play tennis as an end in itself but rather as a means to an end, namely to obtain pleasure. It would be misleading to say this because, if a person gets pleasure from tennis and plays *for that reason*, this is the same as saying that he plays tennis as an end in itself.

From considerations like these, some philosophers have concluded that the game of tennis has *intrinsic value* for the person described above because he values it (places value on it, judges it to be good) for being the kind of game it is, and not for its consequences or its relation to anything else. To generalize: Something has intrinsic value if, and only if, it is valued (or judged to be valuable) because of its "intrinsic" nature and not because of any factors "extrinsic" to it. When we come to point (iv) we shall see why this view of intrinsic value is a plausible one.

(iii) The word "intrinsic" has sometimes led philosophers to view intrinsic value as an objective property belonging to things in the same way that empirical properties belong to them. Suppose we characterize a landscape painted by a Dutch master of the seventeenth century as harmonious in its color scheme and balanced in its composition. In describing the picture this way, we are thinking of those characteristics as objective properties of the painting. If our description is true, the work must actually have the properties being attributed to it. For we are claiming that anyone who is able to perceive the painting's objective characteristics would recognize its color scheme to be harmonious and its composition to be balanced. So also, according to this view, when we assert that the landscape is intrinsically good, or that it has intrinsic value as a painting, we are asserting that its goodness or value is one of its objective properties. And our assertion is true if the painting does have this objective value-property; otherwise it is false.

This theory of intrinsic value is sometimes called "nonnaturalism" because intrinsic value is being thought of as a property of things, but a property which *cannot be known empirically*. A nonnatural property (such as being intrinsically good) is contrasted with a natural property (such as having harmonious colors) as follows. Any statement attributing a natural property to an object expresses an empirically verifiable proposition — one whose truth or falsity can be determined on the basis of the evidence of our sense perceptions and inductive inferences from such perceptions. A proposition of this kind states a matter of fact. A value judgment, on the other hand, is an assertion or statement attributing a nonnatural property to an object. To call the property nonnatural is to say that the proposition in which the property of an object is predicated is *not* empirically verifiable. Its truth or falsity cannot be known either by direct sense perception or by inductive inference. How, then, can it be known? One answer to this question proposed by nonnaturalists is that we have the capacity to know the presence of a nonnatural property in an object by means of *intuition*. To have an intuition is to be immediately aware of the intrinsic value of something (just as, in sense perception, we are immediately aware of the color of an object). It might require considerable mental training for a person to acquire this ability to intuit the objective value-property of an object. For example, in order to be able to intuit the intrinsic value of a Dutch landscape painting, a thorough study of the history of landscape painting and a disciplined development of sensitivity to aesthetic aspects of works of art may be necessary. But given this ability, a judgment of intrinsic value can be known to be true by direct cognition or awareness of that value as an objective property of the thing being judged.

Putting aside for later consideration (in Chapter Eight) the philosophical difficulties which this view involves, we may focus our attention here on this important point: It is possible to think of intrinsic value in ways other than as an objective nonnatural property of things. In fact, we have already discussed two such ways (under headings (i) and (ii) above) and we shall now proceed to examine a third. In all of these cases it is worth noticing that the term "intrinsic value" does not designate an objective property distinct from the natural or empirical properties of things. Instead, it designates the fact that a thing has empirical properties by virtue of which it fulfills certain standards of value—these standards themselves being justified in some way other than by a direct intuition. (The two standards most frequently proposed by philosophers as standards of intrinsic value, namely pleasure and happiness, will be examined in detail later in this chapter.)

(iv) The final concept of intrinsic value we shall consider may be stated thus: Whenever the value of something does not depend on the value of something else, it has intrinsic value. Take the two examples already discussed in connection with views (ii) and (iii): the intrinsic value of playing tennis and of a landscape painting. Playing the game of tennis has intrinsic value for a person if, according to the present concept, its value is *nonderivative*. This means that the value which the person places on tennis-playing does not derive from the value he places on anything else. Whatever might be the reasons he has for valuing tennis, those reasons do not involve reference to something else that he prizes—such as physical health, or social prestige. If, on the other hand, he judges tennis-playing to be good because it maintains his health or because it gives him some social prestige, then tennis-playing has only derivative value for him, not intrinsic value. Similarly, if someone judges a landscape painting to be good because it is worth a lot of money (and hence would be a good investment to buy), its value for him is derived from the worth of something else (making money) and hence his judgment, "This is a good painting," is not a judgment of intrinsic value. An aesthetic assessment of the painting, on the other hand, in which it is judged to be good *as a landscape painting,* would be a judgment of intrinsic value. The value of the painting would not be derived from anything but the characteristics of the painting itself, taken as an aesthetic object. The fact that something other than the painting (that is, money) is good does not, in this case, make the painting so. Its goodness, independent of the worth of other things, is intrinsic to it. According to the view considered here, then, intrinsic value is simply nonderivative value.

Let us now see how this concept of intrinsic value compares with the others we have been discussing. First, what is the relation between desiring something as an end in itself and judging it to have nonderivative value? It has been shown that they cannot be identical, since the value judgment "X is intrinsically good" does not mean the same thing as the factual statement "X is desired as an end in itself." Yet it would seem that, whenever we desire to have or do something for its own sake, we think of it as *worth* having or doing regardless of the value we place on other things. We might not, of course, actually decide to do something we desire to do as an end in itself, since in a given set of circumstances its consequences might be so bad (intrinsically or instrumentally) that their disvalue outweighs the value we place on the activity itself. Nevertheless, we still judge it to have that value independently of the value (or disvalue) of other things. So if a person judges something to be intrinsically good by considering it to have nonderivative value, he will at the same time have a certain positive attitude toward it and will want it as an end in itself. His judgment of intrinsic value and his desire for something as an end in itself are correlated. His judgment does not *assert* that he has the desire, but such a desire is present whenever he sincerely makes such a judgment.

The second concept of intrinsic value is that it is the value of something that rests on its nature and not on its consequences or on its relation to other things. It can now readily be shown that this second concept is an implication of the fourth (the concept of intrinsic value as nonderivative value). In a judgment of nonderivative value, whatever might be the standard of evaluation being applied, one condition must be satisfied. The "good-making" properties of the object (that is, the properties by virtue of which it fulfills the given standard) must be those belonging to the object itself and not attributes of its consequences or of its relations to other things. For if they were the latter, then what would *make* the object good would be some fact or facts about its consequences and/or its external relations. And in that case its goodness or value would be derivative. What makes something intrinsically (nonderivatively) good, therefore, must be a property or set of properties belonging to the thing itself. In this sense the intrinsic value of something must be *grounded on* its nature.

Finally, with regard to the third concept, it should be clear that it is not necessary to think of intrinsic value as an objective nonnatural property of something if it is defined as nonderivative value. Of course there must be some *empirical* property or set of properties of the object considered intrinsically good which constitute its "good-making" characteristics. That is to say, there must be some facts about its nature which are the reasons for a person's judging it to have intrinsic value. But to assert that it has value is not to add another property, a nonnatural one. It is to evaluate (appraise, assess) the object on the basis of its empirical properties by applying a standard to it. (For a full account of this view of a value judgment, see Chapter Eight.) To call the value of something "intrinsic" is simply to deny that it is derived from the value of anything else. It is not to affirm that it somehow exists "in" the thing which is judged to be intrinsically good.

HEDONISM

We come now to the problem of the *ground* or *standard* of intrinsic value. So far the standards of evaluation that might be applied in making judgments of intrinsic value have not been considered; this discussion has only dealt with the general nature of such judgments. But there has been a great deal of philosophical controversy regarding the standard of intrinsic value. What makes something intrinsically good? By what test can we determine its intrinsic goodness? What is the ground of intrinsic value? Perhaps the most important answer to these questions in the history of ethics has been *pleasure*. The theory that pleasure is the one and only standard of intrinsic value is called "valuational hedonism," or sometimes simply "hedonism." Valuational hedonism should not be confused with (1) psychological hedonism, (2) hedonistic utilitarianism, or (3) egoistic hedonism. Let us briefly consider how valuational hedonism is differentiated from these other views.

(1) Psychological hedonism is a theory of human motivation. It holds that the only thing a person can seek as an end in itself is pleasure. To put it another way, it is the view that the ultimate object of every desire of a person is his own pleasure. If he desires anything else, it is only as a means to pleasure. (This theory was criticized in Chapter Two, where it was discussed in connection with psychological egoism.) It is important not to confuse this theory with valuational hedonism, since psychological hedonism could be false while valuational hedonism is true and the reverse could be equally true. In the first case it would be possible for people to seek ultimate ends other then *their own* pleasure, and yet the intrinsic value of anything might depend on *someone's* finding it pleasant. In the reverse instance, it

would be possible for the test of intrinsic value to be something other than pleasure, even though everyone always aimed at his own enjoyment as an ultimate end.

(2) Hedonistic utilitarianism, as we saw in Chapter Four, is the normative ethical system according to which an act is morally right, or a moral rule of conduct valid, if its consequences produce more pleasure and less pain in the world than would result from any alternative act or rule. This position combines a teleological ethical theory (that right action depends on the intrinsic value of its consequences) with valuational hedonism (that the intrinsic value of the consequences is grounded on pleasure). However, one can accept valuational hedonism and not be a hedonistic utilitarian simply by rejecting utilitarianism or any other teleological theory of moral rightness. Moral value may be entirely different from and independent of intrinsic (nonmoral) value, or it may not be related to intrinsic value as means to an end. It is possible, in other words, to hold that our moral duties derive from deontologically grounded rules (as in a formalistic ethical system) and at the same time hold that a correct *nonmoral* way of evaluating human experiences is by appealing to the standard of pleasure. Such a position would logically separate questions concerning nonmoral values from those concerning moral right and wrong. Thus valuational hedonism must not be confused with hedonistic utilitarianism.

(3) Egoistic hedonism must also be kept distinct in our minds from valuational hedonism. Egoistic hedonism is the view which, in popular talk, is often called simply "hedonism." If someone in everyday life is said to be a hedonist, this usually implies that the person is a pleasure-lover, in the sense that his dominant goal in life is to have as much pleasure as possible. This is closely related to a form of ethical egoism, according to which the best way of life for anyone to live is one that brings the maximum amount of pleasure to that person himself. Such a theory, however, is not only different from, but is actually inconsistent with, valuational hedonism. For if the sole valid standard of intrinsic value is pleasure (valuational hedonism), then whatever experience is pleasurable is intrinsically good, *no matter whose experience it is.* According to valuational hedonism, an experience that *anyone* finds pleasant or enjoyable has intrinsic value just because it is gratifying to *that* person. Thus the theory would imply a denial of the egoistic view that only *one's own* pleasure is to count in calculating the best way of life. The egoist will take into consideration other people's pleasure only if it is a means to the end of increasing his own pleasure. Other people's pleasure will have, for him, instrumental or extrinsic value only. The valuational hedonist, on the

other hand, will consider everyone's pleasures as having equal intrinsic value. Thus he will judge all pleasures equally worthy of being sought for their own sake.

Hedonism (as we shall refer to valuational hedonism from this point on) has been strongly attacked by some philosophers and vigorously defended by others since the very beginning of western philosophy. A closer look at it is in order.

We have defined hedonism as the view that the sole valid standard of intrinsic value is pleasure. This view has four implications:

(a) All pleasures are intrinsically good.
(b) Only pleasure is intrinsically good.
(c) A thing is intrinsically good to the extent that it is pleasurable.
(d) What makes anything intrinsically good is the pleasure it gives to someone.

Proposition (a) means that there are no bad pleasures. Immediately someone will question the hedonist: But what about a sadist who gets pleasure out of torturing people? Are not the pleasures of a sadist bad? The hedonist's reply is that his pleasures are *extrinsically* bad, because they cause pain (the opposite of pleasure) to others. That is, they have intrinsically bad consequences. But the very thing that makes those consequences intrinsically bad mades the sadist's experience itself intrinsically good, namely, the fact that he finds it pleasurable. It would be much better (where "better" refers to the total, overall value of the situation) if he found pleasure in bringing pleasure to others, or at least in lessening their pain. But, argues the hedonist, if we consider only the nonderivative value of his experience, we must admit it to be good. For we are then disregarding its consequences and its relation to other things. In judging intrinsic value it is necessary to abstract an experience from its context. We must not consider its effects either on the person himself or on others. It is only within this limited (but highly important) frame of reference that the sadist's experience is judged to be good.

Proposition (b) means that there is nothing intrinsically good but pleasure. Immediately someone will object, But surely there are many good things in human life besides pleasure. What about knowledge? beauty? friendship? moral virtue? The hedonist will reply, "Yes, I agree that these things are good, but what is it that makes them good? Why do we value them so highly? Is it not that they either tend to increase the amount of pleasure in the world or are themselves great sources of pleasure for those who experience them? Suppose no one liked to know the truth and suppose that knowledge was used only to make the lives of men more miserable. Would we then consider knowledge something worth having? Suppose no one found pleasure in the experience of beauty, or ever enjoyed having friends. Aren't these good things held to be good precisely because they are such deep sources of pleasure for practically everyone? And if we consider moral virtue, we do not have to be utilitarians to see that, whether we take it as a means to an end or as an end in itself, it would have no value if it did not yield pleasure to someone." The hedonist would claim that, though a man may be morally admirable because he seeks to do his duty for its own sake, the inherent value of such a virtuous character lies in the fact that an impartial spectator does find pleasure in contemplating it. If such a spectator disliked the contemplation of moral virtue, and if the virtuous person himself found no satisfaction in doing his duty for its own sake, and if no pleasant consequences of any sort resulted from his being virtuous, would we not withdraw all value from moral virtue?

Proposition (c) means that the degree of intrinsic value in any experience is directly proportional to the amount or quantity of pleasure it brings to the person who has it. The quantity of any pleasure is measured by its intensity and its duration. Of two pleasures that last the same length of time, the more intense has the greater intrinsic value in direct proportion to the degree of its additional intensity. Similarly, of two pleasures having equal intensity, the longer lasting is proportionately of greater intrinsic value. The next section of this chapter will present a famous criticism of this third proposition of hedonism.

Proposition (d) states that the only intrinsically good-making characteristic of anything is pleasure. This follows from the principle that pleasure is the only standard of evaluation to be used in judgments of intrinsic value, since a standard determines what characteristics of a thing are good-making. To say that pleasure is an intrinsically good-making characteristic of X is to say that, so far as the intrinsic value of X is concerned, it is good by virtue of the fact that it is pleasant to someone. Thus it is not a mere accident that every pleasure is intrinsically good, that only pleasure is intrinsically good, and that the intrinsic goodness of something is directly proportional to its pleasantness. Proposition (d) is the logical ground for propositions (a), (b), and (c). The hedonist's justification for proposition (d) is the same as his argument for his basic principle. This principle may be stated thus. In judging whether any experience is intrinsically good or bad we apply only one test, namely, to ask how pleasant or unpleasant the experience is to the person who "lives through" it. In order to be clearer about the nature of this hedonistic standard, and in order to better understand the arguments given in support of it, we must make certain distinctions with regard to the concept of pleasure.

First it is necessary to distinguish two meanings of the term "pleasure." One meaning equates pleasure with *bodily pleasure* or *pleasure of the senses.* When "pleasure" is used in this sense, it is the name of a certain class of sensations or feelings which we get when our bodily organs and nerve endings are stimulated in various ways. Sometimes the terms "animal pleasure" and "sensual pleasure" are used to denote all such sensations and feelings. When "pleasure" is used in this way, its opposite is bodily pain.

The second meaning of pleasure is *any pleasant experience.* We can think of this in the following way. Suppose we were asked to place all of our experiences on a scale, ranging from those which were most pleasant through those which were somewhat pleasant, slightly pleasant, neither pleasant nor unpleasant, mildly unpleasant, quite unpleasant, to extremely unpleasant. Perhaps many of our daily experiences would fall near the neutral center of the scale. These would be experiences that, as far as their pleasure (pleasantness or unpleasantness) was concerned, were indifferent to us. But there would be other experiences that we would unhesitatingly place on either side of the neutral line. Now the word "pleasure" in its second sense is taken to denote the entire class of experiences that fall on the positive side of the neutral line, no matter how they might vary in degree or amount of pleasantness, and no matter what may be the source of their pleasantness. What one person finds to be pleasant another will find to be unpleasant or indifferent; what one person derives great pleasure from another will derive only mild pleasure from, or none at all. Thus the *sources* of pleasure may vary considerably from person to person. But the *hedonic tone* of different people's experiences is common to them all. That is to say, everyone knows the difference among pleasant, indifferent, and unpleasant experiences, however great may be their disagreement concerning the particular things they find to be pleasant, indifferent, or unpleasant.

In common usage we have four terms for referring to the hedonic tone of our experiences: "enjoyment," "liking," "satisfaction," and "pleasure." Examples of typical phrases in which these terms are employed are: "One enjoys X"; "One finds X enjoyable"; One likes (doing) X"; "One finds satisfaction in (doing) X"; "X gives one pleasure"; "X is pleasant to one." When the word "pleasure" is used in its second sense, it is understood to cover all four of these ways of speaking. It is the name of the entire class of experiences which any person enjoys, likes, finds satisfying, or finds pleasant.

In this second sense of the word, the opposite of pleasure is not bodily pain but rather the unpleasantness of any experience, whatever its source. Thus it is possible for bodily pain (that is, the sensations resulting from the stimulation of certain nerve endings) to be pleasant. A certain type of masochist, for example, finds the experience of being whipped pleasant. Here we can say without contradiction that the person finds pleasure in having pain sensations. This means simply that, because of his abnormal emotions (extreme guilt, the need for punishment, etc.), the person gets satisfaction — even thrills — from the experience of bodily pain. A *source* of pleasantness, for him, is for most of us a source of great unpleasantness. It might also be possible — though perhaps it is very rare in actual occurrence — for a person to find bodily pleasure (that is, "pleasure" in the first sense) to be an unpleasant experience. This might happen to a person who was sexually aroused but had extreme guilt feelings about sex. At any rate, if we are careful to keep the two meanings of "pleasure" separate in our minds, we need not think that it is somehow gross or animalistic, and hence degrading or ignoble, to be a hedonist. For a hedonist may advocate, as the sole valid standard of intrinsic value, pleasure in the second sense and not in the first. And this is the sort of hedonism we shall be concerned with here.

It is important not to confuse the sources of pleasure with pleasure itself. The hedonist claims only that pleasure itself (meaning, now, the positive hedonic tone of any experience) is the standard of intrinsic value. He does not claim that intrinsic value depends on any particular source of pleasure. For the hedonist *any* pleasant experience is intrinsically good just *because* it is pleasant, no matter what it is that gives pleasure to the person concerned. There is no reason why the most exalted kinds of experiences, such as reading poetry or attaining a mystical vision, should not be included as sources of pleasure. The hedonist does not say that everyone ought to be a pure sensualist and try to have as much bodily pleasure as possible. Indeed, the so-called "hedonic paradox" is perfectly consistent with hedonism. The "hedonic paradox" states that those who seek pleasure as a conscious goal in life are often those who gain very little pleasure from life. A person who deliberately sought to maximize his bodily pleasures would probably end up having experiences that were less pleasant over the long run than those of a person who found pleasure in a variety of sources and who did not even pursue "a life of pleasure" as a deliberate goal.

QUANTITY VERSUS QUALITY OF PLEASURE

One of the principal criticisms of hedonism is that, even if we distinguish between pleasure itself and its various sources, it seems that the intrinsic value of any source of pleasure depends on something other than the mere quantity of enjoyment involved. We saw above, in connection with proposition (c), that quantity of pleasure is measured in intensity and duration. Now let us imagine a life that contains as much intrinsic value as possible. If the total sum of intrinsic value is solely a function of quantity of pleasure, such a life will be a series of the longest lasting, most intense pleasures a person can experience. It will no doubt include a certain variation in sources of gratification, for no one would continue to get intense joy from the same kind of experience without change over any length of time. Nevertheless, the variation will be entirely dependent upon what changes will add to the total quantity of enjoyment felt by the person. Such variation could well include different types of sensual gratification (eating, drinking, sex, and whatever pleasant sensations could be derived from relatively harmless drugs). It would encompass not only the thrills and excitement of active games, but also the more passive pleasures of spectator sports, entertainments, and amusements. But such a life might embrace nothing that we could describe as a noble achievement — the attainment of a difficult and worthwhile goal after a long struggle. It would not, for instance, include any great challenge to intellectual effort or creative endeavor in the fine arts.

Reflections of this sort led one utilitarian philosopher, John Stuart Mill, to argue that the true test of intrinsic value is not merely quantity of pleasure, but also quality of pleasure. Quantity of pleasure is a matter of *how much* satisfaction or enjoyment one gets from something; quality of pleasure has to do with the *kind* of satisfaction or enjoyment derived. Mill held that, if two pleasures were equal in quantity, one might still have greater intrinsic value than the other. This would be the case if one were of a higher quality than the other. Indeed, if there is a conflict between quantity and quality, so that the pleasure which is greater in amount is of lower grade or the pleasure lower in amount is of higher grade, then according to Mill, quality outweighs quantity as a ground of intrinsic value. Thus he made the well-known statement, "It is better to be a human being dissatisfied than a pig satisfied; better to be Socrates dissatisfied than a fool satisfied." The position here is that one pleasure (or set of pleasures) is more desirable in itself than another, and hence has greater intrinsic value, if higher in quality, even if lower in quantity.

What is the test of the higher or lower quality of one pleasure, when compared with another? Mill's answer is that one pleasure is of higher quality than another when the first is a kind that is *preferred* over the other by people who have experienced both kinds and are therefore competent to judge their comparative worth. If there should be a disagreement in the preferences of such competent judges, Mill said that the best or highest quality pleasure is that which the majority of competent judges prefers over all others.

It might be noted that Mill thought that the highest quality pleasures would, by the foregoing test, turn out to be those of the intellect and the aesthetic sensibility, rather than the pleasures of the body. This, however, is a contingent matter, having to do with what *sources* of high quality pleasure are preferred by people. As far as Mill's definition of the ranking of pleasure is concerned, if a majority of competent judges preferred bodily over mental pleasures, bodily pleasures would be higher in quality.

Is there any reason for accepting Mill's test for high quality pleasure as the ultimate standard of intrinsic value? One might argue in support of Mill that if intrinsic value is the worth we place on something independently of our evaluation of anything else, then the true standard of intrinsic value must be, not any standard used by anyone when placing such nonderivative value on something, but a standard which *competent* persons tend to use when they critically reflect about what value *ought* to be assigned to the object nonderivatively. It is not the actual preferences that anyone happens to have which determine the intrinsic value of our experience, but those relatively stable and firmly held preferences that emerge from the reflective judgment of a person who either has actually undergone, or can vividly imagine, the circumstances and conditions of life whose intrinsic value is being appraised. Perhaps Mill was overly brief in his account of high quality pleasure as measured by the preferences of a majority of competent judges. But his insight concerning the inadequacy of quantity of pleasure as a *sufficient* and *exclusive* test for intrinsic value was not without foundation. If we are looking for an appropriate or justifiable norm for those judgments we make about what things are truly worth seeking as ultimate ends in life, then such a norm might well be that which thoughtful men and women tend to use when they fully understand the nature of those ends. This leaves open the further question of whether bodily pleasure or other kinds (or a combination of both) would actually be judged to have intrinsic value when a justifiable standard so defined was used.

PLEASURE AND HAPPINESS

In the remainder of this chapter, another possible standard of intrinsic value besides pleasure will be analyzed. This is the standard of happiness, which traditionally has been the main rival to pleasure as the sole valid criterion for what is intrinsically good in human life. What is the difference between pleasure and happiness? Is not happiness simply a whole life full of pleasures — perhaps of "high quality" — but nevertheless pleasures? If this were so, then it would be mistaken to say that a person can be happy even when he has experienced much unpleasantness in life. Is this, indeed, mistaken?

It might at first be thought that a happy person is one who has achieved self-fulfillment. But what is self-fulfillment? Until we have answered this, we have not answered the question: What is happiness? even if "self-fulfillment" is a correct synonym for "happiness." Suppose it is suggested that a person has achieved self-fulfillment (and hence is happy) when all his desires are satisfied — if not completely then at least to a large extent. That this does not seem to provide an accurate analysis of the concept of happiness becomes evident when we ask ourselves, Can we not correctly describe someone as being unhappy even when his desires are satisfied? Consider the case of a person who comes to regret his having satisfied certain desires. He even wishes he had never had them in the first place, now that he sees the results in his life of satisfying them. If this kind of disillusionment should happen over and over again, we might well say (and so might the person himself!) that such an unfortunate individual has led an unhappy life, though he was always able to satisfy his desires. Furthermore, it does not appear to express a self-contradiction to say that a man or woman is a profoundly happy person even if there are periods when many of his or her desires remain unsatisfied. If this is so, happiness cannot be simply equated with the satisfaction of desire.

Setting aside for the moment exactly what (if anything) does differentiate happiness from pleasure and from the satisfaction of desire, let us see why philosophers have thought happiness an appropriate standard of intrinsic value. The reason becomes clear when we consider the frequently heard statement, "Everyone wants to be happy." This does not seem to be merely an empirical generalization based on finding out that this person seeks happiness rather than something else, that person seeks happiness rather than something else, and so on for everyone. The statement has the sound of a necessary truth — it seems necessarily to be the case that everyone wants to be happy. To understand why this seems to be so, consider a denial of the statement. If we heard it said about a person that he does not want to be happy, we would be likely to react in either of two ways. We might say, "You mean, he doesn't *think* he wants to be happy, but all the same he *really* wants to be happy." Or we might say, "You mean he doesn't want what most people call happiness, but he is still seeking his own kind of happiness." Both of these reactions show a tendency to make happiness (that is, *true* happiness) something which *by definition* is wanted by everyone. Furthermore, it seems absurd to ask what anyone wants happiness *for*, as if it were merely a means to some further end. We tend to think of happiness as an ultimate end of human life, something which *by definition* is wanted for its own sake.

These considerations show why happiness is a plausible candidate for the sole standard of intrinsic value. For if we value things extrinsically only as a means to something else which we value intrinsically, while what we value intrinsically is not valued because of something else we want, then whatever goal of human life is an ultimate end for everyone must serve as the very criterion of intrinsic value. It is for the sake of that end that everything else is valued, and it is not valued itself for the sake of anything else. Hence its value must be intrinsic to it. And if it is the only such end of human life, it is alone the standard of intrinsic value.

In order to reveal what are the philosophical implications of holding happiness to be the sole valid standard of intrinsic value, three conceptions of human happiness are analyzed below. It should be remarked at the outset that the shift from the concept of pleasure to the concept of happiness as a standard of intrinsic value involves a corresponding shift in the kind of thing that *has* intrinsic value. Implicit in our discussion of pleasure was the assumption that it is *particular experiences* of people that are properly described as being pleasant or unpleasant and hence may possess intrinsic value or disvalue. When we turn to happiness we notice that there are two basic kinds of things that are judged to be happy or unhappy: persons themselves, and their whole lives (or large segments of their lives). It is only by extension that we talk of particular experiences as being happy or unhappy. Thus we say that a certain person is a happy man or a happy woman; and we say that someone has led, or leads, a happy life. Or we say that a man had a happy life until he lost his wife, or until he was wounded in a war, and so on. We say such things as "She had a happy childhood" or "She was very unhappy during her adolescence." Still more narrowly, we make such statements as "It was a happy two-week vacation" and "It was a moment of supreme happiness for them." Generally speaking, however, when we talk of a happy vacation or a happy moment, we mean that some *person* was happy during that time. Certain pleasures that a person experiences may be called "happy moments" or even "happy experiences"; there may be enjoyments, of course, that *contribute to* a person's happiness (even though it may be that pleasures alone cannot *make* a person happy). Nevertheless it is not the pleasures (that is, the pleasant experiences themselves) that are happy, but the person who has them.

When happiness is used as a standard of intrinsic value, then, it will be understood to apply to a person or to a person's whole life (or a large segment of it). As a corollary of this, to judge a person or life as happy, and therefore as having intrinsic value, is to judge it without regarding its effects on the lives of others. A person's life may not only be happy and hence have intrinsic value, it may also bring happiness to others and contribute to the flourishing of a whole community. But in that case it will have instrumental or extrinsic value *additional to* its intrinsic value. Similarly, the intrinsic value of a happy life is not diminished by the fact that it causes unhappiness to another person. (Recall the case of the sadist's pleasures, mentioned earlier.) This is not to deny that a person's *knowledge* of the effect of his life on others may be a factor that increases or decreases his own happiness and is accordingly relevant to its intrinsic value. Such knowledge would then have instrumental value (or disvalue) in relation to the intrinsic value of the person's life. However, regardless of what causes him to be happy or unhappy and regardless of what kinds of experiences comprise his overall happiness, it is the happiness or unhappiness itself that exclusively determines the intrinsic value or disvalue of his life.

Three philosophical concepts of happiness will now be examined to see what implications they have as possible criteria for intrinsic value. They shall be designated "the essentialist conception," "the plan-of-life conception," and "the self-evaluative conception."

(1) The essentialist conception of happiness

This conception has a long philosophical tradition behind it, going back to classical Greece. The two greatest philosophers of that time, Plato (427-347 B.C.) and Aristotle (384-322 B.C.) each developed and propounded an essentialist conception of happiness that has had an undying influence on the history of ethics. We shall here be concerned only with the basic ideas that are common to both their conceptions, since we wish to contrast *any* essentialist conception with the plan-of-life, and the self-evaluative concepts. No attempt will be made to set forth the differences in the specific views of either Plato or Aristotle.

According to the essentialist conception of happiness, a truly happy life is identified with the Good Life for Man. The person who lives such a life is realizing the Human Good, that is, the good of man as man. Happiness (*eudaimonia,* well-being) is the kind of life that is suitable or fitting for a *human* being to live, and a *human* being is one who exemplifies the essential nature (or essence) of man. Thus happiness is not to be identified with any kind of life a person might actually want to live. Instead, it characterizes the kind of life we all *would* want to live if we understood our true nature as human beings. Happiness, then, may be defined as that state of the "soul" or condition of life which all human beings, *insofar as they are human,* ultimately aim at.

This is called an "essentialist" conception because it presupposes that there is such a thing as an essential human nature. This essence of man is not only a set of properties common to all human beings and unique to them (setting them off from all other creatures); it is also a set of attributes which define the good for man as such, a Human Good that is fundamentally different from an animal's good or a plant's. This idea may be clarified as follows. It is not difficult to describe a plant's or nonhuman animal's good. It is a condition of life and growth in which the plant or animal is healthy and strong, living at its highest capacity for adjusting to its environment, maintaining its full range of life-functions unimpaired, and surviving until what, for its species, would be old age. One might say that the happy plant or animal does not merely survive, but thrives and flourishes. (Anyone who has taken care of a plant or an animal will know exactly what is meant.)

Now what would correspond to such flourishing in a human being? The essentialist's concept of the Human Good is not the concept of what is good for a person merely as a biological creature. For a man or woman can be physically healthy and can stay alive a long time, yet live a *kind* of life that is unfit for man, that is, a kind of life that runs counter to what is truly human in man's nature. Essentialist philosophers view the good for man as an ideal of human perfection, a perfection which is uniquely suitable to characteristically human capacities. To the extent that an individual lives in a way not in keeping with this ideal, he remains biologically a human being (that is, a member of the species *homo sapiens*), but he fails to realize his human potentialities. On the other hand, to the extent that he fulfills this ideal he manifests his human nature (as distinct from his mere biological nature). He achieves true human dignity, a kind of nobility of character that sets a model of human excellence that all men really strive for insofar as they are human.

When this conception of happiness is used as the standard of intrinsic value, that standard becomes identical with the essentialist's standard of human perfection or virtue. What determines the intrinsic goodness of a person's life is the realization of an ideal; in living a truly human life, the person is realizing the good for man as man. Not everyone fulfills this standard to the same degree, but to the extent that a person does, his life takes on a worth, a perfection, that gives it value in itself, independently of any consequences it might have in the lives of others.

Exactly how the standard of the Human Good is conceived varies somewhat from philosopher to philosopher. (For the Greek philosophers, the basic element in the Human Good is man's use of reason in the guidance of life as well as in achieving knowledge of ultimate reality.) This matter need not be entered into here, since the aim is to contrast the essentialist view with two other views of happiness, neither of which presupposes an essence of man. Let us now proceed to an investigation of these nonessentialist conceptions of happiness.

(2) The plan-of-life conception of happiness

There are three conditions that must hold true of a person's life if it is correctly to be judged a happy life according to this second conception: (a) It must be a unified, integrated whole in which a person is carrying out a plan of life. (b) The person himself must be the autonomous creator of that plan. (c) During his life the person must have the opportunity and ability to realize his basic goals according to their ordering in his life plan. Let us consider each of these conditions in turn.

(a) A plan of life is, first, a coherent, internally harmonious system of means and ends. It consists of a set of goals that are considered by a person to be worth seeking. The goals may be either self-regarding or other-regarding. That is, they may involve the satisfaction of interests that can be understood independently of the interests and aims of other persons (for example, becoming a good violinist), or they may arise from motives which can be described only by reference to the welfare and objectives of others (for example, being a good friend).

When a person has a plan of life, there is an ordering of goals based on his own judgment of their comparative importance. Thus, when he is in circumstances where he must choose between pursuing one goal or another, his choice is determined by the priority that he assigns each goal in his life as a whole. The ordering of means and ends therefore reflects the individual's own value system. The ends on which he places greatest value are those he has decided to pursue at the cost of his less valuable ends, when he cannot achieve all of them at once. In this manner a plan of life is integrated into a unified whole. With regard to such integration of goals, however, two points should be kept in mind. First, it need not be a hierarchy consisting of one supreme goal or ultimate end to which all other ends are subordinate. There may be a plurality of ends that are judged equally worthy of realization. In cases of choice among those ends, the person may sometimes pursue one and sometimes another, depending on the unfolding over time of his life plan. At various stages in his life, different priorities may prevail among the several highest goals. But at any one moment, the order of his life plan enables the person to make a rational choice of ends and means—of ends to aim at and of means to use in achieving them.

The second point is this: A plan of life is not chosen once and for all. It gradually emerges and develops as the individual confronts the ever-changing situations of life. The ordering of the plan is a dynamic ordering which is open ended, constantly subject to revision and modification. Thus a happy person, according to the conception under study, is one whose plan of life gradually unfolds as a reflection of his own choices and value judgments made at different stages of his life. The goals of the plan are goals he has set for himself, in the light of his other aims and interests and the available opportunities found at each moment in the changing circumstances of his life.

(b) The second condition of happiness may be put this way: A person's plan of life must be the authentic expression of his own conception of himself. This means that the ordering of the plan must be the outcome of the person's own decisions, made in the light of his self-chosen system of values. A happy life is not only an integrated life, making it possible for one to pursue long-range as well as short-range goals; it is also self-directed, a life of self-determination at every moment. A person's happiness, in this respect, stems from his being the master of his own existence. His plan of life is a kind of *model of selfhood* which he has himself created as an autonomous being, that is, as one who can determine his own nature.

We are now in a position to compare the second conception of happiness with the first. According to the essentialist view, man's nature or essence sets limits to the goals it is proper for him to pursue. Insofar as he is human, he seeks one ultimate end: the Human Good. Unless he is realizing the Human Good in his life, he cannot be truly happy. The second conception, on the other hand, denies that human happiness is determined by man's essential nature. Indeed, it holds that there is no such thing as an essential human nature. Man is conceived as a being who creates himself; he has the capacity to define his own nature by making autonomous decisions. It is these decisions which constitute, for a happy person, a plan of life. Thus according to the plan-of-life conception of happiness, each individual must *choose* what kind of person he is to be at each moment, there being no limits to the goals he sets for himself. There is no ideal founded on his nature that tells him what kind of person he ought to be, or must be if he is to be happy. On the contrary, he is happy (assuming that condition (c), to be discussed below, holds true) if he has a plan of life that authentically reflects the decision he makes at every moment to define himself in a certain way.

What does it mean to decide to define oneself in a certain way? It means to choose one's own plan of life, first, by setting for oneself those goals that are to be one's ultimate ends, and secondly, by deciding how they are to be weighed against each other in situations requiring a choice between them. In this way the internal structure of each person's plan of life both expresses and determines the kind of being he is, and the coherence of the life plan is precisely the unity of himself as one person.

(c) We have seen so far that a person is happy, in accordance with points (a) and (b), when his life is the unfolding of a coherent order of means and ends, an order which the person himself continuously creates as a self-directed being. To live such a life, however, requires that the person have the *opportunity* to pursue his goals and the *capacity* for making autonomous choices throughout his life. Having the opportunity to pursue one's goals means that one enjoys freedom from interference by others and that the basic instrumentalities for realizing one's ends are available. One must be educated so that certain abilities are developed, and of course one needs the means for staying alive and healthy enough to exercise those abilities. (A person who wishes to become a good violinist will need an instrument, musical instruction, time for learning and playing, a relatively quiet place, et cetera, as well as the ordinary necessities of life.) Finally, one needs the general capacity for autonomous decision-making and the opportunity for a full range of expression in his life (at least to the maximum extent compatible with a like freedom for every other person).

So much, then, for the second conception of happiness. It may be worth noting at this jucture how happiness so conceived differs from the two other definitions of happiness — the maximizing of pleasure and the satisfaction of desire — mentioned at the beginning of this discussion of happiness. With regard to pleasure, there is nothing in the idea of an autonomously chosen life plan that makes it a hedonistic ideal. A person living by his own life plan does not necessarily aim at maximizing pleasure as his one supreme goal, with all other ends being sought as means for achieving this one goal. He may well pursue a variety of activities as ends in themselves, each deemed worthwhile for its own sake as well as for the contribution it makes to the realization of his life plan as a whole. No doubt his being able to accomplish his goals will bring him pleasure, and he will find satisfaction in choosing his own ends as a way of defining himself. But there is no logical or psychological necessity such that an individual *must* seek to maximize his pleasures in choosing a life plan for himself. He need not set for himself the one goal — undergoing as many pleasant experiences as possible — as having the highest priority over all his other goals.

With regard to the equating of happiness with the satisfaction of desire, a person who creates himself in pursuing a self-chosen plan of life does have a complex set of desires corresponding to his various interests and aims. But his active pursuit of his interests and aims should not be understood as the having of *another* aim, namely, the satisfaction of his desires. To take the example mentioned earlier, suppose one of his aims is to become a good violinist. We can then redescribe this by saying, "He desires the state of affairs, being-a-good-violinist"; this means the same as "Being-a-good-violinist is the state of affairs that would satisfy one of his desires." However, "the satisfaction of one of my desires" does not designate for that person a goal which is different from that designated by "being a good violinist." In other words, the satisfaction of desire, as such, is not an end. Furthermore, let us suppose the person never does become a good violinist because he lacks sufficient ability. If he discovers this fact about himself at a certain stage in his life, he will give up the pursuit of that end (though he may continue to play the violin as a relaxing or enjoyable pastime). A desire that he has had is left unsatisfied, but this does not by itself entail that he is an unhappy person or is living an unhappy life. It would depend on whether he was able to accept the fact of his limited ability for violin playing and revise his plan of life accordingly. If the person is, as we have been supposing, a self-directed individual truly in control of his life, he will make such an adjustment. He will experience a certain amount of disappointment, no doubt, and we can then correctly speak of his "being unhappy" about that particular matter. Yet, given the conditions enumerated above (a unified plan, created solely by the individual, who is able to realize it) his life as a whole could still be described as a happy one.

When the plan-of-life conception of happiness is used as a standard of intrinsic value, it has the following implication. We would have to distinguish between what might be called "subjective" intrinsic value and "objective" intrinsic value. Something has subjective intrinsic value when a person places value on it, or judges it to be good, as an end in itself. From his point of view, it has nonderivative value. Within the framework of a given individual's value system and plan of life there will be, at any one time, a number of activities and experiences that have subjective intrinsic value for him. These will be activities and experiences he considers worthwhile doing and enjoying for their own sake. "Objective" intrinsic value, in contrast, will be the value of happiness itself, which is the value of a person's whole life when it satisfies the three conditions of internal coherence, autonomously chosen, and with opportunity to be realized. A happy life so defined has intrinsic value because it is a good thing simply that someone lives such a life; his life is not good just because it serves some further purpose (such as the advancement of science or the overthrow of a dictatorship).

It follows from happiness as a standard of intrinsic value that every happy life possesses a distinct kind of goodness precisely because it is the sort of life it is. It has an intrinsic worth (in the sense of "objective" intrinsic value) *by virtue of the fact that it is the authentic manifestation of an individual's autonomous choice of his own selfhood.* The social and historical consequences of someone's living such a life at a particular time may lead us to say that it was good that he lived as he did. We would then be judging his life as having instrumental value in affecting the lives of others or in contributing to the progress of a whole society. But this value judgment, even if true, takes nothing away from the goodness of happiness which attaches to that life itself. That goodness, being a nonderivative value, is intrinsic to that kind of life. At least, this is how we would have to view the matter if we used the plan-of-life conception of happiness as our standard of intrinsic value.

(3) *The self-evaluative conception of happiness*

The third conception of happiness is to be distinguished from the other two in several important ways. In the first place, according to this third view, to assert that someone is a happy person or leads a happy life is not to *describe* the person or his life; it is to *evaluate* it. In the second place, an ascription of happiness in the first person ("I am happy") is primary, while such an ascription in the second or third person ("You are happy," "He/she/they are happy") is secondary. It is only on the basis of understanding what the first-person ascription means that we can meaningfully predicate happiness of someone else in a second- or third-person ascription. Thirdly, there is a sense in which only the person himself knows whether he is really happy. Each individual is, as it were, the final authority on his own happiness (or unhappiness). Let us see how these three aspects of happiness ascriptions support one another and yield a coherent conception of happiness.

When a person, without self-deception, sincerely asserts that he is happy, he is expressing the outcome or "verdict" of an assessment he has made of his life as a whole. This assessment has two basic characteristics: It leaves out nothing important (that is, nothing which is important *to the person himself*), and it takes priority over every other assessment. A brief look at each of these characteristics will bring out the self-evaluative nature of happiness assertions.

To assert that one is happy is to make a value judgment about one's total condition of life. This value judgment consists in the claim that, with respect to what is really significant in life, one's life is good. The standards used in this assessment define one's own idea of what makes for a generally satisfactory existence, as far as the important things in life are concerned. Even the criteria of what is "important" or "really significant" in life are themselves part of the individual's own value system in terms of which the happiness assessment is made. If the person in question thinks that certain things in life which others consider trivial or shallow are very important, then it is his own values that must be taken into account, not those of others, in judging his happiness or unhappiness. We might sum this up by saying that a happiness assertion is the *broadest* or *most comprehensive* assessment one can make of life on the basis of one's own values.

A happiness assertion is, secondly, the *highest* evaluation one can make of life. It takes priority over every other evaluation—at least as regards nonmoral goodness and badness. This follows from the very logic of the concept of happiness. Thus we say such things as: It is better to be happy and poor than to be unhappy and rich; better to be ill but happy than have excellent health yet be unhappy; and so on for all the other components that make up a satisfactory existence according to one's own standards of value. The general principle involved here may be stated thus: If an individual is basically happy although his life lacks something whose presence would make it even more satisfactory, then he is better off, all things considered, than he would be if he possessed that good thing but was otherwise not happy. This is a logical consequence of the fact that a happy life is a life which is judged to be good on the whole, as one views it within the framework of one's total nonmoral system of values. From this standpoint the concept of happiness is identical with the concept of the *summum bonum* (the highest good).

Given this way of looking at happiness assertions, it can now be seen why a first-person ascription of happiness is logically prior to a second- or third-person ascription. Until we have grasped what it means to be happy or unhappy ourselves, we cannot understand what it means for others to be happy or unhappy. The reason for this is that only in the light of our own values can we make a judgment about the happiness or unhappiness of life *as we experience it*. In other words, we must be able to know what it is to apply our own standards to our life experiences if we are to understand what being happy or unhappy *means*. Only then are we in a position to understand another person's evaluating life as *he* experiences it in terms of *his* standards. When we say "You are happy" or "He/she/they are happy," we presuppose that we understand what it means for a person to be happy, and we can understand this only when we know what the statement "I am happy" means. For in saying "You are happy" we are in effect saying, "In terms of your values, your life as you experience it is good on the whole." We can assert this meaningfully only when we already know what it is to evaluate life as a person experiences it directly, and to evaluate it on the basis of standards or values one has accepted for oneself. It may be the case that, when we do make such an appraisal of our own life, it is *not* judged by us to be "good on the whole," but rather to be "bad on the whole." Then we know not only what "I am unhappy" (a true statement) means. We also know what "I am happy" (a false statement) means. For if our own standards are clear to us, we can conceive of the sort of life that would fulfill them, even though our actual life does not. Both the true and the false statement express evaluations based on our own accepted standards. As such, both are primary in relation to our ascribing happiness or unhappiness to others on the basis of *their* accepted standards.

In line with this conception of happiness, a further point can now be made. Unless some exceptional condition holds, each person is the best judge of whether he is happy. This derives from the fact that to call a person happy is to evaluate the total condition of his life in the light of his value system, and it is normally the person himself who knows best what his own value system is. Moreover, it is the individual himself who knows his life experiences firsthand and is directly aware of their relative significance or insignificance in his total scheme of things. Now suppose someone judges himself to be unhappy, while another person claims that the first individual is "really" happy. We would tend in that case to doubt the second person's claim. For we imagine such a case as applied to ourselves, and we realize that other people often do not know what our own values are, or are misled by outward appearances about our true condition of life. The situation where one person is judged by someone else to be "really" unhappy when the person himself declares (outwardly or inwardly) that he is happy is a more uncertain one. For often a person will deceive himself into thinking he is happy, or want to make himself and others believe he is, because he does not wish to face the reality of his own misery. So a person is not always an *infallible* judge of his own happiness. Nevertheless, if he is able to avoid self-deception, his sincere judgment (which may not be expressed to others) is generally to be taken as authoritative, for the reasons given.

It is worth noticing how the self-evaluative conception of happiness .as it has been presented here is in fundamental disagreement with the essentialist view of it, but is compatible with (though not identical to) the plan-of-life conception. According to the self-evaluative view, happiness is correctly ascribed to a person only on the basis of his own standards of value. It follows that what is a happy life to one person will not be a happy life to another, when each is using a different value system in judging his life experiences. The essentialist view, on the contrary, entails that an individual's assessment of his life as a happy one might be correct as far as his own value system is concerned, but that estimate will not tell us whether the individual in question is *truly* happy. For it is the set of standards embodied in the ideal of the good life for man as man (which is necessarily the same for all humans) that determines true happiness. If the standards used by an individual are not in accord with this universal Human Good, then the essentialist holds that there is a discrepancy between the individual's *apparent good* and his *real good*. His apparent good is defined by the standards he has accepted—whatever they might happen to be—as part of his system of values. His real good is the Human Good, that is, the realization of his truly human potentialities as defined by his essential human nature. When such a discrepancy between one's apparent and real good occurs, a person might think he is happy (because he achieves his apparent good) but not really be happy (because he fails to realize his real good).

When we compare the plan-of-life conception of happiness with the self-evaluative conception, a different sort of relationship emerges. In both conceptions, a person's own value system is central to any judgment of his happiness or unhappiness. But according to the plan-of-life view, an individual is truly happy only when he can live by fulfilling his plan of life, which is based on a value system he has autonomously chosen as his way of defining himself. It is only under this condition that a person's value system can correctly serve as the ground for a happiness assertion. The self-evaluative conception does not place such a restriction on the value system used in a happiness assertion. Furthermore, the two conceptions differ with regard to the function of a happiness assertion (as distinct from its ground). According to the self-evaluative conception, when one makes such an assertion one is *evaluating* a life—specifically, the life of the person who makes the assertion. From the standpoint of the plan-of-life view, however, when one makes such an assertion one is *describing* a life, which may or may not be the life of the person who is making the assertion. Now it is possible for someone to both evaluate and describe his own life—as being happy or unhappy—in one and the same assertion. If the evaluating is done in accordance with the conditions specified in the self-evaluative view and if the life being described satisfies the three conditions (a unified whole, autonomously created by a person with the ability to realize his goals) as defined by the plan-of-life view, then "I am happy" could be accepted by both views as a correct happiness assertion made by a given individual concerning his own life. Thus the two views are consistent with each other. However, because of the differences between them that have already been mentioned, they are not to be considered as expressing but one conception of happiness.

At this point it is pertinent to examine the implications of the self-evaluative view with respect to using happiness, rather than pleasure, as the standard of intrinsic value. Suppose a choice has to be made by someone between obtaining a pleasure while risking a chance of unhappiness and giving up a pleasure to help bring about or maintain a state of happiness. It would seem that a rational person will choose the second alternative. The reason for this has to do with the concept of happiness itself. According to the self-evaluative view, a happiness judgment is the highest evaluation one can make of one's own life taken as a whole. This implies that it is better to be happy but poor than be unhappy and rich, and does so for every other good thing which might form a part of happiness or a means to achieving it, but is not that state itself.

Bringing this consideration to bear on the relation between happiness and pleasure, we might admit that pleasure is a good thing, not merely because it contributes to one's happiness but because it is good in itself. We might grant, in other words, that any pleasure has some intrinsic value, just by virtue of the fact that it is a pleasure. But we can now see that, whatever degree of intrinsic value it may have, it is always outweighed by the intrinsic disvalue of the whole life of which it is a part, when that disvalue is measured in terms of unhappiness. Thus, it is better to be happy and in pain than to experience pleasure and be unhappy. Indeed, a whole life full of pleasures is not worth leading an unhappy life. The argument for this does not require our imagining two sorts of lives and trying to weigh their relative merits. One simply has to think clearly about what a happiness assertion means. For according to the conception being examined here, to say that someone is happy is to say that, in his judgment, his life is good on the whole, when everything of importance is taken into account. So no matter how much pain a person suffers, if he correctly assesses his own life to be a happy one, it must be better when compared with avoiding the pain but being unhappy. It is true that someone might in fact choose to lead a life of avoiding pains and pursuing pleasures rather than a happy one (assuming such alternatives were open to him). But that cannot be a rational choice, since he is choosing the alternative that is worse *as judged by his own system of values*. Therefore, happiness appears to be a more appropriate standard of intrinsic value than pleasure.

As a final consideration regarding happiness and pleasure, let us assume that a teleological ethical system is true and ask ourselves, Which is more appropriate as an ultimate end of morality, pleasure or happiness? A teleological ethical system, we recall, holds that morally right conduct has instrumental value in bringing about an intrinsically good end. Now it would seem that the use of pleasure as the sole standard of intrinsic value (that is, valuational hedonism) leads to a paradox. For example, suppose that a person finds pleasure in deceiving and exploiting people, or in torturing animals. It would then follow from a teleological ethical system that, given these sources of pleasure, the ultimate purpose of morality is to bring about an immoral state of affairs.

Does happiness fare any better with regard to the same issue? To answer this it is necessary to distinguish the second and third conceptions of happiness from the first. In the case of the second (plan-of-life) view and the third (self-evaluative) view, there is nothing in the concept of happiness itself that would rule out what would ordinarily be judged to be an immoral life. For, given the second conception of happiness, a person might autonomously choose a plan of life such that it would be desirable for him to take unfair advantage of others, interfere with their freedom, or otherwise benefit himself at others' expense. Psychologically this may be improbable, but it is not logically impossible. Similarly, if we use the third conception of happiness as our standard of intrinsic value, we again do not rule out the possibility that a person might correctly assess his own life as happy in terms of his own value system, even when it involves immoral conduct on his part. The first conception of happiness, according to which a person is happy when he is realizing in his life the Human Good, escapes this difficulty. But this is due to the fact that it includes a moral concept itself as part of the meaning of happiness. For the essentialist holds that the Human Good can only be realized by one who possesses both intellectual and moral virtue. The essentialist conception of happiness, in other words, presupposes an *ethical* system of some sort and consequently cannot be used as a purely nonmoral standard of intrinsic value.

It may be the case, however, that all teleological ethical systems are mistaken. If this is so, our present problem does not arise. For a deontological or nonteleological ethical system would imply that there is a logical independence between moral rightness and intrinsic goodness. Given that logical independence, either pleasure or happiness could serve equally well as (nonmoral) standards of intrinsic value, since neither would itself provide a ground for moral judgments. Either pleasure or happiness may be what makes something intrinsically good, but what is intrinsically good can be, at the same time, what is morally bad or wrong.

Suggested Reading

Basic works of classical Greek ethics:

Plato, *Gorgias; Philebus; Protagoras; The Republic.*
Aristotle, *Nicomachean Ethics.*

Studies of the concept of intrinsic value:

Baylis, Charles A., "Grading, Values and Choice," in *Mind,* LXVII, 268 (1958), 485-501. Reprinted in *Problems of Moral Philosophy: An Introduction to Ethics,* Second Edition, ed. Paul W. Taylor. Belmont, California and Encino, California: Dickenson Publishing Co., Inc., 1972.

Beardsley, Monroe, "Intrinsic Value," in *Philosophy and Phenomenological Research,* XXVI (1965), 1-17. Reprinted in *Readings in Ethical Theory,* Second Edition, ed. Wilfrid Sellars and John Hospers. New York: Appleton-Century-Crofts, 1970.

Lewis, Clarence Irving, *An Analysis of Knowledge and Valuation.* Book III. LaSalle, Ill.: Open Court Publishing Co., 1946.*

Moore, George Edward, *Ethics,* Chapters I, II, and VII. London: Oxford University Press, 1912.*

———, *Principia Ethica,* Chapters III and VI. Cambridge: Cambridge University Press, 1903.*

Sesonske, Alexander, *Value and Obligation: The Foundations of an Empiricist Ethical Theory.* Chapter IV. New York: Oxford University Press, 1964.*

Stevenson, Charles L., *Ethics and Language,* Chapter VIII. New Haven: Yale University Press, 1944.*

Works on hedonism and the concept of pleasure:

Blake, Ralph Mason, "Why Not Hedonism? A Protest," *International Journal of Ethics,* XXXVII, No. 1 (1926), 1-18. Reprinted in the Bobbs-Merrill Reprint Series in Philosophy. Indianapolis: The Bobbs-Merrill Co., Inc.*

Bradley, F. H., "Pleasure for Pleasure's Sake," Essay III of *Ethical Studies.* London: Oxford University Press, 1927. Reprinted in James M. Smith and Ernest Sosa, eds., *Mill's Utilitarianism: Text and Criticism.* Belmont, California: Wadsworth Publishing Co., Inc., 1969.*

Brandt, Richard B., *Ethical Theory: The Problems of Normative and Critical Ethics,* Chapter 12. Englewood Cliffs, N. J.: Prentice-Hall, Inc., 1959.

Cowan, J. L., *Pleasure and Pain.* London: The Macmillan Co., Ltd., 1968.

Gosling, J. C. B., *Pleasure and Desire: The Case for Hedonism Reviewed.* London: Oxford University Press, 1969.

Moore, George Edward, *Ethics,* Chapters II and VII. London: Oxford University Press, 1912.*

———, *Principia Ethica.* Chapters III and VI. Cambridge: Cambridge University Press, 1903.*

Nowell-Smith, P. H., *Ethics,* Chapter 10. Baltimore: Penguin Books, Inc., 1954.*

Perry, David L., *The Concept of Pleasure.* The Hague: Mouton and Co., 1967.

Ryle, Gilbert, "Pleasure," *Proceedings of the Aristotelian Society,* 28 (1954), 135-146. Reprinted in *Moral Concepts,* ed. Joel Feinberg. London: Oxford University Press, 1970.*

Schlick, Moritz, *Problems of Ethics,* Chapters VI and VIII. New York: Dover Publications, 1939.

*Available in paperback

Sidgwick, Henry, *The Methods of Ethics,* 1874. Sixth Edition, Book I, Chapter IV, and Book II. Chicago: University of Chicago Press, 1962.

Von Wright, Georg Henrik, *The Varieties of Goodness,* Chapter IV. New York: Humanities Press, 1963.

Recent studies of happiness and related concepts:

Austin, Jean, "Pleasure and Happiness," *Philosophy,* 43 (1968), 51-62. Reprinted in Smith and Sosa, op. cit. This article is an important source of the self-evaluative conception of happiness.

Fried, Charles, *An Anatomy of Values: Problems of Personal and Social Choice.* Cambridge, Mass.: Harvard University Press, 1970. This excellent book contains a very careful and thorough study of the concept of an end-in-itself. It also sets forth a systematic analysis of the idea of a plan of life.

Kenny, Anthony, "Happiness," *Proceedings of the Aristotelian Society,* 66 (1965), 93-102. Reprinted in *Moral Concepts,* ed. Joel Feinberg. London: Oxford University Press, 1970.* An analysis of the concept of happiness, with special reference to Aristotle's views.

Olafson, Frederick A., *Principles and Persons: An Ethical Interpretation of Existentialism.* Baltimore: The Johns Hopkins Press, 1967.* Includes excellent studies of the concepts of autonomy, defining one's nature, authenticity, and value.

Rawls, John. *A Theory of Justice.* Cambridge, Mass.: Harvard University Press, 1971.* The most important contemporary work on the relation between the right and the good. It includes the idea of a plan of life, which Professor Rawls originated.

Smart, J. J. C., "An Outline of a System of Utilitarian Ethics," Sections 3 and 4, in *Utilitarianism: For and Against,* by J. J. C. Smart and Bernard Williams. Cambridge: Cambridge University Press, 1973.*

Von Wright, Georg Henrik, *The Varieties of Goodness.* New York: Humanities Press, 1963, Chapter V. Propounds a nonessentialist view of the Good of Man, with an associated conception of happiness.

*Available in paperback

VII

Moral Responsibility and Free Will

One of the most important and yet one of the most difficult problems in the whole of ethics centers on such questions as: Is freedom of the will a reality or only an illusion? Can human beings rightly be punished or blamed for their wrongdoings? What does it mean to say that a person is morally responsible for what he does? These questions have preoccupied thinkers since the very beginnings of philosophy, and they remain to this day a source of great perplexity. The purpose of the present chapter is not to provide final answers to these questions, but to point out the first steps toward a philosophical understanding of the many different concepts and issues involved in answering them. In this way the basic problems will have been clarified and the reader will have made an orderly start on his own reflections about them.

EXCUSING CONDITIONS

Suppose we have accepted a normative ethical system according to which certain acts are right and others wrong. (It does not matter for present purposes what specific norms make up the system, or whether the system is utilitarian, formalistic, or of some other kind.) If we then judge that a particular act performed by someone was not the right thing for him to do in the given situation, we can always ask the further questions: Should he or should he not be held responsible for doing it? Was the act excusable or inexcusable? Is the person at fault for having carried it out?

The conditions under which we normally excuse a person and do not believe he should be held morally responsible for an act he has committed are of four kinds: (a) excusable ignorance of the nature or consequences of an act; (b) the presence of a constraint which forced the person to do the act

146

and which was of a degree of strength no ordinary amount of will power could overcome; (c) the circumstances in which the action was taken were beyond the person's control; (d) the absence of either the ability or the opportunity, or both, to perform an alternative act that would be the right thing to do in the given situation. Let us consider each of these in turn.

(a) Excusable ignorance

In the first sort of case we excuse a person because he could not reasonably be expected to have known the wrong nature of his action, or to have foreseen the bad consequences that in fact resulted from it. For example, a young man or woman accepts a job with an apparently legal and respectable company which is actually a front for organized crime. Or, to take an instance of excusable ignorance concerning consequences, the driver of a car picks up a friend to take him to the store. A minute later another car, with a drunken driver, crashes into the car on the side where the friend is seated, seriously injuring him. In these situations actions occurred that can be correctly described as "aiding criminals" and "causing harm to come to a friend," yet we do not blame the persons who did such acts. This is because we would think it unreasonable to expect that the agents involved would *know* that those descriptions applied to their actions. If we look at their beliefs and motives at the time of doing the actions, we see that they intended to do what they had every reason to think was the right thing.

(b) External or internal constraint

The second condition of excusability occurs in a situation in which we say of a person, "He did not do the act of his own free will," or "He could not help it," or "It was not a matter of his own choice." Here there is either some *external coercion* being exerted upon the person or he feels driven by an *inner compulsion* to do something he believes wrong but finds beyond his power to control. In the first kind of case, we say that the act was committed against the person's will; he did not want to do it but was forced to. An example would be a man's being compelled to participate in a bank robbery because the robber threatens to kill him if he does not do as he is told. We withdraw our condemnation of the man and consider him innocent when we discover that his act was done under coercion. In this way we contrast his case with that of someone who helps the robber "of his own free will," desiring a share of the cash.

In the second form of constraint, the compelling element comes from "inside" rather than from someone else. The person cannot help behaving as he does because he feels driven by an uncontrollable impulse or craving. An example is the overwhelming desire for a drug which the addict experiences if he has not been able to get his usual amount at the usual time. It should be noted that we do not always excuse an addict who commits a crime to obtain his drug. It would depend on whether the formation of his habit was itself excusable under one or more of the four conditions considered here. If the formation of the habit was in the beginning a matter of the person's free choice and if it would be reasonable to expect him to have known the probable consequences of cultivating it, we might consider him at fault for *putting himself in the position* of being subject to an uncontrollable craving that leads him to commit a crime. It may happen, however, that a neurotic or psychotic person will do something wrong from an inner compulsion, a compulsion that did not develop from choices he had freely and knowingly made in the past. The shoplifting of a kleptomaniac is a case in point. Such a person keeps repeating the act of stealing even when he knows he will be caught and despite his conscious judgment that he is doing something wrong. His behavior exemplifies a rigid pattern which is beyond his power to change. In this kind of situation we tend to think of the individual as mentally or emotionally ill, in need of special therapy to get rid of his obsessive impulse to steal. Thus, we distinguish his case from that of a bank robber who has carefully and cooly planned his crime over many weeks and feels no inner drive to carry it out. Unlike the kleptomaniac who cannot stop himself from stealing no matter how hard he tries, the bank robber can decide to give up his plan and refrain from carrying it out, as is shown by the fact that he does precisely this when something he had not anticipated occurs (such as a reinforcement of police protection for the bank).

(c) Circumstances beyond the agent's control

A third condition of excusability holds when the circumstances in which an action is done, as distinct from an external or internal constraint upon the doer of the action, are beyond a person's control. There are many such clearly recognized excuses which we accept as legitimate reasons for failure to fulfill an obligation or carry out a duty. Illness, accidents, the unexpected call of higher obligations are typical instances. In each case, however, the circumstances that prevent the person from fulfilling his obligation must be beyond his control at the time and must not be due to his own voluntary acts in the past. Thus we do not excuse a person who misses an appointment because he got into a traffic accident as a result of his own reckless driving, nor do we excuse him if the accident was the result of an automobile breakdown which could have been avoided had he taken ordinary care of his car beforehand.

(d) Absence of ability or opportunity

Finally, there are situations in which a wrong act is done or a right act left undone because the person lacks either the ability or the opportunity to do the right one. If someone cannot swim, we do not blame him for not jumping in to save a drowning man (though we would hold him responsible if he did not call for help or throw the man a life preserver when one was available). On the other hand, a person might be able to swim but fail to save a drowning man because he sees him only when it is too late. In the former case there is absence of an ability, in the latter the absence of an opportunity. In either case we say that the consequences were unavoidable, since it was not within the power of the person to prevent their happening.

There are two important points to realize about all four of these conditions of excusability. The first is that, insofar as any actual situation satisfies one or more of these conditions, it can significantly be contrasted with an opposite situation, where these conditions are not satisfied. The second is that circumstances of both kinds do occur in everyday life. Thus, just as there are cases where a person cannot have foreseen the harmful consequences of his acts, there are others where someone does foresee such effects and still chooses to take the step. (A man who intends to murder someone not only foresees that his victim will die but wants this to happen.) Just as there are acts done because the agent is forced by others to do them, so there are acts committed when no such coercion is present. A government official who accepts a bribe from a business firm may have decided to do it entirely by himself and have acted under no external constraint. It is possible, indeed, to act in opposition to a considerable amount of outside pressure. Whenever a person commits a crime he does so in spite of, rather than because of, such external constraints as threat of punishment, fear of the police, and general social disapproval. Again, consider the case in which an internal urge or drive compels a person to act independently of his own will. This kind of case is contrasted with that of a person freely choosing to do something after carefully deliberating about it. A man might be in full control of himself as he works out a scheme to embezzle funds and feel under no compulsion as he calmly carries out his plan. In connection with the third type of excusing condition, just as we sometimes are prevented from doing what we ought to do by circumstances beyond our control, there are other situations where we don't do what we ought simply because we don't want to. We sometimes try to avoid our obligations when we find them onerous. Finally, although in a given situation we may lack the ability or the opportunity to do what would be right, just as often we have the capacity and the chance to choose any number of available alternatives and yet we knowingly choose to do what is wrong. For example, the man who does not accurately report his income to avoid paying a tax certainly has the ability and opportunity to make out an accurate report and knows that this is the right thing for him to do.

DETERMINISM AND EXCUSABILITY

In everyday life, then, there are occasions when we excuse a person and occasions when we hold someone morally responsible for what he does. The problem of free will arises when the theory of determinism, or universal causation, is applied to human choice and conduct. Determinism is the principle that every event has a cause. This principle is used by the sciences of psychology, sociology, and anthropology in explaining man's behavior. Although these sciences have developed only recently, they have already made impressive achievements in our understanding of why people act, feel, and choose as they do. As these sciences progress, our ability to account for human feelings, motives, and beliefs will greatly increase, and along with such knowledge will develop our ability to give causal explanations for human decisions and conduct. Accordingly, many people are beginning to think about man the way they think about animals and machines. They take the same scientific point of view toward all of them, and in doing so see their activities not as chance events occurring in a haphazard or unpredictable manner, but as events that happen in an orderly way. This order is discovered when scientists are able to explain the events in terms of causal laws. It is true that the laws by which human behavior is to be explained may be far more complex and far more difficult to discover than the laws of the inanimate world and of the plant and (lower) animal world. But this does not mean that the human world is any the less explainable by causal laws. Man is a part of nature, and nature is an order of causes and effects which the sciences are gradually revealing to us. Everything in nature happens in accordance with this order, and the choices of individual men must be understood in this light.

The principle of determinism, that every event has a cause, is accepted by all scientists with regard to the subject matter of their particular science, since the aim of their science is to find a causal explanation for anything that happens within the domain of that science, and to look for such an explanation is to assume that the happening is caused. What is a causal explanation? This is a difficult question to answer; it gives rise to many subtle disputes in the philosophy of science. Here we can only suggest an answer sufficient to bring out the relevance of determinism to free will and moral responsibility. To give a causal explanation of an event is to show how the event is related to other events by a causal law. Every causal law is of the following form: Given certain conditions in space and time and a set of changes occurring at a certain time, a new set of changes will take place under the given conditions. For example, when a gas is heated it will expand (certain conditions remaining constant). A chemist may thus explain the expansion of a gas as the effect of an increase in its temperature, along with the law that relates, in a functional equation, the temperature, pressure, and volume of a gas. Causal laws are always universal statements; they apply to all events of a certain kind *whenever* they occur, not just to a particular set of events that occurred at a particular time in the past. If we know the causal law according to which events of a certain kind are followed by events of another kind under certain conditions, then we are able to predict, when the first set of events occurs under the stated conditions, that the second set of events will follow. In this way predictions of future events are based on the very same laws by which we explain present and past events. The definition of "cause" and "effect" may then be given as follows: If any law holds true of two sets of changes in the world such that, whenever changes of the first set occur under certain conditions, changes of the second set will follow, the events making up the first set are the *causes* of the events making up the second set, and the latter are the *effects* of the former. Thus the set of events that are the causes of an effect constitute a *sufficient condition* for the occurrence of the effect. If at a certain time the sufficient condition for an event occurs, the event must then occur. It will be causally or physically impossible for the sufficient condition to occur without the event following it. Hence given the causes, the effect must follow.

A *causal explanation* of any event consists in specifying the causal law which states a universal connection between events of the kind to be explained and a set of events which they invariably follow when certain conditions remain constant. Thus the principle of determinism may be taken to mean: There is a causal explanation for every event occurring in the universe. To say this, however, is not to say that anyone *knows* the causal explanation for any given event. It only says that such an explanation is theoretically possible. The ideal goal of the empirical sciences would be to find a system of causal laws in terms of which every event in the universe could be explained. Such an ideal, of course, can only be approached gradually as scientists obtain more and more knowledge of the world; it may never be reached. But the determinist is not bothered by this fact. He merely claims that, however ignorant of causal laws mankind may remain, those laws are nevertheless in constant operation and no exception to them ever occurs.

What has determinism got to do with conditions of excusability and moral responsibility? The true answer to this question may be, "Nothing whatever," but many people have thought otherwise. They have believed that there is a contradiction between determinism and moral responsibility, so that if it is legitimate to hold people morally responsible for at least some of their acts, we must reject the principle of determinism. The kind of freedom which is necessary for moral responsibility, they argue, is the freedom of *indeterminism*. A person's "will" must be undetermined at the time of choice if he is to be held responsible for what he does. And this means that no causal explanation will account for his choice. Thus the question, When is a person morally responsible? has come to be hinged upon the question, Is determinism true?

The usual argument that moral responsibility is incompatible with determinism runs as follows. Let us consider only cases where the four types of conditions of excusability discussed above do *not* hold, since it is only in these situations that we ordinarily believe it is justified to hold people responsible for their acts. Now in such situations, although a person may not appear to be under external or internal constraint, and may appear to have the ability and opportunity to do a number of alternatives open to his choice, these appearances are mere illusions if his choice and subsequent action are causally determined. For suppose they are determined. Then, given the causal laws operating in his situation of choice, only one "alternative" course of action can possibly occur, namely, the one which will be the effect of the previous causes that are occurring in the situation. The act that the person finally chooses to do is inevitable, since there was some set of events which was a sufficient condition for his choosing to do that particular act and, given the occurrence of the sufficient condition, the choice of that act must take place. No other act could occur in the world as it was at that time, for the world at that time included the events which were sufficient for the occurrence of the given act. And that is just another way of saying that the act the person finally chose to do was *caused*.

The argument then continues in the following way. In a deterministic universe (that is, a universe in which every event is caused) the future is not really open. When someone thinks he has a number of alternative courses of action open to him, any one of which can be brought about as a result of his decision to do it, he is under an illusion. Actually only one of these imagined alternatives is going to be realized. It will be the one which must occur as the effect of the causes that are operating in the situation at that time. It does no good to argue that among these causes must be the person's own choice to do the act. For even though it is quite true (when conditions of excusability are absent) that a person's own choice is the cause of one act being done by him rather than another, this choice itself is the effect of previous causes, and these in turn are the effects of still earlier causes, and so on until we get back to the formation of the individual's personality and character in his childhood. In other words, if there is a causal explanation for the person's act in terms of his deliberation and choice, there is equally a causal explanation of why he deliberated and chose the way he did. This causal explanation may be very complex, but however difficult it may be to discover it (given the present state of the science of psychology), the causes are operating so as to bring about every thought and every feeling that goes into the deliberative process and emerges in the specific choice.

The conclusion drawn by the determinist is this. Since there was in fact only one possibility for action, given the past causes and surrounding conditions of the person's choice, he was not really able to choose any other alternative. His ability to *do* other alternatives and his opportunity to choose them *if he wished* are not to the point, since he, being the kind of person he was, could in fact only choose one of the acts. Similarly, the absence of external and internal constraints only gives him the false belief that he is free to choose among the alternatives. He *feels* free when he chooses because he does not feel any inner compulsion or external constraint upon him, and it is perfectly true that there is no such compulsion or constraint. Still, only one of the alternatives can in fact be chosen by him, and this one alone is the single possibility open to him, regardless of what he might feel or think at the time of choice. Now suppose the act he finally chooses to do is something he and others believe to be morally wrong. Then, the determinist goes on, he cannot be held responsible for it, since he could not have done otherwise. It was the only thing he could have done in the situation, given the kind of person he was and the circumstances of his life at that moment of choice.

LIBERTARIANISM

Some philosophers have been convinced by the foregoing argument and have thought that, to preserve moral responsibility in human life, it is necessary to deny determinism. Confronted with the choice between determinism and no responsibility or responsibility but not determinism, they have opted for the latter. They have held·that a human being is not a mere *personality* entirely explainable in causal terms; he is also a *moral agent,* having the power to choose between right and wrong. Thus it is up to the individual himself whether he does, or fails to do, what he ought. It is he himself, as moral agent, who determines which of the possibilities open to him are to be realized in the actual world. Accordingly, he can correctly consider himself answerable or accountable for what he does and, when the four excusing conditions mentioned earlier are absent, he can justifiably be held responsible for his actions.

A position of this sort is called *libertarianism.* In holding that the actions we perform as moral agents are not merely the inevitable effects of past causes, it claims that such actions are not amenable to causal explanations. The kind of freedom we exercise when we choose between good and evil—the only kind that, in the libertarian's view, is consistent with the concept of moral responsibility—is a creative power to initiate changes in the world and thereby determine what shall in fact occur as far as our own actions are concerned.

How is the moral agent when so understood related to the formed character or personality of an individual, in light of the findings of contemporary psychology concerning the causes of people's actions and choices? Libertarians argue that causal factors operating on the character or personality of an individual set certain directions or tendencies for the individual's choice, but do not completely determine it. At a given stage in one's personality development, there is a *probability* that one will choose to do certain kinds of acts and not others. But this is a probability only, not a certainty. An individual's motives, desires, beliefs, and feelings will limit the possible choices open to himself as a moral agent. For an individual with a certain kind of personality, it will be psychologically improbable (if not impossible) to commit murder; for someone with another kind of personality, such an act will be quite possible, and at particular moments in his life might even become highly probable. But this, the libertarian insists, does not mean that he *must* choose to commit murder. It only means that he has a tendency to do so, and if he is aware of the moral aspects of the act, he can exercise his capacity as a moral agent and counteract this tendency by refraining from it. Indeed, this is exactly what happens to anyone who is faced with a choice (when no excusing conditions hold) between doing what he believes to be right and doing what he knows is wrong but finds strongly tempting. "The conflict between duty and interest," as such a choice is often called in ethics, is just the area where our "moral self" comes into play as a determining factor in our deliberation and conduct. The "moral self," for the libertarian, is simply the person insofar as he can function as a moral agent: one who has the capacity to think out the moral considerations relevant to a choice and to act on the basis of those considerations.

The libertarian then draws the following conclusion. No matter in what direction—toward good or toward evil—the tendencies of an individual's personality might pull or push him, it is his moral self that finally makes the choice between doing his duty and yielding to his interest. As long as a person has a sense of duty or a sense of responsibility, he can use self-control and willpower to overcome the personality traits that steer him in the wrong direction. And having a sense of duty or responsibility is itself simply part of what it means to be a moral agent. A moral agent, as has been shown, is defined as one who can recognize the moral aspects of a choice open to him and who can act accordingly. This implies that he can exert the power of self-determination in making his choices, within the limits set by the tendencies of his personality. It is this which distinguishes men and women from small children, lunatics, and (nonhuman) animals. Therefore, unless a human being totally lacks any sense of what is morally right and wrong, he can be considered to be a moral agent and hence responsible (answerable, accountable) for his acts. He cannot cite his personality tendencies as an excuse for failing to do what he himself admits he ought to do. Having a personality, in short, is not one of the conditions of excusability.

Sometimes the moral self is understood by libertarians to be the "soul" of a person, conceived in terms of the traditional metaphysics of Christian theology. The soul is an immaterial substance, created by God and endowed with freedom of the will. It resides in the body until death, after which it continues its existence in some supernatural condition. The freedom of the will is thought of as a God-given capacity or faculty of the soul which operates at the moment of choice between good and evil. When a person knowingly chooses to do evil, he (that is, his soul) is held accountable for his action and is subject to God's punishment. In this chapter the arguments for and against the existence of a soul will not be considered. This would extend into the realms of metaphysics and theology and thus introduce considerations beyond what are essential for present purposes. It will be sufficient to notice here that it is possible to hold a libertarian position on free will without appealing to the idea of a soul-substance. For a libertarian can think of free will in the manner set forth above: simply as a set of capacities or powers which human beings have as moral agents.

It is a fundamental tenet of libertarianism that the choices made by a moral agent are not entirely explainable in causal terms. The libertarian takes this stand because he believes that there could be no such thing as moral responsibility in a completely deterministic universe. If every event— including every human choice and action—has a cause, then it would be the inevitable result of past conditions beyond the control of the agent. In that case the agent cannot legitimately be held responsible for those conditions and hence cannot properly be made accountable for the choice or action that resulted from them. In affirming moral responsibility, the libertarian consequently denies the principle of determinism. This is sometimes expressed by saying: Libertarianism entails *incompatibilism,* where "incompatibilism" is taken to be the view that free will and determinism are inconsistent with one another. Now this view has been strongly challenged by a group of philosophers known as compatibilists, reconciliationists, or soft determinists. They believe it is possible (that is, logically consistent) to accept the principle of determinism and at the same time consider persons morally responsible for what they do. They do not think it is necessary to speak of an undetermined "moral self" in order to account for the freedom of choice presupposed in judgments or moral responsibility. Nor do they think that a person's exercising his capacities as a moral agent is causally unexplainable. In their view, free choice and free action are empirical concepts exemplified in everyday life and perfectly consistent with universal causation.

To see how this position of soft determinism (or compatibilism, or reconciliationism) can be plausibly defended, we begin with a brief account of the ordinary use of the word "free" as applied to human choices and actions. This account will reveal not only how a soft determinist conceives of freedom, but also why he separates the question: Do persons ever act freely? from the question: Is determinism true?

THE COMPATIBILIST CONCEPT OF FREEDOM

What does it mean to say that someone freely chooses to do an action, or acts of his own free will? The first thing which the soft determinist points out is that freedom and its absence are matters of degree. A free action is one that is *comparatively* free. There is a continuum or gradation of acts, ranging all the way from clear-cut cases in which we would ordinarily say there is very little freedom or none at all, to equally clear-cut cases of what all of us would usually call free acts. Thus a man in jail is not free to get out; a person whose life is threatened if he disobeys someone with power over him is not free; and so on for other cases in which, in everyday life, we would say there is little or no freedom. Similarly, we say that a person did something of his own free will when he was not forced or compelled to do it and when he could just as easily have done something else instead. But this does not require us to claim that there are "absolutely" free acts that have nothing in common with unfree acts or with conduct which we would describe as being partly or somewhat free.

If freedom is a matter of degree, argues the compatibilist or soft determinist, an important conclusion follows: *The question of whether a given act is or is not free cannot be the same as the question of whether the act is or is not determined.* For determinism and indeterminism are not matters of degree. Here it is all or nothing: either there is a sufficient condition for the act to occur or there is not; either the act is determined or it is not. Even if someone argues that there is a "tendency" in a person to do a certain act, as long as this tendency is not sufficient to cause the person to do the act the question remains, Is the act determined or not? And this means, Would any causal explanation completely account for the person's doing the act in the given circumstances? If the answer is yes, then the act is absolutely determined, and there is no point in saying that a "high degree" of causal determination is operating in this instance, or that the act is "mostly" determined. If the act is not completely determined, then it is simply not determined. In that case there is no sufficient condition for the occurrence of the act and no causal explanation will be able to account for the person's doing the act.

In reply to this it might be argued that causal explanations are always only probable, never certain, and that probability is a matter of degree. But this argument confuses the two very different statements: (1) All human acts are determined. (2) Act X is determined by such-and-such causes. Statement (1) is the claim that *some* causal explanation can provide a completely adequate account of why any human act has occurred. Statement (2) is the entirely different claim to have knowledge of the specific causal explanation for the occurrence of a particular act, X. Now it is true that our knowledge of specific causal explanations is never more than probable, since it involves reference to causal laws or empirical generalizations, and these can never be established with certainty. So no one can know with certainty the true causal explanation of any particular act. But this in no way throws doubt upon the issue of whether every act is determined. The causal explanation of a given act might be totally unknown to us, yet such an explanation, if known, could provide a complete and true account of why the act was done. For it would specify the events that constituted at that time a sufficient condition for the act's being done. Indeterminism (which is entailed by libertarianism) is the denial that there is any such sufficient condition for the act. Hence with regard to an undetermined act, the indeterminist and the libertarian must hold that there is no causal explanation, *known or unknown*, for that act. The soft determinist takes the view that, whether or not a statement of type (2) above is known to be true, statement (1) is in fact true.

According to soft determinism, then, degrees of freedom are not to be thought of as being in inverse proportion to degrees of determinism. There are no degrees of determinism. What, then, are the conditions whose fulfillment in varying degrees is the test for varying degrees of freedom? This is the question the soft determinist must answer if he is to define the terms "free" and "unfree" as applied in everyday life to human choices and actions. The way to discover such conditions, he claims, is as follows. First, consider clear-cut cases or paradigms of what are ordinarily called free choices and acts. Next, consider paradigms of what are commonly recognized as unfree choices and acts—cases we would all agree (before knowing anything about determinism or indeterminism) to place at the other end of the continuum. Then notice the properties or characteristics which these two groups of cases do *not* have in common, and especially those properties we ourselves point out when we are asked about a member of the first group. "What *makes* that a case of freedom of choice or action?" and which we point out when asked about a member of the other group, "*Why* do you call that an unfree choice or action?" Finally, after specifying these properties, turn to the unclear and problematic cases, those which tend to fall near the center of the continuum. Regarding these cases, ask yourself, "What is it about them that makes it difficult for me to decide whether they are free or unfree?" We shall then find that all these problematic cases exemplify some of the properties which we noticed in the clear-cut cases of freedom and at the same time have other properties in common with our paradigms of unfree choices and acts. By bringing out these properties, we make clear to ourselves the conditions which define degrees of freedom. That is, we come to understand what criteria or tests must be satisfied in varying degrees by human choices and acts if we are to say that they are free or unfree in varying degrees.

What are these criteria of free actions and choices? Compatibilists or soft determinists offer the following, subject to revision by anyone who can think of other criteria actually implicit in the common usage of the word "free." An action is free if, and only if, first, it occurs only because a person chooses or decides to do it, and second, that choice or decision is itself free. A choice or decision made by a person (P) to do an action (X) is free to the extent that:

   (i) P has the physical and mental ability to do X and hence could do it if he wanted to.
  (ii) P has the physical and mental ability to refrain from doing X and hence could so refrain if he wanted to.
 (iii) In the given situation P has the opportunity to exercise ability (i) and also the opportunity to exercise ability (ii). That is, the given situation is such that nothing will hinder, prevent, or otherwise interfere with P's doing X if he so chooses, nor will anything hinder, prevent, or otherwise interfere with his refraining from X if he so decides.
  (iv) If P does X it is because he has reasons for so doing, and if he refrains from X it is because he has reasons to refrain from it.

Now suppose all four of these conditions are true of a person P and suppose that, under these conditions, P in fact performs action X. Then the only explanation for P's doing X is that he *decides* to do it in light of the reasons he has for doing it. And that decision is itself free *to the degree that* conditions (i) through (iv) are satisfied. For when (and only when) an action is performed under those conditions, claims the soft determinist, do we ordinarily describe it as having been done freely. Only then do we speak of a person's doing something "of his own free will."

A more precise formulation of the problem of moral responsibility and free will is now possible: (1) Are the defining criteria of free choices and actions given above consistent with the principle of determinism? (2) Are these criteria such that we are morally justified in holding people responsible for their choices and actions *to the extent that they are free?* Compatibilists or soft determinists hold that both questions are to be answered in the affirmative. They maintain that the kind of freedom necessary for moral responsibility is perfectly compatible with determinism. This position is to be contrasted with a view that combines determinism with incompatibilism, a view which is sometimes called simply "determinism" and sometimes "hard determinism" to distinguish it from soft determinism. Hard determinism consists of the following three propositions: First, whatever may be the criteria by which we distinguish in everyday life between free and unfree actions, they are *not* such as to justify our holding people "morally respon- sible" in the way this has traditionally been conceived. Second, the necessary conditions for moral responsibility in the traditional sense are not compat- ible with determinism. Third, determinism is true. Thus hard determinists deny the traditional conception of moral responsibility and the kind of freedom they think is presupposed by it. Toward the end of this chapter we shall discuss the traditional view of moral responsibility and also consider a different view of holding people responsible that has been proposed by some hard determinists themselves as being the only view that can be justified, given a deterministic universe.

SOFT DETERMINISM AND HARD DETERMINISM

An examination of the central issue between hard and soft determinists regarding free will follows, starting with the soft determinist's claim that free action is compatible with universal causation. The argument in defense of this position may be stated thus. Suppose that determinism is true and that, consequently, all actions are caused. This does not mean, says the soft determinist, that every action is necessitated in the sense of being *unavoid-able,* for something is unavoidable when it is beyond our control. We can't do anything to prevent it and hence with respect to its occurrence we are helpless. Now it is only when our actions do not result from our own choices that they are unavoidable in this way. We then find ourselves doing things without being able to stop even when we try. However, when our actions result from our choosing to do them, they are within our control and hence are avoidable. They would not occur unless we chose to *make* them occur.

To say that an action is caused, we have seen, is simply to say that there is a sufficient condition for its occurrence. It is not to say anything about the *nature* of that sufficient condition. Now consider the case in which the sufficient condition for the occurrence of an action includes, as one of its essential elements, the agent's decision to do it. Then the action's being done is caused, but is not unavoidable. The agent could have prevented its occurrence simply by deciding not to do it and then carrying out that decision by refraining from doing it.

This, then, is the first step in the soft determinist's argument for the compatibility of free will with determinism: Universal causation as applied to actions that are within our control does not entail that the actions are unavoidable (unpreventable). The second and final step in his argument is his reply to the following objection: "We grant that an action may be avoidable in your sense when it depends on an agent's choice. But is his choice avoidable? Although in the kind of situation you have described, the action is indeed caused by the agent's choice, this must also be caused (since you admit that the principle of determinism is true). But if the choice is caused, it follows inevitably from whatever condition is sufficient to have brought it about. Therefore, even though the action is avoidable with respect to the person's choice, it is *not* avoidable with respect to the *cause* of the person's making the specific choice he does. Hence the action is not really free after all, and the person is not to be considered morally responsible for having done it."

The soft determinist replies to this objection by showing that sometimes the cause or sufficient condition for a person's choice does satisfy criteria (i) through (iv) given in the foregoing analysis of freedom. In that case the choice is free (by the very definition of the term "free"), while at the same time it is also caused. And to the extent that it is free, to that extent the person is responsible for the action he chooses to do. If we look again at criteria (i) through (iv), the soft determinist continues, we notice that each condition could hold true of a person at a certain time without contra-dicting the principle of determinism. Thus a person could have the neces-sary abilities and opportunities to perform and to refrain from an action, could have reasons for doing and for refraining from it and could decide to do it or refrain from it *for those reasons.* Nothing said here rules out the claim that, whichever the person elects, to do the act or to refrain from it, there is a sufficient condition for his deciding as he does. As long as that sufficient condition *includes* his reasons for doing or not doing the act, and as long as the other criteria are satisfied, his action is free even though it is caused. Under those circumstances, he does the action "of his own free will."

A simple example will clarify this. Suppose a person has applied for a job at several firms and that two of the firms have offered him positions. One position is that of sales clerk, and the other is driver of a delivery truck. He considers the two jobs, going over in his mind such facts as the type of work involved in each, hours of work, pay, and vacations. He then decides to accept the sales clerk position because the pay is higher and he prefers indoor work, even though the other position has shorter hours and longer vacations. The soft determinist argues that in a case like this a person chooses to do something of his own free will despite the fact that his decision to do it is caused. As long as the person had the *abilities* needed for being a truck driver and for being a sales clerk, then, given his desire to be one or the other, the fact that he chose one rather than the other when offered the *opportunity* to accept either shows that his decision was based on his own reasons. This is precisely the sort of situation of which we say that a person is free in choosing and acting as he does.

The conclusion drawn by the soft determinist is that all three of the following assertions are mutually consistent and true: (1) Some acts are free. (2) All acts are determined. (3) People can rightly be held responsible for their free acts.

The hard determinist's response to the foregoing argument is to raise this question, *Could the person have done otherwise?* According to the hard determinist, when we say in everyday life that someone acted of his own free will or acted freely, we mean that he could have done otherwise than he did. Thus if a person has done action X in a certain situation and if we say he did X freely, we mean that he did not have to do X in that situation but could have done something else instead. The meaning of "free" as applied to human actions, therefore, depends on the meaning of "could" as used in sentences of the form "He could have done otherwise." What, then, does "could" mean in such a context? The answer given by the soft determinist—an answer that is rejected by the hard determinist—is that "could" means nothing more than "would have..., if..." Thus according to soft determinism when we say that, though person P did action X at time T, he *could* have done action Y instead, we mean that P *would have* done Y at time T *if* he had chosen or decided to do Y. The soft determinist then goes on to claim, as we have seen, that the truth conditions for the assertion "P would have done Y at time T if he had chosen to do Y" are compatible with the truth conditions for the assertion "P's doing X at time T was caused." The truth conditions for the former assertion are the very criteria, (i) through (iv) given earlier, which the soft determinist holds to be consistent with the fact that there was a sufficient condition (cause) for P's doing X at time T.

The hard determinist replies to this by pointing out that, if there was indeed a sufficient condition (cause) not only for P's doing action X at time T but also for his choosing or deciding to do that action at that time, then it was impossible, given those sufficient conditions, for anything to happen at time T other than P's doing X. Hence P's doing Y could not have occurred at time T. Therefore, P could *not* have done Y at time T.

In this counterargument the hard determinist is not denying the truth conditions that were said to hold for P at time T, namely criteria (i) through (iv). He is claiming that, though all of those conditions are satisfied, this does not mean that P could have done Y at time T. For the word "could" in this context does *not* mean merely "would have..., if...." The reason it does not is that the "if..." clause might not be fulfilled. In that case, although it is true that when P did X he could have done Y in the sense that he *would have* done Y *if* he had chosen to, in fact he *could not* have chosen to do Y (since there was a sufficient condition for his choosing to do X) and therefore he *could not* have done Y. "Could," in other words, is not a hypothetical or conditional term, but a categorical one. And in this categorical sense of "could," P could not have done Y when there was a sufficient condition for his choosing to do, and hence for his doing, X. In fact, since *every* event has a cause (as both hard and soft determinists assert), it follows that *no one can ever do anything but what he does do.* Hence, the hard determinist concludes, every statement of the form "So-and-so could have done otherwise" is false. But we saw above that "He could have done otherwise" was offered as an equivalent of the assertion "He did the action freely." So if this is the meaning of "free action." no acts are free.

THE INESCAPABILITY OF FREEDOM

It is possible now to consider a further important aspect of the free will problem. For the moment let us assume that determinism is true, leaving open the question of whether it is compatible with freedom (soft determinism) or incompatible (hard determinism). It is assumed, in other words, that our every thought, our every decision, our every action has a causal explanation. The following question can then be asked: Even if this assumption were true, what difference would it make to our actual experience of life? Would it, indeed, make any difference at all? Would we not still be confronted with situations in which we have to decide what we are to do in the future? Would we not still have to make up our minds as to how we should act? Would not "the practical question," that is, What ought I to do? still require an answer from each of us?

It might be claimed that this seems to be so only because it is being assumed that we would be ignorant of the causal explanation of every event.

If we knew all the causes of what occurs, we would see that we never have a real choice about what actions to perform in the future. For we would then know the present causes that would necessarily be followed by their future effects. Hence asking ourselves, What ought I to do? would be futile. Indeed, the question would never be asked, since whatever answer we arrived at in our thinking would be the inevitable effect of known causes that have already occurred. And what we decided eventually to do—if "deciding" has any meaning under those conditions—would always be something we knew we had to do. It would not be open to us to do anything else. So it would be pointless for a person to ask, What ought I to do? as if he had a choice about it. The conclusion then drawn is that it is only our ignorance of causes that makes it sensible to ask and to try to answer "the practical question."

Let us look more closely at the supposition that the causes of all events are known. Some philosophers argue that this supposition involves a contradiction if it is taken to mean not merely that all causes are known to someone, but that they are known to everyone. For, they claim, the causes of a person's future actions cannot be known *by that person himself.* To see the reasoning behind this claim, try to imagine what it would be like to know your own future actions. Suppose, for example, that you are in a restaurant and have been given a menu with a list of desserts to choose from. Now what would it mean to say, "I know that I am going to have strawberry ice cream rather than apple pie"? Would it not mean that, *in the very act of predicting your future action you were thereby deciding to do it?* It is true that a person other than yourself might predict correctly—if he knew you well enough—that you were going to choose strawberry ice cream. This makes perfectly good sense. But then suppose that other person tells you, before the event, that he *knows* that you are going to have strawberry ice cream. Couldn't you falsify his prediction by deciding to have apple pie? Well, if he truly knew your future action, he would presumably know that when he said you'd select strawberry ice cream, you'd be motivated to falsify his prediction by picking apple pie (just to show him up, perhaps, or to assert your inviolable freedom!). In that case, of course, you would not in fact have falsified his *real* prediction. But notice that he had to keep his *real* prediction secret. For if he had told you *that,* it would again be susceptible of being falsified by your decision to do something other than what he predicted. In which case he would not really have known your future action.

The upshot of these reflections seems to be that, even if everything is caused and those causes are known by someone, there must remain a certain class of causes that cannot be known by a certain class of persons. The causes of the future actions of any given person cannot be fully known by that person himself (and so cannot be made fully known to him by others). What follows from this? It would follow that "the practical question"— What ought I to do?—always makes sense. Indeed, the need to answer it is *inescapable*. For we have seen that even if another person were to attempt a prediction of our future behavior, we could still ask ourselves meaningfully, Should I do what he predicts or should I do something else? As long as we are not *compelled* to fulfill his prediction in such a way that we cannot help doing it, we must still *decide* whether or not to do it.

An important conclusion may now be drawn. It is that the truth of determinism (if it is true) does not take away the necessity to think about what we ought to do. Even if it is the case that every action has a causal explanation and is theoretically predictable, we must still consider what reasons we might have for or against doing one thing rather than another. In practical life we would still need to deliberate and arrive at decisions in the light of that deliberation. As long as we are not helpless with respect to our future, that is, as long as the steps we actually take depend upon our reflection and decision, we are confronted with "the practical question" and must find our own answers to it. Determinism, we have seen, does not imply that we are all helpless about our future, that the actions we perform never depend on how we think and decide to act. As far as determinism is concerned, the causal factors that bring about our actions may include our own thoughts and decisions. Thus determinism is compatible with the *efficacy* of our deliberation and choice. The way we reflect and choose can be decisive in causing us to act in one way rather than another. And as long as we cannot know our own future actions, it makes sense to ask ourselves, and to answer as best we can, "the practical question."

Assuming that determinism is true, does the foregoing argument entail soft determinism? It might at first appear to do so, since it seems to make determinism compatible with freedom and responsibility. For if our actions do depend on our decisions and deliberations, it would seem that we are free and can rightly be held responsible for what we do. And since freedom (the necessity to make choices) is inescapable, so is responsibility.

However, a hard determinist could counter as follows. It is not *freedom* that is inescapable; it is *the illusion of freedom* that we can't avoid. We must, it is true, act as if we were free; but this is, in reality, a false assumption. We are not in fact free, even though we think we are. For thinking of ourselves as free is seeing ourselves as being confronted with open possibilities from among which we can choose. But this view stems from our ignorance of the causes of our actions and choices. Granted that those causes cannot be known in advance by the person who chooses and acts, they are nevertheless present and uniquely determine what his decision and conduct will be. Therefore, even when someone does what is morally wrong, he cannot rightly be held responsible for what he does. It was impossible that he could have taken any other action, given the causes for his being the kind of person he was when he deliberated, decided to act, and carried out that decision.

So the problem with which these considerations leave us may be stated thus: Is it freedom (and hence responsibility) that is inescapable? Or is it the illusion of freedom (and hence the denial of genuine responsibility) that is inescapable?

THE CONCEPT OF MORAL RESPONSIBILITY

The problem of freedom of the will concerns the meaning and interrelations of three basic ideas: freedom, causation, and moral responsibility. After the foregoing examination of issues regarding freedom and causation, it is time now to consider the idea of moral responsibility. Here it is important to keep in mind the difference between two questions: (1) What does it mean to say that someone *is* morally responsible for what he has done? (2) Under what conditions is it justifiable to *hold* a person morally responsible for what he has done? The answer to the second question might be, "When the person did the action freely," the concept of a free action being understood in one of the ways we have considered. But this does not provide an answer to the first question. To say that someone is morally responsible for having done an act is not merely to say that he did the act freely. It is to say something like, He is accountable for having done it; or, if it is a wrong act, He is at fault for having done it and so deserves to be blamed. Perhaps we would not think it right to consider a person accountable or blameworthy for his conduct unless he had acted freely. That is, freedom might be a *necessary condition* for accountability or for the justifiability of blame. But the *meaning* of "being accountable" or "deserving blame" is not the same as the *meaning* of "having done an action freely."

In common usage the word "responsible" is sometimes applied to events and to inanimate objects, rather than to persons. Thus we say such things as, "Heavy rains were responsible for the flood" and "Ice on the road was responsible for the accident." In such cases to say that something is responsible for something else is to say that the first thing is the cause, or part of the cause, of the second. Now we can and do use the word "responsible" in this same sense in some of the cases where we apply it to persons and their actions. Thus we say, "It was her shyness that was responsible for her being overlooked for the job," and "His accidentally pushing the wrong button in the elevator was responsible for his meeting the woman who later became his wife." In situations of this sort, no question of accountability or blameworthiness need arise. However, *causal responsibility* (as we may call it) does play a role as one of the necessary conditions for a person's being *morally responsible* for something. A person's action must be a causal factor in bringing about the state of affairs for which he is morally responsible. But causal responsibility is not a sufficient condition for moral responsibility nor is it all of what we *mean* by "moral responsibility." This may be made clear by an example.

A number of years ago one of the most beloved animals in New York City's Bronx Zoo, a walrus, died in agony because it had swallowed a rubber ball that someone had thrown into its cage. It was never discovered who was causally responsible, but whoever it was, unless he had thrown the ball into the animal's cage, the walrus would not have died as he did. Granted that the person who threw the ball was causally responsible, was he also morally responsible? There seems to be a further condition that is necessary for the ascription of moral responsibility to the person. The action, we think, must have been done with the intention of harming the animal. If it was a child who had thrown the ball, thinking that the walrus would enjoy playing with it, and who *for that reason* did the act, we might say it was a tragic or unfortunate mistake but, since it would be quite understandable that a child would think this, we would not believe he deserved to be blamed for his action. The child's having that intention, we might say, was not evidence of a flaw in his moral character. Similarly, if we discovered that the child had been told by his parents to throw the ball into the cage, we would absolve the child from blame. He was obeying his parents, and it was for that reason that he did the act. As before, no weakness in the child's moral character was exemplified in that case. Or suppose the ball had not actually been thrown into the cage, but had fallen into it when someone inadvertently bumped into the person holding the ball and knocked it from his hand. Again, we do not think of the person as being morally responsible, though he was still causally responsible for the death of the animal. However, if it turned out that the ball fell into the cage because someone had carelessly dropped it while leaning over the fence of the cage (thereby breaking one of the well-publicized rules of the zoo), then moral responsibility would be likely to be ascribed. The crucial difference between the last two situations is that in the first there is no flaw in anyone's character being exemplified, while in the second there is.

The conclusion that some philosophers have drawn from examples like this is that the meaning of moral responsibility is analyzable into two basic ideas: that of causal responsibility and that of a flaw or weakness of moral character. To say that someone is morally responsible for a certain state of affairs in the world is to say, first, that his doing a wrong action was a cause (that is, part of a necessary causal condition) for the occurrence of the state of affairs, and second, that his conduct manifested in some way a flaw in his moral character. This is the suggested *meaning* of the idea of moral responsibility. The suggested answer to the question, Under what conditions is it justifiable to *hold* someone morally responsible for a given state of affairs? is connected with that meaning. To this question the proposed answer is that we are justified in holding a person morally responsible (that is, accountable or answerable) for a state of affairs if and only if the wrong action which was causally responsible for the state of affairs was done *under no excusing conditions*. By "excusing conditions" are meant any of the four sets of conditions listed at the beginning of this chapter, where it was pointed out that we tend to absolve a person from guilt whenever we discover that any of these circumstances held at the time the action was done. What unifies all these conditions and makes them the ground of legitimate excuses is that, when any of them holds for an action, the doing of the action by an agent is *not* a sign of something morally bad or objectionable about the agent as far as his character is concerned.

It is relevant here to note that we may hold a person morally responsible even when he does not actually commit a wrong action. This occurs when someone fully intends to do something that is wrong, tries to carry out his intention, but fails. For instance, suppose a man aims a loaded gun at someone he intends to murder and pulls the trigger, but the gun misfires and the intended victim escapes unharmed. Although the law does not punish this would-be murderer as severely as it does an actual murderer in similar circumstances, we might nevertheless claim that, *morally* speaking, there is no difference between the two cases. After all, it was not anything the gunman did himself that made the difference between the life and death of his intended victim. Although he failed to commit a murder, he did everything he could to do so. His "will" was the will of a murderer, though he did not become one. So he is just as much at fault as an actual killer would be. This example shows that it is not the actual consequences of a person's actions that are relevant to his moral responsibility, but rather his character insofar as it is manifested in his intentions, his reasons for action, his "will."

What does it mean to hold a person accountable or answerable for something he has done? Here it is illuminating to consider what it means to hold *ourselves* accountable or answerable. If we have committed an action we believe to be not only wrong but inexcusable (because we think there were no excusing conditions present at the time of the action), we make a moral judgment about ourselves, not merely about our action. We hold a moral standard up to ourselves, as it were, and in its cold, hard light we confront the reality of a weakness in our own character. This is the first step in holding ourselves to account: to face unflinchingly our own true moral nature. The second step has to do with our response to this moral judgment of ourselves. In holding ourselves accountable or answerable for what we have done, we commit ourselves to doing something that will make up for it. If we have harmed someone, we do our best to make reparation for that harm. If we have done something that cannot be corrected or taken back, we may try to compensate for our wrongdoing by reforming both our inner and outward life. Feelings of guilt and remorse, no doubt, will accompany such responses. But to hold oneself accountable for something one has done involves a great deal more than feeling guilty about it. It is not primarily a matter of feelings at all, but a matter of making a sincere, objective judgment of oneself and committing oneself to the performance of actions deemed appropriate in the light of that judgment.

Sometimes holding oneself responsible or accountable will require placing oneself in a position of being *publicly answerable*. This would happen if a person had done some wrong which involved the deception of others. His holding himself publicly answerable would then mean that he owns up to what he has done and is willing to face social condemnation (and all that that might entail in his practical life).

Common to all the various kinds of responses that are appropriate to a judgment of moral accountability or responsibility is the idea of *returning to a moral equilibrium*. The doing of the wrong, inexcusable act is understood as upsetting the balance of justice that holds between oneself and others. To think of oneself as being morally responsible is to acknowledge a special obligation to right this imbalance—an obligation one has brought upon oneself as the result of doing the act. Hence the need to make amends, to repair the damage, to set things right by compensating for the wrong. It is a requirement of justice: One judges that one deserves to be blamed for the past action and must make up for it to reach the point of balance again where one can wipe the slate clean and no longer be blameworthy. When this point is reached — and perhaps it is only one's own conscience that can tell when — the moral equilibrium is restored. Justice has been done.

Essentially the same analysis can be made of holding another morally responsible. Society, generally, holds individuals morally accountable in the same way a person can hold himself accountable. Thus, there are conventional judgments of moral character which form part of a society's moral code and are expressed in praise and blame. Society deems individuals at fault when they act so as to violate moral rules in circumstances that are not recognized socially as excusing conditions. And with regard to compensatory actions, society expects such conduct of an individual as his public acknowledgment of moral responsibility. The sorts of behavior expected of offending individuals are required, in the society's view, to meet the demands of justice. A person is expected to perform such an action, because it is seen as a duty that he has himself incurred by his own wrong conduct done in the absence of the generally recognized excusing conditions. The fulfillment of that duty is the socially approved way by which the individual is able to restore the moral equilibrium and so again be accepted without further stigma into the moral community.

This, then, is one way to understand what it means to be morally responsible for an action. It can be called the *traditional* concept of moral responsibility. Earlier in this chapter it was seen that hard determinists believe that this view of moral responsibility is not compatible with the principle of determinism. It is left to the reader to decide for himself whether hard determinists are right about this. Much will depend on whether moral responsibility, when so understood, presupposes a kind of freedom that is inconsistent with an action's being caused. In the remainder of this chapter, a sharply contrasting view of moral responsibility will be considered, one which hard determinists have sometimes advocated as the only concept of moral responsibility that is consistent with determinism. It will be designated the *future-oriented* concept of responsibility, to contrast it with the traditional concept.

According to the future-oriented view, stating that a person is morally responsible for an action is to say that it is justifiable to blame or otherwise condemn him for having done it. Whether it is justifiable to blame or condemn a person is held to depend on whether such sanctions will have some good effect upon his future conduct, in particular, whether they will prevent his repeating the same kind of action as that for which he is being censured. If blaming or condemning him will have this effect, then he is to be considered morally responsible. Otherwise he is not, and the only way to deal with him is to forget the wrong he has done and try to "condition" him in some other way to refrain from such actions in the future.

The traditional view, on the other hand, makes moral responsibility a matter of judgment of moral character and the obligation to fulfill a duty of (retributive) justice that was originally incurred by a person's own wrong-doing. Thus, an ascription of moral responsibility does not depend on whether the person in question will or will not repeat the same kind of act in the future. As far as his responsibility for the past action is concerned, his future conduct (beyond the duty of restoring the moral equilibrium) is irrelevant.

Hard determinists have proposed the future-oriented concept because, even if no actions are done freely and no one is at fault for having committed a wrong act, this does not mean we must let people do anything they please. Moral conduct is essential to a stable social order in which the rights of individuals are respected. Hence, we need to hold people responsible in order to ensure social stability and prevent the violation of people's rights. But holding someone accountable cannot be justified if it presupposes a kind of freedom that is inconsistent with causal necessity. Therefore, the only way to justify holding someone responsible is by showing that this is a *cause* that will bring about a certain *effect*, namely, getting the person to refrain from wrongdoing in the future.

Several criticisms of the future-oriented view have been raised by contemporary philosophers. One criticism is that the future-oriented view takes away an essential aspect of moral responsibility: its *rationality*. Thus, it is argued that a person can be held responsible only if he understands what it means to be answerable for what he did, and this requires that he understand the reasons why he was at fault. He must recognize and acknowledge to himself the *grounds* on which the moral judgment that condemns him is made. Otherwise he merely sees himself as a target of others' blame or finds himself experiencing guilt feelings that make his life unpleasant. Now the conditioning process which, according to the future-oriented view, is a device for changing a person's behavior need not appeal to the person's reason at all. It may do so, but only if this is the most effective way to cause the change. If nonrational techniques of persuasion could be used more effectively, then reasoning with the person would not be justified. Thus, moral responsibility is reduced to a way of manipulating people, on a par with any method, however devoid of reason, for producing changes in human behavior. This makes nonsense of the whole notion of moral responsibility.

A second criticism is that the future-oriented view does not enable us to distinguish between nonhuman animals and human beings. Thus we might "blame" a dog in order to change his future behavior and we might succeed, but even the hard determinist would admit that we don't hold dogs morally responsible for what they do.

A third criticism is based on reflections about situations in which we hold *ourselves* responsible. Do we believe we are justified in doing so only when we expect that this will tend to restrain us from similar actions in the future? This seems not to be the case. We often believe we ought to hold ourselves responsible for a past act, regardless of what we expect the future consequences to be of taking such an attitude toward ourselves. We think we are justified in holding ourselves responsible whenever we acknowledge that we had no legitimate excuse for our past conduct. Now the point is this: We would continue to think this even if we knew we were about to die and thus be unable to change our future conduct. Indeed, our confrontation with imminent death might well lead us to make a final judgment of ourselves, a "summing up" of our lives in which our acceptance of responsibility for what we have done has a fundamental place.

Finally, the future-oriented view overlooks the difference between moral training and moral maturity. When we express our disapproval to a small child because he has done something wrong, we might do this in order to get him to change. If that is our reason, our disapproval is part of the moral training of the child. We are then *not* treating the child as a responsible moral agent. Indeed, the whole point of the training process is to help the child become morally adult, so that he will be able to stand on his own two feet and act as a morally responsible being. But if all moral responsibility is a matter of conditioning, we are forever training people. We are never dealing with them as mature, fully developed moral persons, capable of acting responsibly as members of the moral community. The future-oriented concept thus entails the absurdity that moral training is not aimed at the forming of a capacity which renders further training unnecessary!

The hard determinist's reply to all such criticisms is in the form of a counterattack. To reject the future-oriented view and accept the traditional concept faces one with the dilemma of determinism. How can it be justifiable to hold people accountable for what they had no choice in doing? It is as unfair and cruel to do that as it is to punish a person for something he could not help. If someone does commit a wrong, any response of others or of the person himself to that fact should lead to some good effect. Otherwise one's judgments and attitudes serve no purpose but to create more pain and misery in the world.

So these questions, then, are left: Does the principle of determinism require us to give up the traditional concept of moral responsibility? Or can there be a kind of freedom, even in a deterministic universe, which allows man to conceive of himself as a responsible agent, morally accountable for his own actions?

Suggested Reading

Classic works:

Aristotle, *Nicomachean Ethics,* Book II, Chapters 1-5; Book III, Chapters 1 and 5.
St. Augustine, *On Free Will.*
St. Thomas Aquinas, *Summa Theologica,* Part I, Questions 82, 83; Part II, First Part, Question 6.
John Locke, *Essay Concerning Human Understanding,* Book II, Chapter XXI. 1690.
Jonathan Edwards, *Freedom of the Will.* 1754.
David Hume, *Treatise of Human Nature,* Book II, Part III. 1739. *Inquiry Concerning Human Understanding,* Section VIII. 1748.
Baron d'Holbach, *System of Nature,* Chapters XI, XII. 1770.
John Stuart Mill, *An Examination of Sir William Hamilton's Philosophy,* Chapter XXVI. 1865. *A System of Logic,* Book VI, Chapter 2. 1843.

Each of the following volumes contains a collection of writings on the free will problem or on some particular aspect of it:

Berofsky, Bernard, ed., *Free Will and Determinism.* New York: Harper and Row, Publishers, 1966.*
Brand, Myles, ed., *The Nature of Human Action.* Glenview, Ill.: Scott, Foresman and Company, 1970.*
Enteman, Willard F., ed., *The Problem of Free Will: Selected Readings.* New York: Charles Scribner's Sons, 1967.*
Ezorsky, Gertrude, ed., *Philosophical Perspectives on Punishment.* Albany: State University of New York Press, 1972.*
Feinberg, Joel, *Doing and Deserving: Essays in the Theory of Responsibility.* Princeton, N. J.: Princeton University Press, 1970.

*Available in paperback

Hart, H. L. A., *Punishment and Responsibility: Essays in the Philosophy of Law.* New York: Oxford University Press, 1968.*

Hook, Sidney, ed., *Determinism and Freedom in the Age of Modern Science.* New York: Collier Books, 1961.*

Lehrer, Keith, ed., *Freedom and Determinism.* New York: Random House, Inc., 1966.*

Morgenbesser, Sidney and James Walsh, eds., *Free Will.* Englewood Cliffs, N. J.: Prentice-Hall, Inc., 1962.*

Pears, D. F., ed., *Freedom and the Will.* New York: St. Martin's Press, 1964.

White, Alan R., ed., *The Philosophy of Action.* London: Oxford University Press, 1968.*

Three different defenses of libertarianism in recent philosophy:

Ayers, M. R., *The Refutation of Determinism: An Essay in Philosophical Logic.* London: Methuen and Co., Ltd., 1968.

Campbell, C. A., *In Defence of Free Will, with Other Philosophical Essays,* Essays I-III. New York: Humanities Press, 1967.

Franklin, R. L., *Freewill and Determinism: A Study of Rival Conceptions of Man.* New York: Humanities Press, 1968.

Two defenses of soft determinism, especially recommended for their studies of the concept of moral responsibility:

Baier, Kurt, "Responsibility and Action," first published in *The Nature of Human Action,* ed. Myles Brand. Glenview, Ill.: Scott, Foresman and Company, 1970.*

Glover, Jonathan, *Responsibility.* New York: Humanities Press, 1970.

Arguments intending to show the incompatibility of determinism and freedom are set forth in the following:

Broad, C. D., "Determinism, Indeterminism, and Libertarianism," in *Ethics and the History of Philosophy.* London: Routledge and Kegan Paul, 1952. Reprinted in Berofsky, op. cit., and in Morgenbesser and Walsh, op. cit.

Ginet, Carl, "Might We Have No Choice?", first published in Lehrer, op. cit.

O'Connor, D. J., *Free Will.* New York: Anchor Books, Doubleday and Co., Inc., 1971.*

Taylor, Richard, *Action and Purpose.* Englewood Cliffs, N. J.: Prentice-Hall, Inc., 1966.

An excellent analysis of what it means to say that a person at a certain time has the mental and physical ability to do a number of different kinds of actions (the basis for a soft determinist view of freedom):

Duggan, Timothy and Bernard Gert, "Voluntary Abilities," *American Philosophical Quarterly,* IV, No. 2 (1967), 127-135. Reprinted (slightly revised) in Brand, op. cit.

*Available in paperback

VIII

Values and Facts

Normative ethics is concerned with what ought to be, not with what is. Its task is to tell us how people ought and ought not to act, not how they do in fact behave. It holds up ideals for us to strive for, ideals that are not shown to be false merely because we fail to live up to them. Furthermore, to describe how individuals do act is not to show how they ought to. The fact that most people do a certain thing does not make it right. Even the moral code actually accepted by a given society only tells us what some believe to be right; it does not tell us what is right. In other words, it informs us about morality as it is, not about morality as it ought to be. Thus, the difference between the "is" and the "ought," between the real and the ideal, between facts and values, underlies the whole domain of normative ethics. Indeed, it is just this difference that separates ethics from sociology, psychology, and anthropology. Ethics is not one of the social sciences; yet it is not entirely unrelated to them. Ethics is not psychology; yet it can make use of the findings of psychology (for example, in predicting the probable consequences of acts or rules with regard to people's happiness), and in the last chapter we saw how the findings of psychology have a direct bearing on the ethical problem of free will and moral responsibility. Although facts and values are (at least at first glance) different from one another, they are nevertheless related, and no discussion of the problems of ethics can omit a consideration of their relation.

This chapter will be concerned with three fundamental questions: (1) What is the difference (if there be any) between facts and values? (2) How are they related to each other? (3) What is a value judgment?

175

NATURALISM AND NONNATURALISM

We shall begin by considering two opposite theories regarding the relation between facts and values: naturalism and nonnaturalism. According to naturalism, values are one kind of fact; according to nonnaturalism, values and facts are separate kinds of things, absolutely irreducible to one another. We can best understand what is meant by these claims if we take a "fact" to be an empirically verifiable statement about events and objects in the real world, and if we let "value" designate a value judgment, that is, a statement concerning what ought or ought not to be, or an assertion that something is good or desirable or right. When we state a fact we assert that some object exists or some event occurs, or else we describe the properties and relations of objects and events. When we utter a value judgment we are evaluating, appraising, or assessing the value of something. Consider the difference between the statements "Mohandas Gandhi was assassinated in 1948" and "Mohandas Gandhi was a good man." The first expresses a fact about, but does not evaluate, a certain event in history. The second evaluates a person; it compares him favorably with most men and rates him high in an order of merit. Facts are empirical assertions, purporting to give us correct information about the real world; we can determine whether they are true or false by appeal to experience. Values are normative assertions; they tell us whether something is good or bad, right or wrong, desirable or undesirable. How can we determine *their* truth or falsity? The basic contradiction between naturalism and nonnaturalism lies in the different answers they give to this question.

Naturalism holds that value judgments are empirically verifiable, just as facts are. The philosophical naturalist argues this point as follows. Consider any typical value judgment, such as "War is evil" or "It is right to aid those who are destitute." Statements of this kind express a proposition in which a value-predicate ("evil," "right") is applied to a subject ("war," "aiding the destitute"). Now according to naturalism, all value-predicates can be defined in terms of factual-predicates, that is, in terms of predicates that stand for empirical properties. Different naturalistic theories offer different definitions of value-predicates, but they all give meanings which analyze value-predicates in empirical terms. For example, a natur-alism of the *subjectivist* type may define "evil" as meaning "disliked by the person who makes the statement" and "right" as meaning "approved of by people in the given society." A naturalistic theory of an *objectivist* type may define "evil" as "causing pain" and "right" as "productive of the greatest amount of happiness." A theory of value (that is, a theory about the meaning and justification of value judgments) is naturalistic, then, if it defines a value-predicate in empirical or "naturalistic" terms, or in other words, in terms of properties whose presence in anything can be determined by tests that rest on direct experience.

If we were to accept a naturalistic definition of a value-predicate, we would see at once that every value judgment in which the predicate occurred would necessarily express an empirically verifiable proposition. That is to say, every such value judgment would be a statement of fact. For given the naturalistic definition, to apply the value-predicate to something would be to claim that the object or action was characterized by an empirical property or set of properties, namely, those that define the value-predicate in question. Take one of the foregoing examples, "It is right to aid the destitute." If a subjectivist type of naturalism were correct, this judgment would be equivalent to "Aiding the destitute is approved of in our society." Now either this is true, as a matter of fact, or it is false. It can be discovered to be one or the other by ascertaining the attitudes of people in the given society to see whether they do indeed favor aiding the destitute. If they do, then the value judgment is true. The property, "being approved of by the given society," does characterize the action type, "aiding the destitute." The empirical method of verifying the value judgment would involve such procedures as observing people's behavior toward the destitute in the given society, sampling their opinions and feelings by means of carefully constructed questionnaires, and using other techniques developed by the social sciences in recent years for determining what people's real attitudes are.

In the view of the nonnaturalist, on the other hand, a value judgment is not a factual assertion about people's attitudes, nor indeed is it an assertion about *any* empirical fact or set of facts. He agrees with the naturalist in holding that value judgments are propositions in which a value-predicate is applied to a subject, but he disagrees with the naturalist about the definability of value-predicates in naturalistic terms. The nonnaturalist claims that value-predicates, such as "good" and "right," are names of special value-properties of things, and value properties cannot be reduced to empirical properties. Thus, he maintains that when we utter a value judgment of the form "Object X is good" or "Action Y is right," we are asserting that object X is characterized by the property, "being good" or simply goodness, and that action Y is characterized by the property, "being right" or rightness. These properties (one might call them "objective values") are ultimate and irreducible. That is, they cannot be analyzed into—or defined in terms of—some other property or set of properties which are empirical. A value judgment is true when the subject of the judgment (object X, action Y) does have the objective value-property which is named by the predicate of the judgment (goodness, rightness). Otherwise the judgment is false.

How do we *know* whether a given value judgment is true or false, according to nonnaturalism? Since the presence or absence of an objective value-property cannot be determined by empirical tests, such knowledge is not based on sense experience. How, then, can it be obtained? There are two answers that nonnaturalists give to this question: by *intuition* and by *self-evidence*. According to the first answer, we know the truth of a value judgment by means of intuition, which is a direct way of apprehending or being aware of an objective value-property in something. It is important not to confuse intuition with instinct. An intuition is not an unlearned response or an innate ability, with which human beings are born. Developing the capacity to be immediately aware of the objective value-properties in things may require much education and experience of life. But once an individual gains this ability, then his knowledge of what is right and wrong, good and bad, is a matter of intuiting—that is, being immediately conscious of, or directly aware of—right and wrong, good and evil, as those properties are exemplified in actions and objects. The nature of this "immediate con-sciousness" or "direct awareness" can be clarified by comparing intuition with sense experience. How do we know that something is yellow? We *see* the color yellow directly on the surface of the object. How do we know that a lemon is sour? We experience the sourness directly by *tasting* it. How do we know that a stone is hard? We touch it and *feel* its hardness. So, in the case of a value judgment, we know that something is good by directly *intuiting* its goodness. Suppose someone makes the value judgment, "Breaking your promise is wrong." We can know that this assertion is true, according to the nonnaturalist (or, as he is sometimes called, the intuitionist), by directly apprehending the wrongness of breaking one's promise. We are simply aware that it is our duty not to break our promises. If a person were not aware of this, he would be morally blind; he would be lacking in the knowledge most of us gained in our moral upbringing. Although we do not see, touch, hear, taste, or smell the quality of wrongness in the act of promise-breaking, we nevertheless immediately grasp the truth of the state-ment that it is wrong to break a promise, for we are directly aware of the wrongness of that kind of act.

The second answer of the nonnaturalist to the question, How do we know the presence of objective value-properties? is that the truth of certain value judgments — in particular, fundamental moral judgments — is *self-evident*. We do not have to use a method of reasoning to go from the factual proposition, "This is an act of breaking a promise," to the moral judgment, "This act is wrong." There is a necessary connection between promise-breaking and wrongness that makes it self-evident that every action, insofar as it breaks a promise, is at least prima facie wrong. This means that unless an instance of promise-breaking also has some positive moral property, it is necessarily wrong. This is not because "wrong" is *definable* as "promise-breaking." To claim *that* is the mistake of the naturalists (since it would define a value-predicate in empirical terms and so commit the naturalistic fallacy, as will be seen below). Rather, if we have reached a certain level of moral development, we just "see" the necessary connection between the (factual) property of promise-breaking and the (value) property of wrongness.

Nonnaturalism (or intuitionism) may at first strike the reader as a very peculiar theory. Why does anyone hold it? And if someone does hold it, is that not simply a reflection of his ethnocentric bias? In claiming that one has an intuition into the objective rightness or wrongness of an action or that the truth of a moral judgment needs no proof because it is self-evident, isn't the nonnaturalist merely putting forth his own moral beliefs as absolute truth? Indeed, what is an intuitive, self-evident moral judgment but merely an unquestioned opinion which is held with an inner conviction that makes the believer absolutely certain of its truth? And if this is so, then no method of *knowledge* is being provided by either intuition or self-evidence. For someone from a different culture might well have contrary "intuitions." Judgments that are self-evidently true to one nonnaturalist may be self-evidently false to another. Unless one of the intuited or self-evident judgments could be *proven* to be true, no claim to have moral *knowledge* can correctly be made. But if a method was used to prove the truth of one of the moral judgments, then *this* method would be the ultimate way of knowing, not intuition or self-evidence. For it would have to be assumed as a method by which one could correct, or validate, the claims of intuition and self-evidence. Hence, intuition and self-evidence would not *by themselves* constitute ways of knowing objective values. Such a conclusion would undercut one of the basic principles of nonnaturalism.

In order to understand the appeal that nonnaturalism has had for some philosophers, it is helpful first to notice an important feature of moral language, its *objectivity*. By the objectivity of moral language is meant the fact that, when we utter moral judgments and discuss moral matters in everyday life, we appear to be making claims that are either true or false.

Our use of language presupposes that there is a real difference between merely believing that an action is right and knowing that it is right. We think that it is possible for people to be mistaken in their moral beliefs and that there is some way to correct such mistakes. Thus, we might think that a person who sees nothing wrong in driving his car recklessly in heavy traffic lacks an awareness of the moral aspects of his conduct. We might even say that he is "morally blind," meaning that he fails to realize what is objectively or actually wrong about his action. Whether or not he subjectively "in his mind" thinks of his action as being wrong, it nevertheless *is* wrong. This way of talking, which is a perfectly ordinary use of language in moral situations and does not stem from a special philosophical theory, presupposes a difference between "Doing X is wrong" and "Doing X is believed (by someone) to be wrong." It allows for the possibility of something being objectively wrong without someone's knowing, recognizing, or acknowledging it to be so. It is in this sense that the feature of objectivity is implicit in our everyday moral discourse.

There is another respect in which the objectivity of moral language makes itself evident. This is the fact that questions of morality (concerning what actions are right, what motives are good, when a person should be absolved from blame, et cetera) are not considered to be matters of taste. When we express our subjective preferences, our likes and dislikes ("Hiking is more fun than water-skiing"; "This steak would be better if it were not so well done"), we do not distinguish between what we like and what is good, or between believing that something is good and knowing that it is so. For in matters of taste, declaring that something is good is to say that one likes it — that it "appeals to one's taste." If we correctly express our preferences, there is no way in which our judgments of taste can be false. We cannot be mistaken in what we like. Thus, once we understand that in calling something "good" an individual is merely expressing his personal preferences, we do not try to argue with him, even if his preferences are different from our own. "Concerning tastes there is no disputing." We get a completely different picture, however, when we consider disagreements regarding a moral matter. Thus, suppose a manufacturing company is polluting a river so that the ecological balance of an entire region is being destroyed. We do not think the judgment that the company is doing something wrong merely expresses our distaste for that sort of thing or reflects our dislike for the people who do it. If someone were to defend the company's action by asserting that it is not wrong to pollute the river, we certainly would not cease making our judgment on the ground that "it is foolish to argue about the question, since it's all a matter of taste." We think that our assessment of the case is impersonal, one that would hold true of any similar situation. Above all, we do not believe it is our dislike of pollution that makes the act of fouling a river wrong. We think that an appeal to some moral principle is appropriate in this kind of situation, and by invoking such a principle we consider ourselves to be making an objective claim. For we appeal to a principle (such as a principle of conservation or one of fairness to future generations) which we believe ought to be accepted by any rational person. In other words, we presuppose that some justification can be given for the principle, and that this justification consists of reasons that all can recognize as good reasons in this kind of case.

Moral language, then, is imbued with the characteristic of objectivity. What account can be given of this? The answer that might first come to mind is that moral judgments are objective for the same reason that factual judgments are; they are assertions about matters of fact and hence are either empirically true or empirically false. This is, indeed, exactly what a *naturalistic* theory of value judgments does maintain. However, naturalism has come under strong attack in twentieth-century philosophy. In fact, it was the nonnaturalists who originally launched this attack, leading them to argue that their own views provide the only adequate account of the objectivity of moral language. They admitted that naturalism is correct insofar as it preserves the feature of objectivity in moral judgments. But, they claimed, it fails to explain the crucial differences between moral language and the language of fact, between normative statements and descriptive statements, between "ought" propositions and "is" propositions. It is necessary now to look into this nonnaturalist criticism of naturalism, for it is based on one of the most famous and influential arguments in ethical theory. It was this argument that convinced many philosophers not only of the falsity of naturalism but also of the truth of nonnaturalism. Quite apart from this historical fact, however, this reasoning is still a central topic of philosophical discussion and is vital to understanding contemporary studies of the relation between facts and values. The argument consists in a refutation of naturalism on the ground that all naturalistic theories commit what is called "the naturalistic fallacy."

THE NATURALISTIC FALLACY

The argument that all naturalistic theories commit the naturalistic fallacy was originally stated by Professor G.E. Moore (1873-1958) of Cambridge University. In 1903, Professor Moore published a book that has become a landmark in the history of ethics. In that book, whose title is *Principia Ethica*, Moore did two things. He set forth a nonnaturalistic theory of value judgments, and he constructed the "naturalistic fallacy" argument against naturalism. Moore believed that these two things are logically connected. If one accepts his argument against naturalism, he thought, one must accept his own nonnaturalistic position about values. Many philosophers of his time agreed with him, and hence the rise of nonnaturalism. However, for reasons to be given below, it is possible to accept Moore's criticism of naturalism and at the same time reject a nonnaturalistic theory of value.

The idea of the naturalistic fallacy may be summed up by two propositions, which for convenience shall be called here "the definist fallacy" and "the deductive fallacy." The definist fallacy is the proposition that the meaning of a value-predicate can be exhaustively analyzed into, or reduced to, purely factual terms. The deductive fallacy is the proposition that it is possible to deduce a value judgment from a set of facts, or to put it in a popular way, to derive "ought" from "is." Each proposition will now be considered in turn, along with the argument intending to show that it is a fallacy.

(1) *The definist fallacy.* According to naturalism, as shown previously, a value judgment is one type of empirical assertion, because a value-predicate is held to be definable in purely factual (empirical) terms. Now the nonnaturalist claims that this is an error. A value-predicate *cannot* mean the same thing as any set of factual or empirical properties. The argument in support of this antinaturalist claim is known as *the open-question argument.* It runs as follows. Let us suppose that a naturalistic definition of a value-predicate were true. In a naturalistic definition of a value-predicate, it will be recalled, the meaning of a value-predicate is identical with the meaning of a word or set of words standing for empirical properties. An example already considered was, "Right" means "approved of by our society." Some other examples are: "Good" means "pleasant." "Intrinsically valuable" means "enjoyed for its own sake." "Socially desirable" means "satisfies people's needs." "Bad" means "disliked by the majority." And so on.

What is the test for the truth or falsity of such definitions? If any such definition were true, then whenever the value-predicate so construed occurred in a sentence, we could substitute for it the word or set of words that define it *without changing the meaning of the sentence.* This can be made clear by first taking the sense of a nonvalue word and applying this substitutability test to it. Consider the definition, "father" means "male parent." If this is indeed true, then whenever the word "father" occurs in a sentence, we can substitute for it the words "male parent" without changing the meaning of the sentence. When the substitution is made in the sentence "My father is fifty years old," we get, "My male parent is fifty years old." Since these two sentences do mean the same thing, the definition is true (assuming the substitution in other sentences would yield the same result).

Let us now apply the test of interchangeability to one of the above examples of a value-predicate. Thus if "good" means "pleasant," then the two sentences "Playing tennis is a good experience" and "Playing tennis is a pleasant experience" must mean the same thing. And they do, in fact, appear to have approximately the same meaning. But now consider the following two compound sentences:

Sentence 1: This is pleasant, but is it good?

Sentence 2: This is pleasant, but is it pleasant?

The only difference between these two sentences is that, where the word "good" occurs in one, the word "pleasant" occurs in the other. Therefore, if the definition, "good" means "pleasant," were true, the two sentences should mean exactly the same thing. But it is clear that they do not. The reason is that sentence 2 is a silly sentence; no one would ever utter it, for if we already know that something is pleasant there is no point in asking whether it is. But sentence 1 is not silly. We may know that something is pleasant and still ask seriously whether it is good. We may very well wonder, if someone finds it pleasant to kick others around, whether it is good that he do so. At least it is an *open question* whether something that is pleasant is also good. Yet if "good" just meant "pleasant," then once we knew that something was pleasant it would make no sense to ask whether it was good, for we would then be asking whether it was pleasant.

We can use the same reasoning with regard to *any* naturalistic definition of a value-predicate, referring to sentences 1 and 2 as our models. Thus, "This action is approved of in my society, but is it right?" is a sensible question to ask, but no one would ever say such a ridiculous thing as "This action is approved of in my society, but is it approved of in my society?" Yet if "right" means "approved of in my society," these two questions must mean the same thing, so that if one is ridiculous the other must be equally ridiculous. Since one of the sentences is not ridiculous while the other is, they cannot be identical in meaning and the naturalistic definition of "right" must not be true.

It is important to understand what is entailed by the open question argument. If the argument is sound, then no matter what empirical properties we know something to have, we can always raise the question, Is it a good thing or a bad thing? Whatever consequences might be brought about by an action, we can still ask, Ought a person to do it? Even if it were known that an act would bring no pleasure to anyone and would cause many to suffer, for example, there is nothing in these facts *alone* that determines whether the act is right or wrong. Of course we might all agree that such an act would be wrong, but to say that it is wrong is not just to say that it brings no pleasure and causes suffering. Indeed, with this example in mind we can now see how the open question argument gives rise to a further argument to show that the definist fallacy is, in truth, a fallacy.

Let us call this additional argument *the "reasons for acting argument."* It may be stated in the following way. Suppose everyone does agree that any action which brings no one any pleasure but causes many to suffer is wrong. Suppose, in addition, that everyone judges it to be wrong *because* it brings no pleasure and causes suffering. It would then follow that "Act X is wrong" *cannot* mean the same thing as "Act X brings no pleasure and causes suffering." For if it did mean this, we could substitute the suggested definition of "wrong" in place of that word wherever it occurs in a sentence without changing the meaning of the sentence. Take, then, the statement, "This act is wrong because it brings no pleasure and causes suffering." By substitution, this becomes, "This act brings no pleasure and causes suffering because it brings no pleasure and causes suffering." The former sentence, which states reasons why an act is wrong (and thus gives reasons against doing it), is transformed into a tautology—an empty statement which says nothing. Yet, according to the hypothetical case above, people believe that an act is wrong because it brings no pleasure and causes suffering. This belief, therefore, cannot be expressed if the suggested naturalistic definition of "wrong" is true. Now to say that an action is wrong because it brings no pleasure and causes suffering is to say something important. It is to give reasons against performing, or intending to perform, an action. But the tautology, "This act brings no pleasure and causes suffering because it brings no pleasure and causes suffering," does not give reasons against anything, since it asserts nothing at all. And the same argument can be applied easily to any naturalistic definition of a value-predicate. To take another instance, it is a fallacy—the definist fallacy—to define the word "desirable" as applied to social policies to mean the same as "satisfying people's needs." For it must at least be possible to say that a social policy is desirable because it satisfies people's needs. But this becomes impossible to say if the definition is accepted. Therefore the definition must be rejected. The conclusion drawn from the reasons-for-acting argument is then quite clear. It is the same as the conclusion drawn from the open-question argument: Every naturalistic definition of a value-predicate commits the definist fallacy and must therefore be false. Value-predicates are not, therefore, reducible to empirical properties.

(2) *The deductive fallacy.* The deductive fallacy is the error of deriving "ought" from "is." This can be expressed with greater precision: Any deductive argument is invalid if its conclusion is a value judgment and all its premises are facts. Or, to put it in still another way, no normative (evaluative or prescriptive) statement can be deduced from empirical statements alone. Let us consider an example. It is sometimes argued that parents ought to love their children because children need their parents' love. The argument may be set forth thus:

> Children need the love of their parents.
> Therefore, parents ought to love their children.

In this argument an "ought" statement is derived from an "is" statement. The deductive fallacy involved is quite apparent. The conclusion does not necessarily follow from the premise, since there is no contradiction in saying that children need the love of their parents but parents ought not to love their children. The *fact* that someone needs something is not by itself sufficient for saying that his need *ought* to be satisfied. A person might have a need for something that is bad for him, or that is morally wrong for him to have. (Think of a sadist's need to have a victim!) Thus, for the above argument to be valid, it requires an additional premise, such as, "Being loved is good," or "The needs of children ought to be satisfied." Notice that if either of these statements were added as a premise we would no longer have an instance of the deductive fallacy. For a normative conclusion ("Parents ought to love their children") would be derived, not from a fact alone ("Children need the love of their parents"), but from the fact plus another normative statement ("Being loved is *good,*" or "The needs of children *ought* to be satisfied"). With this additional normative premise, then, an "ought" is being derived from another "ought" or from a "good," not from an "is." Hence no deductive fallacy is committed.

Whenever anyone argues that, because such-and-such facts about the world are true, it follows that we ought to do or not to do certain acts, he is committing the deductive fallacy. He is deducing a normative claim from facts alone. Any argument of this type is invalid, because it is possible to assert the premises (that is, to accept the factual statements as true) and to deny the conclusion (that is, to reject the normative conclusion as false) without contradicting ourselves. To take another — admittedly extreme — case, "Act X ought not to be done" does not follow from "Act X will cause a nuclear war that will destroy every civilization on earth." For there is no contradiction in saying "This act will cause a nuclear war that will destroy every civilization on earth but nevertheless it ought to be done." Such a statement might show that the person who asserts it (assuming he is sincere) is morally vicious, or perhaps utterly insane. But as far as logic alone is concerned, he is perfectly consistent. There is no *logical* error in his position.

It might be thought that there is a legitimate way to avoid the deductive fallacy, namely, by adding a *definition* to the factual premises. Thus suppose the following argument is given:

> If everyone were to do acts of violence, the structure of social life would disintegrate.
> Therefore, it is wrong for anyone to do an act of violence.

In this argument an evaluative judgment is deduced from a statement of fact. It is fallacious as given, since there is no contradiction in asserting the premise and denying the conclusion. One can consistently hold that it is right for a person to do an act of violence even though, if everyone were to do such acts, the structure of social life would disintegrate. However, suppose we add another premise to the argument as follows:

> (1) "Wrong action" means "Any action of a kind such that, if everyone were to perform it, the structure of social life would disintegrate."
> (2) If everyone were to do acts of violence, the structure of social life would disintegrate.
> (3) Therefore, it is wrong for anyone to do an act of violence.

Here we have a valid argument. The conclusion is a value judgment, but it is not deduced from a fact alone. It is deduced from a fact plus a definition of the value term (namely, "wrong") used in the conclusion. Thus the logical form of the argument is correct, and the conclusion necessarily follows from the premises.

What is wrong with the argument is that, if the definist fallacy is a genuine error, then premise (1) is false. For premise (1) is an example of a naturalistic definition of a value-predicate. Hence the argument, though valid, is not sound. (An argument is sound only if it is valid and all of its premises are true.) Here we see the relation between the definist fallacy and the deductive fallacy. To put it simply, the reason why it is a fallacy to deduce a value judgment from a set of facts is that no fact can be shown to be identical in meaning with a value judgment. Thus no contradiction is involved in asserting a set of facts and denying a value judgment that is meant to be deducible from them.

These considerations regarding the naturalistic fallacy have some important implications. They mean, for one thing, that science *alone* cannot solve our value problems. Even if the psychology of human motivation and personality were to advance to the point where we had a fairly complete account of the causes and effects of human conduct, we would still be unable to deduce from such knowledge what the good life for man is, how any human being should live, what our moral duties are, or whether everyone has the same human rights. No amount of sociological, anthropological, or historical knowledge about the development of societies, how they function, what can preserve them or destroy them, what factors lead to social conflict and what bring about social harmony—none of this knowledge can *by itself* tell us which societies are better or worse than others. It cannot tell us what moral code a society should have, or what legal, political, and economic systems are good or bad, just or unjust. Assume, if we will, that it could be shown that a certain social policy would lead to conflict among groups, the eventual breakdown of social order, and finally the destruction of the whole way of life of the society itself. We still cannot deduce from these facts alone that the social policy in question is wrong or bad. We would always have to add the evaluative or normative premise: The destruction of that society and its way of life is something that ought not to take place. The general conclusion is that no amount of scientific knowledge about the world is sufficient to provide the justification of a set of values. To find out what ideals we ought to seek, or what standards and rules validly apply to human conduct, it is necessary to go beyond science and the purely factual enlightenment which it can give us.

What has been called "the autonomy of ethics" is based on these reflections. Ethics, it is said, is not itself a science, nor does it rest entirely on the sciences. It comprises an independent field of inquiry, a discipline concerned with values (the domain of "what ought to be"), not with facts (the domain of "what is"). It seeks moral knowledge and moral truth, just as science seeks empirical knowledge and empirical truth. It has its own autonomous uses of reason for the pursuit of its goal, and these cannot be subsumed under purely scientific ways of thinking. Knowledge of the realm of values is separated from knowledge of the realm of facts by a logical gap.

This does not mean, however, that ethics must consider facts to be wholly irrelevant to values. It may be the case that, though ethics is an autonomous discipline logically independent of the sciences, it can make use of scientific knowledge in its own field of endeavor. It will be demonstrated later in this chapter how one can reasonably maintain that the justification of value judgments *includes* an appeal to facts. But if the naturalistic fallacy is indeed a fallacy, facts by themselves — however well-established by scientific tests — cannot constitute the exclusive grounds on which value judgments logically rest.

Besides "the autonomy of ethics," another conclusion has been drawn by some philosophers from the naturalistic fallacy argument. This is the claim that, since all naturalistic theories of value are mistaken (because they commit the naturalistic fallacy), nonnaturalism must be accepted as the true theory. This was the conclusion drawn by Professor Moore, who first propounded the naturalistic fallacy argument in the form here considered. We shall now see that, contrary to Professor Moore's view, it is in fact possible to reject naturalism and at the same time not accept nonnaturalism. For there is a third theory about values and facts which, if true, would imply that both naturalism and nonnaturalism are false. This is the theory known as "noncognitivism" or "the emotive theory."

NONCOGNITIVISM

To understand how noncognitivism (or the emotive theory) differs fundamentally from both naturalism and nonnaturalism, it is necessary to begin by distinguishing three uses or functions of language. These may be designated the reportive or assertive function, the expressive function, and the dynamic function.

When we use language to make an assertion or report a fact, we are stating what we believe about something. Thus we might say, "It is going to rain," and so communicate to our hearers a belief we have about the weather in the immediate future. We use language to do the same job when we say, "It rained yesterday," or when we say, "Rain falls when there is a change in atmospheric pressure," or when we say, "A drop of rain contains oxygen," and so on. In other words, whenever we express a matter-of-fact belief that something is so, will be so, or has been so, the language we use has a reportive or assertive function. It is only when language is used in this way that we can ask whether what we say is true or false. And only with reference to this function of language can we speak of knowing that something is or is not so.

The second function of language is exemplified most obviously in emotional ejaculations. Here we use words to express our feelings. Touching a hot stove, I yell, "Ouch!" A music lover cries out, "Bravo!" on hearing a beautifully sung aria. We shout, "Hurrah!" when our team is winning. Language in this way evinces or displays our emotion, just as our posture, facial expressions, and nonverbal actions may also reveal our feelings to others. Ejaculations are the simplest expressive use of language. Perhaps the most complex and subtlest expressive use is found in lyrical poetry. But it is important to notice that declarative sentences may also have this function. Each of the following expresses a certain emotion: "This is a splendid day for a picnic." "I'm so relieved they got home safely." "He was absolutely brilliant in that chess game." "It was a despicable thing to do."

The third function of language is its capacity to arouse or evoke the feelings of others, to influence their attitudes, and to change or redirect their behavior. The simplest example is a command or order, and we are all familiar with the subtle (and not so subtle!) techniques of persuasion used in advertising copy and in radio and television commercials. Other examples are proposals ("Let's go to the movies tonight"); requests ("I wish you would not walk on the lawn"); suggestions ("We suggest that you go by plane rather than by car"); advice ("My advice is that you should see a doctor"); recommendations ("I recommend leniency in this case"); prescriptions ("You ought to get more exercise"). In each instance the uttering of the statement is intended to exert an influence on the hearer, and frequently this intended effect is brought about by the utterance. Political oratory, preaching, "pep talks," and didactic literature all have this function. Language is being used to call forth some response on the part of others. Thus we name this the "dynamic" function of language.

Now where do value judgments fit into this threefold division of linguistic functions? When we utter a moral judgment, are we making an assertion that is true or false? Are we expressing our feelings? Or are we trying to guide and direct the conduct of others? The theory of noncognitivism holds that value judgments belong in the last two categories but not in the first. Statements about what is good, bad, right, wrong, desirable, undesirable are not cognitive assertions. That is to say, the person who makes such statements is not expressing a belief; he is not making a claim that is true or false. Rather, he is expressing his attitudes and trying to get others to have the same attitudes he has. Thus when a person says, "Mohandas Gandhi was a good man," he is expressing his approval of Gandhi and is trying to evoke approval of Gandhi in his hearers. Declarative sentences that express value judgments, therefore, are linguistic utterances having an expressive and dynamic function, but not a reportive or assertive ("cognitive") function. Thus they are sharply to be distinguished from declarative sentences, like "Gandhi was assassinated in 1948," that express beliefs and that accordingly are open to verification procedures. Since value judgments are neither true nor false, there is no sense in talking about their verification. Indeed, since moral statements are merely emotive expressions and dynamic instruments of language, there is no such thing as moral knowledge. Hence the name, "noncognitivism." According to the noncognitivist, we should not talk about *knowing* what is right and wrong, good and bad. However, as we shall see shortly, the noncognitivist does speak of moral *reasoning* in a special sense.

Noncognitivism differs from naturalism and nonnaturalism in that both of the latter theories conceive of value judgments as expressing beliefs, capable of being true or false. Both naturalism and nonnaturalism, consequently, are forms of "cognitivism." Both claim that there is such a thing as moral knowledge. For naturalism, value judgments are one type of factual assertion. They are verifiable empirically or scientifically, and moral knowledge is simply one branch of scientific knowledge. For nonnaturalism, a value judgment is an assertion or belief that a value-property characterizes a given object, act, or person. This belief is either true or false, and intuition is the way to find out which it is. Noncognitivists deny both of these views. They reject naturalism for the same reason given by the nonnaturalist, to wit, it commits the naturalistic fallacy. Noncognitivists, indeed, offer an explanation of why the naturalistic fallacy is a fallacy. Naturalism assumes that all declarative sentences have the same linguistic function, which is to be assertive of facts, and hence it overlooks the possibility that value judgments can be expressive and dynamic but not cognitive or assertive.

Noncognitivists deny nonnaturalism because nonnaturalists think of value judgments as assertive of beliefs about the presence or absence of value-properties in things. Thus they take the adjectives "good," "desirable," "right," and the like to be names of properties: goodness, desirability, rightness, and so on. In so doing, they think of value-words as having a descriptive function, the way "yellow," "loud," "heavy," and other such adjectives are descriptive. But, the noncognitivist argues, adjectives may have any of the three different linguistic functions listed above, and value-words like "good," "desirable," and "right" are used only expressively and dynamically in sentences where they occur as predicates. Such sentences, therefore, are misconstrued if they are understood the way ordinary descriptive sentences, such as "It is going to rain," are understood.

The noncognitivist makes an important distinction between two ways in which people can disagree with one another: disagreement in belief and disagreement in attitude. The first kind of disagreement occurs when one person makes an assertion and another denies it. Both persons are using language reportively. They are expressing opposite beliefs about the same thing. The second kind of disagreement occurs when one person expresses a favorable or positive attitude toward something and another expresses an unfavorable or negative attitude toward the same thing. (Two persons might also disagree in the strength or intensity of their attitudes, even when both attitudes are positive or when both are negative.) It is the latter kind of disagreement that occurs in ethics, according to the noncognitivist. When one person says, "This is good" and another says, "No, it is bad," each is expressing his own attitude and trying to get the other to change his attitude and agree (in attitude) with the speaker. Their disagreement is not a contradiction in the usual sense, where one person claims that a belief is true and the other claims it is false. Instead, it is a conflict of attitudes, and attitudes are neither true nor false.

Does this analysis of value language mean that all value judgments are necessarily matters of taste? Does it deny what we earlier saw to be the objectivity of moral language, as that language is used in everyday life? The noncognitivist does try to account for the fact that moral language has the *appearance* of objectivity, and he does not need to hold that all evaluative questions are matters of taste. His position regarding these points is based on his view of *the relation between attitudes and beliefs*. The apparent objectivity of moral language, he would claim, does not mean that moral judgments are themselves beliefs which can be true or false. When we utter a moral judgment we are not making an assertion; we are expressing an attitude. But our attitudes are not all matters of taste, personal preference, mere liking and disliking. There is a way in which our beliefs can shape our attitudes, so that at least some of the attitudes we have are dependent on our beliefs. Indeed, it is possible to change our attitudes (and hence our value judgments) in the light of our beliefs. Let us see how this can occur.

There are times when each of us will approve of something (and so call it "good" or "desirable" or "right") when we do not have correct beliefs about its nature or consequences. Then, as we learn more about its nature or consequences and accordingly change our beliefs, our attitudes will change, either in strength or in direction. For example, we might approve of a proposed law and then, upon learning what would be the probable consequences of its being passed and adopted, change our attitude from approval to disapproval. In this kind of situation, our attitude toward something depends on our beliefs about it. If two people disagree in attitude, it might then be possible for one person to change the attitude of the other by showing him that he has false beliefs about the object in question. Now since scientific method can be used to establish the truth or falsity of empirical beliefs, science has the capacity to enlighten our moral judgments. This would happen if our obtaining scientific knowledge about something caused a change in our attitudes toward it. This causal relationship between facts and values, however, is still very different from the basic thesis of naturalism, namely, that moral knowledge is itself a kind of scientific knowledge since values are a kind of fact.

The foregoing way of looking at the relation between beliefs and attitudes provides the noncognitivist with a certain conception of *moral reasoning*. We have seen that, according to noncognitivism, value judgments are neither true nor false. How, then, can we reason about them? To give reasons in support of a value statement would normally be understood to be a logical process of justifying someone's accepting the statement. The reasons would be such as to show that the statement is true. Likewise, arguing against a value statement would ordinarily be taken as a way of showing the statement to be false and hence an attempt to justify someone's denying the statement. But if value statements are mere expressions of attitudes and neither true nor false, how can there be such a thing as giving reasons for or against them? The noncognitivist answers this question by distinguishing between "reasons for believing" and "reasons for approving." Those relevant to value judgments are reasons for approving, and since they can be given it is possible for attitudes to be justified or unjustified. Specifying such reasons will consist in citing beliefs that have the psychological effect of changing a person's attitude toward the object whose value is being discussed. At least, they will be beliefs that are intended to have such effect. An illustration of this conception of moral reasoning follows.

Suppose someone utters the judgment "Having an abortion is immoral," and when asked "Why?" gives as the reason, "Because a fetus is a human being and to kill it is an act of murder." According to noncognitivism, moral reasoning here consists in asserting a belief (a fetus is a human being) which might influence someone to take a negative attitude toward abortion. The belief would indeed have such an effect if the person already had a negative attitude toward the killing of a human being, which he deemed murder. However, the process of reasoning could well be continued. To the argument so far given, the reply might be made, "I grant that a fetus is a human being, but I deny that killing the fetus is an act of murder." The noncognitivist analyzes this reply thus. The individual giving the answer agrees that the belief, "A fetus is a human being," is true, but he does not take a negative attitude toward killing it because he does not disapprove of *every* action which comes under the description "the killing of a human being." He might, for example, approve of such an action when committed in self-defense, or when necessary to prevent a grave injustice. Now some abortions are, for him, done in circumstances in which he considers the killing of a fetus (and hence of a human being) justified. And this means that, given his beliefs about abortions so performed, his attitude is not negative but positive. Hence his accepting the belief, "Abortion is the killing of a human being," does not effect a change in his attitude.

It is now clear how the noncognitivist accounts for the appearance of objectivity which moral language has. It is due to the cause-effect relation that can hold between beliefs and attitudes. We think we are giving reasons that establish the truth of our moral judgments, but this is a mistake. Moral judgments, being the expression of attitudes, are never true. (Nor are they false.) But they may be influenced by beliefs which a person accepts as being true, and in this sense such attitudes may be justified to the person himself. When he expresses those viewpoints in the language of declarative sentences ("This is my duty," "That ought not to be done," and so on), he appears to be making objective claims. But this appearance of objectivity is an illusion. Once we become aware that declarative sentences may be used expressively and dynamically rather than simply to assert what one believes to be true, we can see through the illusion of objectivity. For we come to understand that all so-called "value judgments" are ways in which we express and evoke attitudes.

STANDARDS OF EVALUATION AND THE MEANING OF "GOOD"

Noncognitivism is a theory that not only has been held by a number of philosophers in the present century but has also gained some acceptance in popular thinking. It is now fairly common to hear people say, "Oh, that's just a value judgment," as if a value judgment were something quite arbitrary and unfounded, a matter of how we happen to feel, rather than a true or false assertion, which can be analyzed and discussed impartially. The foremost proponent of noncognitivism in the world of academic philosophy is Professor Charles Stevenson of the University of Michigan. In his book

Ethics and Language (1944) Professor Stevenson set forth the theory in its most complete form. In the last thirty years, however, the theory has undergone major changes and revisions under the impact of careful philosophical research into the uses of language. The words and sentences in which we carry on moral and other evaluative discourse have been analyzed with great subtlety. From this research has emerged a new doctrine which has become the center of recent philosophical discussion in the field of analytic ethics. This theory, now called "prescriptivism," was developed and propounded by Professor R.M. Hare of Oxford University in his books, *The Language of Morals* (1952) and *Freedom and Reason* (1963). Prescriptivism shares some of the views of noncognitivism—in particular, its rejection of both naturalism and nonnaturalism—but it adds important ideas of its own. We shall now examine the basic principles of prescriptivism, compare it with noncognitivism, and then see what criticisms have been raised against it.

Prescriptivism, like noncognitivism, separates values from facts on linguistic grounds. The reason why the naturalistic fallacy is a fallacy, according to Professor Hare, is that by making value judgments a kind of factual assertion, naturalism takes away the evaluative meaning of value words. The evaluative meaning of a value word is its *commending* or *condemning* function. Thus when we say "Mohandas Gandhi was a good man" we are commending or praising him; we are not merely describing him or reporting a fact about him. Similarly, to judge someone to be evil or vicious is to condemn him, not to give neutral information about him. Therefore a value statement is not simply a statement of fact. In uttering the former we are *evaluating* the subject being talked about; in uttering the latter we are *describing* it.

So far, it would seem that Hare's view is just like noncognitivism. But this is not correct. Although a value word has a commending or condemning function, this function does not consist merely in expressing a positive or negative attitude on the part of the speaker and in evoking a similar attitude on the part of the hearer. When a person says that something is good or bad, according to Hare, he is doing two additional things besides expressing and evoking attitudes, and these two additional things are what distinguish value judgments from ejaculations, commands, exhortations, and other expressive and dynamic uses of language. First, the person who commends or condemns something on the basis of an evaluation of it is *guiding choices by appeal to a universal principle*. Second, he is *making an assertion that*

must be supported by reasons, and these reasons must be of a certain sort.
Let us consider each of these points in turn.

(1) In order to understand what a value judgment is or what it means to evaluate something, we must distinguish between the *meaning* or a value-word and its *criteria*. Take the word "good," for example. There are many kinds of things we call good: good painters, good mathematicians, good fountain pens, good cars, good books, and so on. In calling any of these things good we are evaluating them positively and hence commending them. This function or use of the word is common to all its applications, no matter what kind of thing the word is being applied to. But if we ask, concerning the thing to which the word is applied, "What makes it good? What is good about it?" we see immediately that there will be different answers, according to the different classes of things being called good. Hare names the class of things with which some object is being compared in evaluating it the "class of comparison." The characteristics or properties of a thing which we point out in answering the questions What makes it good? What is good about it? are called "good-making characteristics." Thus, while the meaning (use, function) of the word "good" remains constant throughout all classes of comparison (the commending function), the set of characteristics that are good-making varies with each class of comparison. The properties that a painter must have to be a good painter will be entirely different from the properties that make a mathematician a good mathematician. (It is possible, of course, for one individual to have both sets of properties.) Similarly, what makes a fountain pen good will be very different from what makes a car good; and so for the other classes of comparison.

For each class of comparison, how do we know which of the characteristics belonging to a member of the class are its good-making characteristics? The answer lies in the *criteria* of goodness or *standards* of evaluation which we implicitly appeal to whenever we make a value judgment. Consider, for instance, a person whom we judge to be a good mathematician. Suppose he has the following properties: blue eyes, six feet tall, born in Chicago, 190 I.Q., does not believe in God, has proven theorems in topology no one else has proven, has three children, has written a book used by other mathematicians in their research. Only three of these characteristics, we would say, are *relevant* to his being a good mathematician. How do we know that these characteristics are relevant and that the other ones are irrelevant? The answer is that these are the characteristics in virtue of which the person *satisfies our criteria* for anyone's being a good mathematician. His high I.Q., his ability to prove theorems, and his being the author of an authoritative book in his field are characteristics which, when present in a person, tend to enable him to fulfill (to some degree) the conditions that define an ideal mathematician. We may therefore speak of the criteria of the word "good" as distinct from its meaning. The criteria of a good fountain pen, to take another example, will be the standards by which we judge fountain pens to be excellent, good, mediocre, poor, terrible, and so on. A good fountain pen will be a fountain pen that fulfills the conditions of excellence to a higher degree than a mediocre or poor pen. And the good-making characteristics are those properties of a pen that enable it to fulfill these conditions to the degree indicated. Such properties are: it does not leak; it does not need frequent refilling; it does not scratch or blot; it is easy and comfortable to hold; it continues to write after many years of hard use; and so on.

We now have four concepts necessary for a complete analysis of a value judgment: (a) *the meaning of a value-word* (its commending or condemning function); (b) *the criteria of a value-word* (the standards of evaluation being referred to when the value-word is applied in each case); (c) *the good-making or bad-making characteristics* (the properties of the object in virtue of which it satisfies or fails to satisfy the criteria to a certain degree); and (d) *the class of comparison* (the class of objects whose different values are determined by one set of criteria). A value judgment may consequently be defined as follows: A value judgment is the commending (condemning) of an object because it has those good-making (bad-making) characteristics which enable it to fulfill or fail to fulfill to a certain degree, in comparison with other objects in the given class of comparison, those criteria which are accepted as standards for evaluating all members of that class of comparison.

We are now ready to see how a value judgment guides choices by appeal to a universal principle, which we said above is one of the two basic aspects of evaluation in Hare's analysis. Suppose I am trying to decide what fountain pen to buy, within a given price range. If someone points to one of the pens I am looking at and says, "That is a good pen," he is directly guiding my choice. Assuming that he and I both accept the same criteria for evaluating pens, I know that if he is telling me the truth I should buy that pen (unless he states that some other pen is even better). For in saying that it is a good pen, he is implying that it has the good-making characteritistics which I also want a pen to have. Furthermore, I know that any other pen similar to this one (in relevant respects) will also be a good pen, since it will have the same good-making characteristics and so will fulfill the criteria to the same degree. The universal principle in accordance with which the value judgment is made is the principle that, if any pen in the given price range (that is, any member of the class of comparison) is like this one in the relevant respects (that is, has the same good-making characteristics), it will be a good pen. Thus, as Hare puts it, "All value judgments are covertly universal." A value judgment tells us not only the value of a particular object, but the value of any object relevantly similar to it. The judgment can guide anyone who is confronted with a choice between such an object and other objects in the class of comparison. This is one reason why the noncognitivist analysis of a value judgment is incorrect, according to Hare. For noncognitivists do not mention standards of evaluation, and do not recognize that such standards make every value judgment a universal guide to choice.

(2) A second reason why the noncognitivist theory of value is mistaken, in Hare's view, is that it fails to account for the way reasons support value judgments. On this point it is enlightening to contrast Hare's analysis of the justification of value judgments with the analysis given by the noncognitivists. According to noncognitivism, as we have seen, the relation referred to by the word "because" in a sentence like "This is good because it satisfies a human need" is a *causal* relation, not a *logical* relation. To make a value statement ("This is good") is to express an attitude. To give a reason for the value statement ("Because it satisfies a human need") is to give a fact, belief in which *causes* a person to have the particular attitude which is expressed in the value statement. We saw earlier that reasoning for the noncognitivist is a psychological matter concerned with how changes in beliefs bring about changes in attitudes. Attitudes may be influenced by beliefs, but there is no kind of reasoning which can show that one attitude is more *appropriate* or more *justified* than another. It cannot be shown by reasoning, for example, that one *ought* to approve of what satisfies a human need. It is purely a contingent, psychological matter whether a person's belief that something satisfies a human need causes him to approve of it.

Hare's prescriptivism offers a very different analysis of the justification of value judgments. According to Hare, whenever a person makes a value judgment by saying, for example, that something is good, we can always demand, What are your reasons for saying it is good? or simply, Why is it good? Now these questions can be rephrased as, What makes this good, in your judgment? or, What do you think is good about it? And these questions, we have seen, are requests for the person to specify the *good-making characteristics* of the object. Thus the reasons that support a value judgment are statements that point out the good-making charactertistics of the thing that is being evaluated. These are empirical assertions concerning its properties, and here is the place where facts are related to values. Empirical statements about an object may be relevant or irrelevant to a judgment of its value. They are relevant if they are about the properties of the object in virtue of which it fulfills the standards of evaluation being applied in the given judgment; otherwise, they are irrelevant. Thus the reasons that justify the judgment that Mohandas Gandhi was a good man will not merely be those beliefs about Gandhi that have an influence on our attitudes toward him, as the noncognitivist would claim. They will be, instead, facts about Gandhi which show that he had those characteristics (such as benevolence, honesty, and courage) that make him a good man, according to the moral standards we are using to judge all men.

One further element in Hare's theory should be noted. The *complete* justification of any value judgment goes beyond the statement of relevant facts about the object being judged. This is only the first step in justifying a value judgment, and it consists in showing that the object does fulfill the given standards to a certain degree. But suppose someone challenges those standards. If this happens, then the person who makes a value judgment on the basis of those standards must justify his use of them in evaluating objects in the given class of comparison. This is the second step of justifying a value judgment. Thus someone might say, "I agree with you that this object is good if you judge it by standards A, B, and C, but it would be bad if it were judged by standards X, Y, and Z. Unless you can show why one ought to use A, B, and C and ought not to use X, Y, and Z as standards for judging this object, you have not established the truth of your judgment that the object is good." This raises the question, How can standards of evaluation be justified? What sort of reasons can be given to validate them? Professer Hare's answer is given when he discusses not only value judgments made by applying standards to objects but also value judgments made by applying rules of conduct to acts. While standards tell us what things are good or bad, rules of conduct tell us what acts are right or wrong. Standards and rules are collectively called "principles" by Hare. Principles serve to guide our choices and decisions, since we appeal to them whenever we want to know what is the best thing to choose, or what we ought to do when we have alternatives among which to decide.

One step of moral reasoning is the application of principles to guide our choices and decisions. Hare points out that this step of moral reasoning can be put in the form of a syllogism or deductive argument, the first or major premise being a statement of the principle, the second or minor premise being a factual statement about the act and its circumstances, and the conclusion being the value judgment about what we ought to do. An example would be:

Major premise (Principle):	Never say what is false.
Minor premise (Fact):	To say X in these circumstances would be to say what is false.

Conclusion (Value judgment): I ought not to say X.

The same kind of reasoning takes place if we are applying a standard of evaluation to an object, thus:

Major premise (Principle):	Any man who is benevolent, honest, and courageous is a good man.
Minor premise (Fact):	Mohandas Gandhi was benevolent, honest, and courageous.

Conclusion (Value judgment): Mohandas Gandhi was a good man.

Decisions and choices, then, are justified on the ground of principles. But how can principles (the major premises) themselves be justified? What kind of reasoning would yield good reasons for accepting one principle rather than another?

Hare explores this question in some detail. He first shows that principles are things we ourselves *decide* to use. Even if we derive them from our culture, they have no power to guide our choices unless we make a "decision of principle" to adopt them as our own. It is our own decision to accept a principle that enables it to operate as a major premise in the syllogism of moral reasoning. So the question, On what grounds do principles rest? becomes the question, What reasons would justify a person's decision to adopt a principle as a guide to his own choice and conduct? In order to answer this question, Hare examines the way principles are adopted, changed, and given up in the ordinary circumstances of life. He considers how we learn principles in childhood, and how we come to reject them, make exceptions to them, or modify them as we use them in everyday experience. In doing this he shows how it is the *effects* or *consequences* of our using principles that determine whether they are justified. When the effects of our principles are unsatisfactory in some way or are unsuitable to our changing environment, we judge these effects to be undesirable. This judgment is a value judgment and, like any other, must be made on the basis of a principle. Thus we reject or modify our original principles on the ground of new principles. These new principles, in turn, are judged by *their* effects or consequences, and so on until we have exhausted all the principles that make up our whole way of life. Hare then considers the question of whether there is any kind of reasoning by which a whole way of life can be justified.

Since he holds that all reasoning involves an appeal to principles, Hare believes that there is no kind of reasoning by which it can be shown that one way of life, taken as a whole, is better than another. A way of life includes all the principles on which evaluative reasoning is grounded. We must simply *decide* to commit ourselves to a way of life. In so doing, we make a profound and far-reaching decision, for we thereby place our reasoning within the framework of a certain set of principles in accordance with which all our evaluations and choices will be made. However, our decision so to commit ourselves need not be arbitrary or capricious. Indeed, if we are fully enlightened about what it means to live by one set of principles rather than another, our decision is as justified as it can possibly be for we have brought to bear upon it all relevant knowledge and experience. We know what we are doing when we choose a way of life as our own, because we understand what living in accordance with its principles means, and we know what the ways of life which we reject are like. Given this enlightenment about the sets of ideals from which we make our choice, nothing further is required to justify that choice. Nevertheless, if another person were to decide to commit himself to a different way of life and were completely enlightened in making his decision, then no method of reasoning can tell us which of the two ways is better. Each decision is as justified as it can be.

DESCRIPTIVISM AND PRESCRIPTIVISM

Hare's prescriptivism has come under philosophical criticism in recent years. This criticism has given rise to a theory, known as "descriptivism," which has been claimed to provide a more adequate account of the relation between facts and values than does prescriptivism. Professor Philippa Foot of Somerville College, Oxford, has been among those who defend this claim, and we shall examine one of her arguments here. The aim of the argument is to show that the prescriptivist is wrong in making a complete logical gap between the facts about an object and an evaluation of it. Professor Foot reasons that there are limits to the kinds of things which can meaningfully be judged to be good and therefore the standards or criteria used in such value judgments are not a matter for us to *decide* independently of our knowledge of facts. We cannot take a positive attitude toward anything regardless of how it is described. There is a connection between our descriptions of things and our evaluations of them. Thus the descriptivist claims that if we look carefully at our actual use of value terms we shall see that there is no logical gap between the factual premises and the evaluative conclusion of our reasoning when we attempt to justify a value judgment. The following paragraphs trace the development of this argument.

Consider the concept of *danger*. If we describe something as being dangerous, we are already taking a negative attitude toward it, as something unwanted, to be avoided or eliminated. We are not logically free to take a positive attitude toward what is dangerous, because the very meaning of "danger" implies that it is a possible source of harm or injury, and "harm" and "injury" are themselves negative value words. It is not that the description of something as being dangerous *entails* a negative evaluation of it. Descriptivism does not commit the naturalistic fallacy, since the descriptivist would admit that no logical contradiction is involved if someone says "This is dangerous but it is good." Nevertheless it would be irrational for someone to take a positive attitude toward what is dangerous just *because* it is dangerous. A person might like to engage in dangerous activities because he welcomes a challenge to his survival skills or simply because he enjoys the excitement (as in boxing, bullfighting, or making a free fall from an airplane). But it is not the danger itself, as danger, that the person likes, but rather the testing of his courage and the excitement.

Why danger itself cannot be something wanted or liked is that the concept of danger is logically connected with other concepts like harm and injury, and these are not evaluatively neutral. No sane person can seek harm or want to be injured just for the sake of being hurt. And this is not because such a thing is a psychological impossibility. Rather it is that we would not *describe* something by means of the words "harmful" or "injurious" if it is something we seek, want, or value positively. Thus, suppose someone must have his leg amputated because gangrene has developed in it and unless it is removed he will lose his life. In such a situation it would be erroneous to describe the amputation, however painful it may be, as "harming" or "injuring" the person. This example shows that our descriptions of the facts are often value-laden. Given a description of something as "dangerous," then, we are not completely free to take a positive attitude toward it (or more accurately, toward that which is dangerous about it).

The general conclusion drawn by the descriptivist is that describing something in a certain way is not always logically separate from evaluating it in that way. Some descriptions actually function as reasons for taking a positive (or negative) attitude toward a thing. Thus, given the fact that a certain description is true of an object, only some attitudes toward the object will be justified or appropriate. Others will be unjustified or inappropriate. When we believe that a positive attitude is warranted, we call the object "good." When we think a negative attitude is appropriate, we call it "bad." Value judgments, therefore, are not logically or conceptually independent of descriptive statements. Professor Foot is not claiming that value words can be defined in terms of factual predicates. She is not *reducing* value judgments to a kind of fact. For this reason it would be misleading to call her position a form of "naturalism." But she does claim that the argument showing that the naturalistic fallacy is a genuine error should not be taken to imply that a complete logical divide separates values from facts.

Descriptivism has been challenged on the ground that it overlooks the framework of normative principles—the system of standards and rules— within which attitudes are justified when certain descriptions are applied to objects. The logical connection between values and facts that the descriptivist thinks he has found is actually only the result of the tacit assumption of the principles of some way of life. What the descriptivist has shown is that many descriptions of events and objects are themselves value-laden, and hence are conceptually linked with value judgments. "X is harmful" is a way of describing X, but it is not valuationally neutral. Such a description of X does not leave open the question of whether X is to be judged good or bad. To call something harmful is already to think of it as bad. And in thinking this, one considers a negative attitude toward it to be appropriate or justified. The prescriptivist, however, could grant all this without being inconsistent. But he would claim that the descriptivist has not taken into account the reason why a thing is described in the first place by means of a value-laden term. Thus, his reply to the descriptivist may be stated as follows.

If a person applies the descriptive term "harmful" to an object, it is not because he has empirical knowledge of certain effects of the object, those effects being understood in a purely *factual* or *neutral* way. It is because he considers those effects to be *bad*, when judged by his own standards of evaluation. Unless he implicitly made such a value judgment on the basis of his standards, he would not use a value-laden term like "harmful" to describe the object. Thus what will count, for that person, as a "harm" and hence as something "bad" (toward which it is appropriate to take a negative attitude) does not depend wholly on any set of neutral empirical facts about the thing in question. It depends on those facts *plus* a set of standards or principles which he has accepted as part of his way of life.

Consider, for example, an event which can correctly be described in *neutral* terms as "causing the loss of part of one's body." This description of the event is value-free (that is, not value-laden) and can be verified by ordinary empirical tests that rest on sense perception. That X causes the loss of part of one's body is, then, a neutral fact. Now whether X will also be described as a "harm" or "injury" (and hence will be thought of as something warranting a negative attitude) does not follow from, or logically depend on, the neutral fact that X causes the loss of part of one's body. For suppose that, according to a society's way of life, a young man's initiation into adulthood requires his left ear to be cut off. Then a young man in that society would not consider harmful, or describe as a "harm," the amputation of his left ear during the initiation rites. Not conceiving it as a harm done to him, he would not think it appropriate to take a negative attitude toward it. On the contrary, he would approve of it as an act by which he achieved something *good,* namely, being admitted into the adult community. For a person in our own culture, of course, the loss of one's left ear will be considered a harm or injury, since it will be judged a bad thing.

The above analysis shows that a neutral fact (X causes the loss of part of one's body) is connected with a value judgment (X is bad) by way of a value-laden description (X is harmful) *only against a background of principles that make up a certain way of life.* Thus it seems that descriptivists cannot escape the necessity of what prescriptivists call "making a decision of principle" in arguing from facts to values. No matter how value-laden might be such descriptions as "harmful," "dangerous," "injurious," et cetera, there is no way to know what particular things are to be described by these terms without presupposing a set of standards or principles. It is appropriate for someone to take a negative attitude toward X not merely because X is described in a certain way, but because that description applies to X in virtue of the fact that X fulfills (or fails to fulfill) the normative principles of a way of life. Unless a person has adopted that way of life and so committed himself to its principles, he cannot know what descriptions apply to X nor what attitude it is appropriate to take toward X. An argument about the value of something, then, cannot be settled merely by appeal to value-laden descriptions of the thing, for what descriptions are or are not to be accepted is the very point at issue, and to resolve *that* issue it is necessary to refer to principles. Nor can such an argument be settled by appeal to neutral facts, even when all parties to the dispute agree about what neutral facts are empirically true of the object in question. There is a logical gap between any set of neutral facts about X on the one hand and the value of X on the other, a gap that can be bridged only by commitment to a set of principles.

This, then, is the way a prescriptivist will reply to his descriptivist critics. Whether his reply is satisfactory will depend on whether he has correctly understood the relation between facts and values. And this is a question still being debated in contemporary moral philosophy.

Suggested Reading

Two excellent studies of the general problem of values and facts:

Harrison, Jonathan, *Our Knowledge of Right and Wrong*. New York: Humanities Press, 1971.
Hudson, W. D., *Modern Moral Philosophy*. New York: Anchor Books, Doubleday and Co., Inc., 1970.*

A well-organized collection of articles concerned with the relation between values and facts:

Hudson, W. D., ed., *The Is/Ought Question: A Collection of Papers on the Central Problem in Moral Philosophy*. New York: St. Martin's Press, 1969.*

Good discussions of the naturalistic fallacy (in addition to the articles in the collection edited by W. D. Hudson, cited above):

Foot, Philippa, ed., *Theories of Ethics*. Essays I-VIII. London: Oxford University Press, 1967.*
Hare, R. M., *The Language of Morals*. Chapters 1-5. London: Oxford University Press, 1952.*
Harrison, Jonathan, *Our Knowledge of Right and Wrong*, Chapter V. op. cit.
Hudson, W. D., *Modern Moral Philosophy*, Chapter 3. op. cit.*

*Available in paperback

Moore, George Edward, *Principia Ethica,* Chapter I. Cambridge: Cambridge University Press, 1903.* The original statement of the naturalistic fallacy is to be found here.

Searle, John R., *Speech Acts: An Essay in the Philosophy of Language.* Chapters 6 and 8. Cambridge: Cambridge University Press, 1969.*

Naturalistic theories of value and various forms of ethical naturalism:

Dewey, John, *Theory of Valuation.* Chicago: University of Chicago Press, 1939.*

Lewis, Clarence Irving, *An Analysis of Knowledge and Valuation,* Book III. LaSalle, Ill.: Open Court Publishing Co., 1946.*

Perry, Ralph Barton, *General Theory of Value: Its Meaning and Basic Principles Construed in Terms of Interest.* Cambridge, Mass.: Harvard University Press, 1962.

Sesonske, Alexander, *Value and Obligation: The Foundations of an Empiricist Ethical Theory.* New York: Oxford University Press, 1964.*

Taylor, Richard, *Good and Evil: A New Direction.* New York: The Macmillan Company, 1970.*

Von Wright, Georg Henrik, *The Varieties of Goodness.* New York: Humanities Press, 1963.

Warnock, G. J., *The Object of Morality.* London: Methuen and Co., Ltd., 1971.*

Nonnaturalism (ethical intuitionism):

Ewing, A. C., *Ethics,* Chapters 5-7. New York: The Free Press, 1953.*

Moore, George Edward, *Principia Ethica.* op. cit.*

Ross, William David, *Foundations of Ethics.* London: Oxford University Press, 1939.

——, *The Right and the Good.* London: Oxford University Press, 1930.

Criticisms of nonnaturalism:

Harrison, Jonathan, *Our Knowledge of Right and Wrong,* Chapters IV and V. op. cit.

Hudson, W. D., *Ethical Intuitionism.* New York: St. Martin's Press, 1967.*

——, *Modern Moral Philosophy,* Chapter 3. op. cit.*

Nowell-Smith, P. H., *Ethics,* Chapters 1-4. Baltimore: Penguin Books, Inc., 1954.*

Noncognitivism (the emotive theory):

Edwards, Paul, *The Logic of Moral Discourse.* New York: The Free Press, 1955.*

Stevenson, Charles L., *Ethics and Language.* New Haven: Yale University Press, 1944.*

——, *Facts and Values: Studies in Ethical Analysis.* New Haven: Yale University Press, 1963.*

*Available in paperback

Criticisms of noncognitivism:

Harrison, Jonathan, *Our Knowledge of Right and Wrong*, Chapter XII. op. cit.
Hudson, W. D., *Modern Moral Philosophy*, Chapter 4. op. cit.*
Urmson, J. O., *The Emotive Theory of Ethics*. New York: Oxford University Press, 1968.*

Prescriptivism:

Hare, R. M., *Essays on the Moral Concepts*. Berkeley: University of California Press, 1972.
————, *Freedom and Reason*. London: Oxford University Press, 1963.*
————, *The Language of Morals*, op. cit.*
————, *Practical Inferences*. Berkeley: University of California Press, 1972.

Criticisms of prescriptivism (other than the articles listed under "descriptivism," below):

Beardsmore, R. W., *Moral Reasoning*. New York: Schocken Books, Inc., 1969.
Hudson, W. D., *Modern Moral Philosophy*, Chapter 5. op. cit.*
Trigg, Roger, *Reason and Commitment*. Cambridge: Cambridge University Press, 1973.*

Descriptivism:

Foot, Philippa, "Goodness and Choice," *Proceedings of the Aristotelian Society*, Supplementary Vol. XXXV (1961). Reprinted in *The Is/Ought Question: A Collection of Papers on the Central Problem in Moral Philosophy*, ed. W. D. Hudson, op. cit.*
————, "Moral Arguments," *Mind*, LXVII (1958): 502-513. Reprinted in *Ethics*, ed. Judith J. Thomson and Gerald Dworkin. New York: Harper and Row, Publishers, 1968.* Also reprinted in *Contemporary Ethical Theory: A Book of Readings*, ed. Joseph Margolis. New York: Random House, Inc., 1966.
————, "Moral Beliefs," *Proceedings of the Aristotelian Society*, Vol. 59 (1958-59): 83-104. Reprinted in *Theories of Ethics*, ed. Philippa Foot. London: Oxford University Press, 1967.* Also reprinted in *Ethics*, ed. Judith J. Thomson and Gerald Dworkin, op. cit. and in *The Is/Ought Question: A Collection of Papers on the Central Problem in Moral Philosophy*, ed. W. D. Hudson. op. cit.

Criticisms of descriptivism:

Beardsmore, R. W., *Moral Reasoning*. op. cit.
Hare, R. M., *Essays on the Moral Concepts*, Essays 5-7. op. cit.
Hudson, W. D., *Modern Moral Philosophy*, Chapter 6. op. cit.*
Phillips, D. Z. and H. O. Mounce, *Moral Practices*. New York: Schocken Books, Inc. 1969.

*Available in paperback.

Contemporary theories of value that do not easily fit into the foregoing class-
ifications:

Becker, Lawrence C., *On Justifying Moral Judgments*. New York: Humanities Press,
   1973.
Fried, Charles, *An Anatomy of Values: Problems of Personal and Social Choice*.
   Cambridge, Mass.: Harvard University Press, 1970.
Rawls, John. *A Theory of Justice*, Part III. Cambridge, Mass.: Harvard University
   Press, 1971.*
Rescher, Nicholas, *Introduction to Value Theory*. Englewood Cliffs, N. J.: Prentice-
   Hall, Inc., 1969.*

Contemporary theories of practical reason (other than prescriptivism and descriptivism) that have important implications for understanding the relation between
values and facts:

Baier, Kurt, *The Moral Point of View: A Rational Basis of Ethics*. Ithaca: Cornell
   University Press, 1958.
Gauthier, David P., *Practical Reasoning: The Structure and Foundations of Pruden-
   tial and Moral Arguments and Their Exemplification in Discourse*. London:
   Oxford University Press, 1963.
Harrison, Jonathan, *Our Kowledge of Right and Wrong*, Chapters XIII-XVI.
   op. cit.
Kemp, J., *Reason, Action and Morality*. New York: Humanities Press, 1964.
Murphy, Arthur E., *The Theory of Practical Reason*. La Salle, Ill.: Open Court
   Publishing Co., 1964.
Nagel, Thomas, *The Possibility of Altruism*. London: Oxford University Press, 1970.
Norman, Richard, *Reasons for Actions: A Critique of Utilitarian Rationality*.
   Oxford: Basil Blackwell, 1971.
Richards, David A. J., *A Theory of Reasons for Action*. London: Oxford University
   Press, 1971.

*Available in paperback

IX

The Ultimate Question

THE DEMAND FOR A JUSTIFICATION OF MORALITY

There is one problem of ethics that perhaps deserves, more than any other, to be called the Ultimate Question. It is the question of the rationality of the moral life itself. It may be expressed thus: Is the commitment to live by moral principles a commitment grounded on reason or is it, in the final analysis, an arbitrary decision?

The Ultimate Question is not itself a moral question. That is to say it does not ask what we morally ought to do or even how we can discover our moral duty. It is, instead, a question about the justification of morality as a whole. Why, it asks, should we be concerned with morality at all? If living by moral principles can at times be so difficult, if our moral integrity may, in some circumstances, require the sacrifice of our happiness or even of our life, why not simply reject the whole moral "game" and live amorally? In short, why be moral?

It is important to see exactly why this is not a moral question or a question about what actions are morally right. When a person asks why he should be moral, he assumes he already knows what "being moral" means. He could not understand his own question when he asked, "Why should I do what is morally right, especially when it conflicts with my self-interest?" unless he understood the meaning of doing what is morally right. Moreover, if his question concerns a *particular* case of conflict between moral duty and self-interest, then it is assumed that the questioner accepts the fact that, in the specific circumstances referred to, a certain action *is* his duty. He recognizes it as an action which, from the moral point of view, he ought to perform. But he also recognizes it as conduct which, from the standpoint of his self-interest, would be irrational. He then asks, Why, after all, should I do it? In effect he is asking, Why should moral duty *outweigh* or *override* self-interest when there is a conflict between them?

208

The Ultimate Question, then, is not a moral question but rather a demand for reasons that would show why anyone should live by moral principles instead of some other principles, such as self-interest. The final justifiability of the moral life itself thus becomes a subject of ethical inquiry. The issue is a fundamental one: Is a person's commitment to live the moral life ultimately an arbitrary choice on his part, a preferring of the moral to the amoral life with no reason whatever for such a preference? If it were, then it seems that a person would be quite justified in ignoring the demands of morality whenever he could thereby gain some advantage or benefit for himself. Assuming that a person's commitment to being moral may involve, at least in some situations, the frustration of his own interests, it would seem that the most sensible thing for anyone to do would be simply to ignore moral principles and live amorally.

The demand for an ultimate justification of morality was first stated in its classic form in Plato's *Republic*. Glaucon and Adeimantus, two of the figures participating in the dialogue, challenge Socrates, the protagonist, to justify the living of a morally upright life. Their challenge is presented in the form of the following story, which is known as The Myth of Gyges.

According to the tradition, Gyges was a shepherd in the service of the king of Lydia; there was a great storm, and an earthquake made an opening in the earth at the place where he was feeding his flock. Amazed at the sight, he descended into the opening, where, among other marvels, he beheld a hollow brazen horse, having doors, at which he stooping and looking in saw a dead body of stature, as appeared to him, more than human, and having nothing on but a gold ring; this he took from the finger of the dead and reascended. Now the shepherds met together, according to custom, that they might send their monthly report about the flocks to the king; into their assembly he came having the ring on his finger, and as he was sitting among them he chanced to turn the collet of the ring inside his hand, when instantly he became invisible to the rest of the company and they began to speak of him as if he were no longer present. He was astonished at this, and again touching the ring he turned the collet outwards and reappeared; he made several trials of the ring, and always with the same result—when he turned the collet inwards he became invisible, when outwards he reappeared. Where-upon he contrived to be chosen one of the messengers who were sent to the court; where as soon as he arrived he seduced the queen, and with her help conspired against the king and slew him, and took the kingdom. Suppose now that there were two such magic rings, and the just put on one of them and the unjust the other; no man can be imagined to be of such an iron nature that he would stand fast in justice. No man would keep his hands off what was not his own when he could safely take what he liked out of the market, or go into houses and lie with any one at his pleasure, or kill or release from prison whom he would, and in all respects be like a God among men. Then the actions of the just would be as the actions of the unjust; they would both come at last to the same point. And this we may truly affirm to be a great proof that a man is just, not willingly or because he thinks that justice is any good to him individually, but of necessity, for wherever any one thinks that he can safely be unjust, there he is unjust. For all men believe in their hearts that injustice is far more profitable to the individual than justice, and he who argues as I have been supposing, will say that they are right. If you could imagine any one obtaining this power of becoming invisible, and never doing any wrong or touching what was another's, he would be thought by the lookers-on to be a most wretched idiot, although they would praise him to one another's faces, and keep up appearances with one another from a fear that they too might suffer injustice. (Plato, *Republic,* Book II. Translated by B. Jowett.)

Here is a classic statement of the case against morality. Socrates' attempt to reply to it, which forms the main argument of Plato's *Republic,* consists in trying to show that moral virtue is its own reward and that only the just (morally upright) man is truly happy. Thus, in effect, Socrates claims that in the long run there is no real conflict between duty and self-interest. Philosophers have been disputing about this ever since.

In order to see exactly what is at stake in trying to answer the question, Why be moral? we must recognize how it differs from a question about the nature of moral reasoning. For the question, Why be moral? arises the moment when someone realizes that, if he commits himself to the principles of moral reasoning, he may find himself in circumstances where his reasoning leads to the conclusion that he ought to do an act which entails some inconvenience, unpleasantness, or frustration for himself. It might even lead to the conclusion that in the given situation confronting him he must give up his life. He then wants to know why he should follow the rules of moral reasoning.

It should be noted that this problem does not arise for the ethical egoist, who *identifies* moral reasoning with prudential reasoning. As we saw in Chapter 3, ethical egoism is the view that each person ought to do whatever will most further his self-interest in the long run. If this is taken as an ultimate moral principle then the question, Why be moral? becomes the question, Why seek the furtherance of my self-interest in the long run? Such a question would only be asked by someone who did not want to give up his pleasures or who was satisfied with pursuing short-range goals in life, and who realized at the same time that his long-range interests might not be furthered by his continuing to live in the way he had been living. The answer to his question, of course, would be that, if he is not willing to put up with inconveniences and discomforts and if he is not able to discipline himself to sacrifice his short-range goals when his pursuit of them prevents him from achieving lasting satisfactions in life, then he will not in fact be happy. But for the ethical egoist, no sacrifice of his self-interest *as a whole* would ever be justified and no such sacrifice would ever be morally required of him.

Since the Ultimate Question arises only when it is logically possible for there to be a conflict between the demands of morality and the pursuit of self-interest, we shall be concerned from this point on with nonegoist moral principles only. We are not assuming that morality is superior to self-interest, but only that it is possible for them to be in conflict. Under this assumption, then, the next point to realize is that the Ultimate Question lies outside the framework of the logic of moral reasoning itself. For the logic of moral reasoning tells us what a good reason in ethics is. It defines the method of reasoning a person should use *if* he were to commit himself to trying to find out what he morally ought to do. In asking, Why be moral? on the other hand, one is challenging the reasonableness of being committed to trying to find out what one morally ought to do. It is a challenge to the whole enterprise of moral reasoning and moral conduct. The challenge can be put this way: Suppose there is a valid method of moral reasoning and suppose, by following it, I do find out what I morally ought to do. Why should I bother to act in accordance with this knowledge? Why shouldn't I follow my self-interest instead? In other words, granted that there is a logic of moral reasoning, why should I choose to let this logic outweigh the logic of self-interest or prudence when there is a conflict between them? In making this challenge the person is not questioning the validity of moral reasoning. Rather, he is asking why such reasoning should guide his conduct when he could just as well choose to have his conduct guided by another set of rules of reasoning, namely, the furtherance of his own self-interest. Thus, he is demanding a justification for morality (the commitment to use moral reasoning as a guide to conduct) *as a whole*.

In order to find an acceptable answer to the Ultimate Question, it is necessary first to consider the logic of moral reasoning. Only then can we determine whether there are reasons of some kind that justify anyone's decision to follow that logic in thought and action.

THE LOGIC OF MORAL REASONING

Moral reasoning takes place whenever someone deliberates about whether he morally ought to do one thing rather than another in a situation of choice, and whenever someone tries to show that another's action, or a past action of his own, was the morally right (or wrong) thing to do, given the circumstances that held at that time. There are, in other words, two contexts in which moral reasoning occurs: deliberation and justification.

We deliberate when we are uncertain about what we should do when confronted with alternative courses of action. The aim of deliberation is to arrive at a true answer to the question: What ought I to do? Our deliberation consists in thinking about the reasons for, or against, doing each of the alternatives. A reason *for* doing an act will be a reason which, in our own judgment, would justify anyone's doing the act in circumstances like those in the present case. It will be a reason in support of the moral judgment "This is a right act (or a good act)." Similarly, a reason *against* doing an act will be such that it justifies a person's refraining from doing it in the same sort of circumstances. It will be a reason in support of the moral judgment "This is a wrong act (or a bad act)." Thus moral deliberation is the process of going over the pros and cons concerning each alternative open to choice with the purpose of arriving at a conclusion about what one ought to do in the given situation, after all the pros and cons have been taken into account.

Moral deliberation is one context in which moral reasoning takes place. The other context is that of moral justification, and the reasoning process is exactly the same. Whereas we *deliberate* about acts open to our own choice, we *justify* the acts of others, or acts done by ourselves in the past, or the acts that anyone who is in a certain set of circumstances ought to do. The term "justification" is here used to cover not only reasons for doing an act but also reasons against doing an act. To show that an act is justified, whether done by ourselves or by others, we must give reasons in support of the moral judgment that the act is right or good. To show that an act is unjustified (and that refraining from it is justified) we must give reasons in support of the judgment that the act is wrong or bad. To state *why* an act is right or wrong, good or bad, is to give reasons for or against doing it. Thus moral reasoning is the same whether we are justifying the acts of others or are deliberating about what we ourselves ought to do in a situation of choice.

What is meant by the "logic" of moral reasoning? We can best answer this question if we first realize that all reasoning is guided by certain principles. In a course on logic one studies the principles of deductive and inductive reasoning. These principles are rules of inference or forms of argument which tell us when we are reasoning correctly (following the rules) or incorrectly (breaking the rules). We sometimes think we are reasoning correctly in everyday life when in fact we are not, and we can test whether our reasoning is sound by applying the principles or "laws of logic" that govern the kind of reasoning we are engaged in. The logic of moral reasoning is the set of principles that governs our reasoning in moral deliberation and justification, when we are not only giving reasons for and against different acts, but are trying to give *good* reasons—reasons that actually do show that an act is justified or unjustified. When this is the case, our aim is to reason correctly, and we must then appeal to a set of principles of valid reasoning. These principles are such that, if our reasoning is carried on in accordance with them, we can claim that we are rationally justified in making the moral judgments which we draw as our conclusions. We can claim to *know* that a certain act is the right or wrong thing to do in a given situation. Moral knowledge is possible only when there is a method for giving good reasons in justification of moral beliefs or, in other words, only when there is a logic of moral reasoning.

Any method of moral reasoning must be intersubjectively valid. This means that its principles must be binding universally, so that if R is a good reason for one person to accept moral judgment M, it must also be a good reason for everyone else to accept M. Of course there may be good reasons for rejecting M as well as good reasons for accepting M. In that case the principles that constitute the logic of moral reasoning must enable anyone to decide which of these reasons outweigh others. But here again intersubjective validity must hold. If in one man's thinking reason R1 outweighs reason R2 and if his thinking conforms to the logic of moral reasoning, then in anyone else's thinking R1 should outweigh R2. Furthermore, the intersubjective validity of moral reasoning requires that it be logically independent of moral beliefs. That is, it must always be possible for a moral belief which is tested by the method to turn out false. If a person were to set up principles of moral reasoning that he could control in such a way as always to justify his own beliefs, it would not be a genuine method of reasoning. Let us suppose, for example, that we are trying to decide whether it was right for President Truman to have ordered the dropping of an atomic bomb on Hiroshima. First we notice that, though this is a case of moral justification and not moral deliberation, nevertheless the very same reasons that now show his decision to have been justified (or unjustified) are reasons that he should have taken into account in deliberating about the alternatives confronting him. What *we* want to know is whether his decision was right or wrong; what *he* wanted to know was which decision would be right for him to make. If R is a good reason for *us* to believe he was right in ordering the bomb to be dropped, then R was a good reason for *him* to decide to give the order. And it would be a good reason for a Japanese living in Hiroshima at the time (however unlikely it would be for him to accept it as a good reason). Similarly, suppose we now have a good reason to think that President Truman made the wrong decision. Then this would have been a good reason at that time for President Truman not to order the dropping of the bomb, regardless of whether he ever thought of this reason or, if he did, whether he accepted it as a reason. And however strongly one might now be convinced that his decision was wrong (or that it was right), one must be willing to "follow the argument wherever it may lead" and accept the outcome of reasoning about the decision, even if the conclusion turns out to be contrary to one's present convictions. For the process of reasoning about the decision is the process of trying to determine which judgment is true: "President Truman's decision was right." "President Truman's decision was wrong." We engage in this process when we seek knowledge about what was morally right or wrong in the given case. Now to seek such knowledge is to presuppose that such knowledge is possible; that is, that there is a method of reasoning which is intersubjectively valid in the domain of ethics. This means that anyone who is willing to be rational in seeking the truth about the morality of President Truman's decision is bound by the rules which define the method.

There have been moral philosophers, however, who have denied any intersubjectively valid method of reasoning in ethics. They have taken the position either of ethical skepticism or of ethical relativism. Ethical skepticism makes the double claim that there is no such thing as genuine moral knowledge and that it is impossible for there to be such knowledge. Ethical relativism (when understood as either normative ethical relativism or meta-ethical relativism, as defined in Chapter Two) holds that moral knowledge is relative to a given culture, in the sense that, although we can justify moral judgments by reference to the standards and rules of conduct adopted in a given culture, no (cross-cultural) reasons can be found to justify those standards and rules. This amounts to a denial of intersubjective validity at a cultural level.

When the Ultimate Question is asked, the person who asks it assumes that there *is* a logic of moral reasoning and that moral reasons *are* intersubjectively valid. He is not an ethical skeptic or an ethical relativist. What the questioner wants is a justification for committing himself to using the universal, intersubjectively valid logic of moral reasoning as a guide to his conduct. His question would not arise if there were no method of moral reasoning that could make a claim to intersubjective validity.

In the foregoing chapters of this book, a number of ways in which philosophers have conceived of the logic of moral reasoning have been examined. In Chapter Four it was shown that utilitarianism proposes an ultimate principle of morality (the principle of utility) as a test either of a right action or of a rule of conduct that determines right action. In either case an account of moral reasoning is implied. For act-utilitarianism, a moral reason is a fact about the consequences of a particular action. A person has a moral reason for the action in that it will bring about more intrinsic value and less intrinsic disvalue than any alternative. For rule-utilitarianism, moral reasoning is a logical process consisting of two steps: evaluation of rules of conduct by appeal to the principle of utility, and application of a utilitarian rule to a particular case falling under the rule. A person's moral reason, then, for doing an action would be that it is in accordance with a rule itself grounded on utility. In Chapter Five we saw how a formalistic ethical theory sets forth, in terms of "universalizability" in its various meanings, a sufficient condition for the duty of every moral agent as such. Moral reasoning then consists in applying the various tests of universalizability to action-types to see if they conform to the Moral Law. A moral reason for doing a *particular* action would be that it belongs to an action-*type* such that the requirement that all moral agents do actions of that type is universalizable. Still other views of moral reasoning were stated or implied by the theories of naturalism, noncognitivism, prescriptivism, and descriptivism, as discussed in the preceding chapter.

So far in the present chapter, the general nature of moral reasoning as a background for examining the question, Why should one be moral? has been considered. This question involves the idea of moral reasoning because it can be interpreted to mean, Is a person's decision to *use* moral reasoning as a guide to his conduct itself rational or is it arbitrary? It is now appropriate to investigate the precise meaning of the Ultimate Question, as well as its answerability.

IS THE ULTIMATE QUESTION AN ABSURDITY?

One view that has been taken by philosophers regarding the Ultimate Question is that it cannot be answered because it is absurd. It has been seen that a person who asks why he should do what is morally right already presupposes that he knows, or at least believes, that certain acts *are* right. In asking his question, therefore, he is not asking what he morally ought to do. He already has an answer to this. What, then, does he want to know? It seems that he wants to know why he should do what he knows to be right. It is as if he is saying, "I know what my moral duty is—now tell me why I ought to act in accordance with this knowledge." This, however, is absurd. For if the person knows that something is his duty, then he already knows why he ought to do it, namely, *just because it is his duty.*

When it is understood in this way, the Ultimate Question cannot be answered. But the reason it cannot is that no real question is being asked. For suppose we try to answer it by showing the person why he ought to do a certain action. We are then giving him moral reasons for doing that particular action. This, however, will not be accepted by him as an answer to the question he is asking. *His* question is, Why should I do what is right?, not, Why is this action the right thing to do? So if we show him that it is the right thing to do, he will not be satisfied. He will still ask for reasons for being *committed to doing* what he *acknowledges* to be something he ethically ought to do. Therefore it is no answer to give him moral reasons for doing the action in question. One cannot cite moral reasons for being moral (that is, for being committed to do what one believes to be right). Someone who wants to justify being moral is asking why he ought to use moral reasons as actual guides in his practical life. To give him such reasons is to assume that he will accept them as reasons for action. But this is the very thing he is questioning.

Once we become aware of this, however, we can see that there is a deep confusion behind the question "Why be moral?" when it is interpreted as a demand for reasons for doing what one acknowledges to be morally right. A moral reason is, by its very nature, a *"reason for acting."* It is not merely a "reason for believing," that is, a reason for accepting or acknowledging the truth of a proposition such as, Act X is morally right. To show why act X is morally right is to give moral reasons why a person should actually perform it. At the same time, it justifies accepting the statement "Act X is morally right" as true. It has been pointed out that the person who asks, Why be moral? is asking (under the present interpretation), Why should I *do* what I *believe* to be morally right? It can now be seen that he is confused in asking this. For he is assuming a separation between moral belief and moral action that isn't possible. To *believe* that an action is morally right is to have a reason for *doing* it, namely, that it is morally right. It is this confusion that explains why his question cannot be answered by giving him moral reasons for being moral. The point is that, once a person accepts moral reasons for *believing* that some action ought to be done, he has all the basis he needs for *doing* it, to wit, those very reasons for believing it ought to be done.

Given this interpretation of the Ultimate Question, it can be dismissed as resting on a mistake. It is not worth trying to answer, since a clear-thinking person would never ask it.

THE MEANING OF THE ULTIMATE QUESTION

Does the foregoing argument successfully dispose of the Ultimate Question? Some philosophers are convinced that it does not. They claim that there is a genuine question behind the apparent oddity of asking why one ought to do something while acknowledging that a moral person would have good reason to do it. The true significance of the question, they say, has to do with a choice or decision to be made between two sorts of reasons: moral reasons and reasons of self-interest. To hold that a person who asks why he ought to do what is morally right already knows why (namely, because it *is* morally right), is to miss the real point of the Ultimate Question. It is true that one cannot give moral arguments for being moral, just as one cannot give prudential arguments for being prudent. Nevertheless there may be moral reasons *for,* and prudential reasons *against,* a certain action, and there may be moral reasons *against* and prudential reasons *for* another action. In situations of that sort, one must act either morally or in one's self-interest; one cannot do both. How is one to decide?

It is here that the question, Why be moral? does not seem at all absurd. This was why Socrates took seriously the challenge to morality expressed in the Myth of Gyges. He realized that, in normal circumstances of life, we do not ask for a justification of morality because society sees to it that it is generally in a person's self-interest to be moral. It pays to avoid social disapproval and to maintain a good reputation. But the philosopher cannot be satisifed with this, since it is possible to imagine a case where a person has the power (as described in the Myth of Gyges) to act immorally and escape social sanctions. Why, then, should he not act immorally? Unless there is a *reason* for his not doing so, morality reduces to the self-interested avoidance of social disapproval. Conformity to the actual moral code of one's own society would then be one's highest duty. This entails, of course, normative ethical relativism. The norms of each society would determine what is right and wrong in it, and no society's code as a whole could be shown to be unjust or evil. But to take the Ultimate Question seriously is to seek a reason for being moral even when it doesn't pay, and even when being moral involves a clash with what is socially approved.

So let us now interpret the Ultimate Question as asking, When moral reasons and reasons of self-interest are in conflict, why should one follow the first rather than the second (assuming that one had the power to do either)?

One possible response to the question so understood might be to try to strengthen in the questioner the desire to be moral, so that he will in fact act morally even when it is contrary to his self-interest. The Ultimate Question is then being taken as a demand for *motivating* reasons (reasons that will actually move a person to act) rather than as a demand for *justifying* reasons (reasons that show why an act ought to be done). Now it may sometimes be true that a person who asks, Why be moral? in real life does want to be motivated to such conduct. We then answer him, not by presenting him with a sound philosophical argument, but by trying to persuade or influence him so that he will feel inspired to do what is right. We try to reinforce his moral motives and strengthen his sense of duty. If he is a child we give him a moral upbringing. We not only try to instill in him a desire to abide by moral rules (of honesty, fairness, nonmaleficence, et cetera), we also try to develop his capacity and inclination to reason morally for himself. If we are successful in this, he will not feel the need to ask the question, Why be moral? in later life. He will have been motivated to be moral and thus not find it psychologically necessary to ask to be motivated.

The philosopher, however, is not interested in engaging in this kind of response. For him the Ultimate Question is a demand for a justification for being moral, not a request to be motivated to be moral. The difference is not always easy to grasp. (Indeed, there is a whole theory in psychology—the behaviorism of Professor B. F. Skinner—which overlooks the difference!) A person's motivation, we have seen, has to do with his desires, his actual tendencies to aim at certain ends or goals. Here the relevant questions are, Does this individual have a desire to be moral, and if so, how strong is that desire? In particular, is it strong enough to overcome the motive to pursue his self-interest in cases of conflict between what he believes to be morally right and what he believes will serve his own interests? Justification, on the other hand, has to do with reasons, not with desires. To justify being moral is to vindicate the belief that moral reasons outweigh or override reasons of self-interest when they conflict. It is to show why moral reasons take priority over, and hence are superior to, prudential reasons. Now the idea of one sort of reasons taking priority over, or being superior to, another sort is not to be confused with the idea of one sort of reasons having greater motivational strength than another sort. A person's believing that moral reasons are better or weightier grounds for an action than prudential ones does not imply that he will always be more strongly motivated to do what is moral than what is prudent. If there is such a discrepancy in a person between justifying reasons and their motivational effectiveness, the person is said to have "weakness of will," and he may even recognize this in himself as a flaw in his character. It is then possible for him to consider an action *unjustified* (because it is morally wrong though prudentially expedient) and still actually do it. In that case his desires and actions are simply not consistent with his moral beliefs.

To justify anyone's being moral, as distinct from motivating some particular individual to be moral, is to give a sound argument in support of the claim that moral reasons take priority over reasons of self-interest whenever they conflict. If we were able to discover, or construct, such an argument, it would follow that everyone ought to be motivated by moral reasons for acting rather than by prudential reasons for acting in cases of conflict. Whether any given individual will in fact be so motivated depends on the strength of his desires, not on the soundness of an argument. Even if a person's desire to be moral were indeed strengthened by his reading or hearing such an argument, thus motivating him to be moral, this is irrelevant to the question of whether the argument actually showed the moral reasons to be superior to those of self-interest. Similarly, the argument might not convince someone intellectually, nor persuade him to act morally, nor reinforce his moral motivation. But the failure of the argument to bring about such results in any given individual is strictly irrelevant to the philosophical acceptability of the argument's content.

Suppose, then, that the Ultimate Question is understood to mean, Why do moral reasons outweigh prudential reasons in cases of conflict, rather than the other way around? Now it will not do to reply, Because morality *by definition* is that set of principles which outweigh all other principles that might conflict with them. This is not an acceptable answer because a person might decide to make reasons of self-interest *his* highest overriding principles. Then, by the given definition, self-interest would become morality in his case, and there could be no conflict between moral reasons and prudential reasons. In short, he would be an ethical egoist, and we saw earlier that the Ultimate Question presupposes that ethical egoism is false. (If ethical egoism were true, the whole issue would cease to be a meaningful problem.)

It has now become clear where the crux of the matter lies. The Ultimate Question places before us a challenge that concerns our *ultimate normative commitments*. It asks: Are there any reasons that would justify our commitment to moral principles as being the supreme overriding norms of our practical life (where "moral principles" are not by definition supreme and where it is logically possible for them to be in conflict with prudential principles)? We shall take this as our final formulation of the Ultimate Question. What answers might be proposed for it when it is understood this way?

TWO PROPOSED ANSWERS TO THE ULTIMATE QUESTION

(1) The first answer is that there are reasons that justify *everyone's* commitment to the priority of moral principles over self-interest. For suppose *everyone* took the opposite position and made a commitment such that, whenever self-interest and morality conflict, considerations of self-interest are to override moral considerations. The consequence would be the total collapse of any social order. Each person would be out for himself and would know that every other person was out for himself. Thus, each could have no confidence that others would refrain from harming him. Everyone would live in continual fear of everyone else, since all would realize that no constraints upon self-interest would be operative (even when such constraints were required by moral principles of fairness and respect for life). A world where the priority rule, "Self-interest is to take precedence over morality," was generally accepted would be a world where no one could attain his goals. Each would lack the basic security of being able to count on others not to interfere with his pursuit of his own ends.

The conclusion is evident. The whole point of any individual's committing himself to the supremacy of self-interest over morality is to promote his own welfare. But if this commitment were made by everyone, each would be unable to promote his self-interest to as great a degree as he would when everyone made the opposite commitment. This is the paradox of universal selfishness. No one would be as well off as he would be under universal conformity to moral rules. The very purpose of universal selfishness, in other words, is undermined by its practice. The priority of self-interest over morality is therefore a self-defeating commitment. It frustrates its own purpose and is consequently irrational. Commitment to the priority of morality over self-interest, on the contrary, is self-fulfilling. Its purpose is to create a social order where everyone benefits from mutual trust. This trust is only possible under the condition that everyone makes a firm commitment to the supremacy of such moral principles as justice and nonmaleficence. For only under that condition can each person count on others not to harm him or interfere with his pursuit of his own goals.

Is this an acceptable answer to the Ultimate Question? Does it provide a sound argument to justify being moral? It seems not, for it is open to the following objection. The answer that has been proposed overlooks an important distinction, which can be brought out by comparing these two questions: (a) Why should I be moral? (b) Why should people in general be moral? The argument given above is an adequate answer to (b), but not to (a). And it is (a) that is the Ultimate Question. The person who asks, Why be moral? is asking why he, *as an individual*, should commit himself to the priority of moral principles over his self-interest. If such a person were given the argument stated above, he would reply, Yes, I agree that if *everyone* were to commit himself to the supremacy of self-interest, it would lead to the frustration of my own as well as everyone else's self-interest. So I agree that it would be irrational for everyone to do this. However, this does not show that it would be irrational for *me* to make such a commitment. For in the world as it is (where others are at least sometimes committed to being moral), by making the commitment to self-interest over morality I would thereby gain a major advantage for myself. This would be especially true if I kept my commitment a secret from others. My self-interest would be promoted by such a commitment on my part, and hence it would not be self-defeating, but quite the contrary. So how can it be shown to be irrational?

When the person who asks the Ultimate Question takes this stand, it is true that the answer to (b) will not provide him with an answer to *his* question, which is (a). But a new aspect of the situation has now come to light; we see that such a person is assuming that his case is an exception to a general rule. The argument against everyone's making a commitment to self-interest, he claims, does not hold for him. Why not? Because his commitment to self-interest can be self-fulfilling only when others do not make a similar commitment. We can then ask him, Why should your case be considered an exception? What is so special about you that makes your commitment justifiable when those of others, in circumstances similar to yours, are not? Indeed, by your own argument you can be justified in making your commitment only on the condition that others do *not* make the same commitment. Now unless you can show that you deserve to be treated as a special case, you have provided no justification for considering yourself an exception.

There is, however, a reply that can be made to this objection—a reply available to the person who asks question (a). He can say, Since I am asking for reasons that support an *ultimate* normative commitment, I am seeking to justify commitment to *any* principle as a supreme one, including the principle that I am not to make my case an exception to a general rule. After all, I can always point to some property that I have and that no one else has as the basis for claiming that my own case is to be treated differently from theirs. That is, I can commit myself to the *principle* (as a supreme one) that having the attribute in question is a relevant difference between one person and another, as far as the promotion of self-interest is concerned. The Ultimate Question can now simply be restated to include this principle, thus: Why ought a person — *any* person — having that property not be considered an exception to the general rule that moral reasons override reasons of self-interest?

To see how such a position is perfectly consistent, consider the property of having six toes on each foot with a wart on each toe. Suppose someone endowed by nature with that property states that he adopts, as an ultimate normative commitment, the principle that *anyone* with such feet is to be permitted to further his interests whenever they conflict with the interest of others. It is not possible, then, to claim that he is making an unjustifiable exception in his own favor (knowing that he alone has the property in question). For he is quite willing to universalize that principle, letting *everyone* commit himself to it and letting it be applied to *all* cases where the property in question is exemplified. Thus he is not claiming that his own case is to be treated differently from others' *merely because it is his own.* Instead, he is committing himself to the principle (as a supreme one) that having the property in question is a relevant difference between persons.

Given this commitment, the Ultimate Question can be rephrased as follows. Instead of asking "Why should I be moral?" the individual now can ask, "Why should I not adopt the principle that anyone having six toes on each foot with a wart on each toe is an exception to the general rule that moral reasons override reasons of self-interest?" This question cannot be answered by asserting that there is no relevant difference between the questioner's case and that of others, for this would simply mean that the one who asserts this does not subscribe to the principle adopted by the questioner. To make such a statement is not to show why the questioner is mistaken, illogical, or unjustified in adopting his principle. It is merely to indicate that one has not made the same ultimate normative commitment that the questioner has. So an adequate answer has not yet been given to question (a): Why should I (as an individual) be moral?

(2) A second way to respond to the Ultimate Question can be seen as emerging from the foregoing considerations. When the Ultimate Question is interpreted as question (a), — Why should I be moral? — what is being asked for are reasons that would justify an individual's making an ultimate choice

of the priority of morality over self-interest. But an *ultimate* choice, by its very nature, cannot be based on reasons, since any arguments given to justify it will themselves presuppose a principle that has already been chosen, from which it follows that the choice being justified is not an ultimate one. Let us set out this argument fully and explicitly.

To give "reasons for choosing" is to show that a person is justified in choosing one thing rather than another when he can do one or the other but not both. Giving such reasons is possible only within the framework of some principle according to which the reasons given do indeed warrant the choice based on them. (That doing X will satisfy a desire is a reason for choosing to do X only because one accepts the *principle,* What satisfies a desire is a good thing to do.) Thus giving reasons for choosing already presupposes commitment to a principle. Now suppose one were to give reasons for choosing one principle rather than another — that is, justification for a commitment to follow one as a guide to conduct rather than another. Then to give reasons for choosing *that* principle would presuppose commitment to some higher principle. And if reasons for choosing this higher principle were offered, commitment to still another at a higher level would be presupposed. And so on, for any higher principle. Therefore, with regard to any choice, if reasons for choosing are given to justify it, it cannot be an *ultimate* choice — the choice of a *highest* principle. Now the Ultimate Question is precisely the demand for reasons for making an ultimate choice. Such a demand is incoherent, as can be seen from the fact that it asks for what is impossible. No reasons can be given for an ultimate choice, for an ultimate choice rules out the possibility of reasons for choosing.

We are now in a position to understand how the challenge expressed in the Ultimate Question is to be met. We simply say to the person who poses the question, "We cannot give you reasons that will show what choice you must make. You must decide for yourself. You cannot avoid this final responsibility. The choice of how you are to live, of the supreme normative axioms of your conduct, is a choice that no one can make but yourself. Even your own reason cannot do this job for you. As we have seen, your acceptance of any reasons for choosing will presuppose some principle that has already been chosen by you. Thus it is a matter, not of your reason, but of your will. You must *decide* what shall be your ultimate commitment, and this requires an exercise of your capacity to make an autonomous, self-directed choice about the kind of life you are to live. In this sort of situation to ask for reasons is actually an unconscious attempt to evade the burden of an ultimate choice. Such an attempt is futile, however, for it is an attempt to deny what cannot be denied: that each individual must finally answer for himself the question of what principles he is to live by."

This line of thought has led some philosophers to the following conclusion. To make an ultimate commitment is nothing less than *to define oneself*. It is to decide to be a certain kind of person. There is no way to escape this choice, the reason being that we *are* at every moment what we choose to *make* ourselves, and we can always choose to create a different self and so define our nature in a new way. Most of our decisions and choices, it is true, are not consciously directed to alternatives of this ultimate kind. But that is because we make most decisions and choices within the framework of a way of life. Our way of life is our mode or "style" of carrying on human existence. It is the expression of our own conception of what it means to be human, and it includes our commitment to the very principles that determine what we accept as reasons for acting and reasons for choosing. Hence, though we make decisions and choices in daily life that are not themselves ultimate, we do so only in terms of the conceptual system embodied in the ultimate principles of our way of life.

Since our way of life is our way of defining ourselves, it is not imposed on us from the outside. Nor is it merely a reflection of the kind of person we already are. For our being a certain kind of person is due to our having chosen to live in a certain way, not the other way around. (This is a logical point about the concepts of a way of life and of personhood, not a psychological account of the origins of our "personality." To exist as a person by choosing to define oneself in a certain way is logically prior to having a "personality" as that is empirically explained and described by the science of psychology.) At every moment, whether we realize it or not, we are choosing our way of life, since at each instant there is some way of life that may be correctly ascribed to us. The fact that we do not change our mode of living from one moment to the next does not show that no choice is being made. For if we do not change, we are choosing to continue to be what we have been. And so we are still creating ourselves, making ourselves in a certain image of man, defining our own nature by living as we do. Thus, whether our way of life is one in which morality outweights self-interest (in cases of conflict between them) or one in which self-interest overrides morality, it is *our* way of life because we have *made* it so. It is we who determine which shall be supreme, ethics or ego. As an ultimate choice, it is a matter of how we decide to live and to define ourselves. And whether our past decisions continue to mold our way of life in the present is something only we have the power to determine. The decision to change or not to change is forever inescapable. We cannot free ourselves from the responsibility to define our selfhood at every moment. At the same time, at every moment we have the "existential" freedom to define our selfhood as we will.

THE COMMITMENT TO BE MORAL

Do these considerations necessarily imply that a person's commitment to the supremacy of moral principles over self-interest is an *arbitrary* decision, like the tossing of a coin? As an ultimate choice it can be called extrarational, beyond reason, neither rational nor irrational. But one can say the same of the contrary choice, by which a person commits himself to the priority of self-interest over morality. Is this all there is to be said?

Something further can indeed be said, but this something further is not the giving of a reason that would justify the choice of one alternative rather than the other. It is, instead, a matter of bringing clearly before one's mind a full recognition of the *nature* of the choice, an ultimate one. Now if it is true that in some sense ultimate choices cannot be avoided — that everyone must make them, and at every moment of life — then making such choices is simply a necessary aspect of one's autonomy as an individual. Thus suppose someone said, "I refuse to make an ultimate choice between morality and self-interest." He would actually be making an ultimate choice, namely, not to commit himself in advance but to wait until he finds himself in a situation of conflict between morality and self-interest and then commit himself on the spur of the moment. His supreme commitment is to whatever principles he chooses to follow as an immediate reaction to particular situations confronting him with the necessity to choose. This is the way he is defining *his* nature. And his decision to refuse to commit himself in advance is itself an exercise of his autonomy as an individual! It seems, then, that there can be no genuine counter-instance to the generalizations that ultimate choices must be made at every moment by each person, and that such choices realize or express the autonomy of each individual.

Now this is of great significance. For if every person, as a person, must bear the responsibility of making his own ultimate choices at every moment of his life, anything that took away or diminished the possibility of someone's exercise of this autonomy would be a violation of the very foundation of rational action and choice in that person's life. In not allowing the person to define himself, it would deny him existence as a person. What is more, to interfere with or destroy someone's capacity for making ultimate choices

would be to negate that person's responsibility to answer the Ultimate
Question for himself. So if the Ultimate Question is not an absurdity and if
one individual can never answer if for another but each must find his own
answer, then, as far as solving the Ultimate Question is concerned, each
person must be unhindered in the exercise of his autonomy as a maker of
ultimate choices.

The necessary conditions for each person's asking and answering the
Ultimate Question are now seen to impose a restriction upon human
conduct: that no one shall deprive another of his capacity to make ultimate
choices, nor interfere with his exercise of that capacity. To put it another
way, each person must respect every other person's autonomy. If, in any
particular set of circumstances, one person's acting from self-interest would
transgress this primary rule of respect for everyone's autonomy, then his
action must not be permitted. To allow him to do it would be to deny the
principle which lies at the very foundation of all rational action and choice.
For the freedom to make ultimate choices is necessarily presupposed by
anyone's having *any* reasons for acting and reasons for choosing, whether
they be moral or prudential reasons.

It seems plausible to hold that respect for the autonomy of persons is
itself a moral principle. If this is so, then the choice between *this* principle
and the pursuit of self-interest, even when it is an ultimate choice, is not
arbitrary. Although one cannot give reasons for choosing this moral principle, one can examine fully the true nature of the choice and recognize that
commitment to the principle in question is a precondition for all ultimate
choices made by anyone, and hence a precondition for anyone's being able
to carry on practical reasoning.

Let us then suppose, as our final consideration, that a person who has
followed the foregoing argument still wants to know why he should be moral
to the extent of respecting the autonomy of others. He admits that he can
meaningfully ask this question only because others are respecting *his* autonomy and that, if he were not to respect *their* autonomy, they would be unable to find an answer, or even seek an answer, to the Ultimate Question.
But he says, "Why should I care whether they seek an answer, or find one?"

There are no reasons that can be given which provide an answer to his
question. He must decide for himself what he is to care about in his life.
The only thing that can be done is to point out to him that this is a decision
of a fundamental kind. It is the decision to be a certain sort of person. Can
he face himself openly and unevasively and still decide not to respect the

autonomy of others, having clearly before his mind the full meaning of such a choice? If he can, then he has determined what conception of being human shall be exemplified in his life and this is all one can say about his decision. No argument can be given to show that his decision is irrational or that it is based on false assumptions.

This, after all, is in keeping with the idea emphasized above: that each person must take upon himself the responsibility for his ultimate normative commitment. In subscribing to the basic principles of his way of life, a person chooses to define himself in a certain way. If he decides to be the kind of person who deprives another of the capacity for an autonomous choice of a way of life, he cannot be said to be inconsistent. One can only ask, Can he make such a decision *authentically*, that is, sincerely acknowledging it as his own and at the same time making the decision, as it were, with his whole being? If he can, he knows what sort of conception of man he chooses to exemplify. And if he is willing to choose to be that sort of person — one who denies the personhood of another in the very act of defining his own personhood — nothing more can be said.

Commitment to moral principles, then, is finally a matter of one's will, not of one's reason. Reason can make clear to us the nature of the commitment and can lead us to a full awareness of the alternatives among which we must choose. But reason alone cannot tell us what choice to make. We must not expect, therefore, that someone might provide us with an argument showing which alternative *ought* to be chosen. There is simply no way to evade the responsibility — a responsibility that rests upon each of us alone — for defining our own selves. It is up to us to answer, each in his own way, that haunting question, Who am I? We give our answer to it by deciding whether our lives shall exemplify, to whatever extent is in our power, the principles of morality, or some other principles. Even to say, "Let each one decide for himself," is to express a doctrine that imposes a restraint upon action. And it is possible for a person to commit himself to some other principle contrary to this one, without being inconsistent. As long as he understands and acknowledges the nature of his choice and does not try to evade the fact that it is *his* choice, such a person cannot be shown to have chosen against the dictates of reason.

It is simply that he decides to be a certain kind of human being. Whether we also decide to be that kind of human being ourselves is a question only we can answer. For no one can escape the necessity to determine for himself what the answer, in his own life, shall be.

Suggested Reading

A good collection of writings on the relation between self-interest, morality, and rationality:

Gauthier, David P., ed., *Morality and Rational Self-Interest*. Englewood Cliffs, N. J.: Prentice-Hall, Inc., 1970.*

Some recent discussions of the ultimate justification of morality:

Baier, Kurt, *The Moral Point of View: A Rational Basis of Ethics,* Chapters 3-12. Ithaca, N. Y.: Cornell University Press, 1958. For a shorter presentation of the argument, see the *Abridged Edition,* Chapters 2-7. New York: Random House, Inc., 1965*

Bradley, F. H., "Why Should I Be Moral?", Essay II of *Ethical Studies.* London: Oxford University Press, 1927. Reprinted in *Ethical Studies, Selections,* ed. Ralph G. Ross. Indianapolis: The Bobbs-Merrill Co., Inc., 1951.* Also reprinted (in part) in *Readings in the Problems of Ethics,* ed. Rosalind Ekman. New York: Charles Scribner's Sons, 1965.*

Carter, Curtis L., ed., *Skepticism and Moral Principles: Modern Ethics in Review.* Evanston, Ill.: New University Press, Inc., 1973.*

Gauthier, David P., *Practical Reasoning: The Structure and Foundations of Prudential and Moral Arguments and their Exemplification in Discourse,* especially Chapters 6, 7, and 8. London: Oxford University Press, 1963.

Gert, Bernard, *The Moral Rules: A New Rational Foundation for Morality,* especially Chapters 5, 6, and 10. New York: Harper Torchbooks, Harper and Row, Publishers, 1973.*

Nielsen, Kai, "Is 'Why Should I Be Moral?' An Absurdity?", *Australasian Journal of Philosophy,* XXXVI, No. 1 (1958), 25-32. Reprinted in *Readings in the Problems of Ethics,* ed. Rosalind Ekman, op. cit.*

————, "Why Should I Be Moral?", *Methodos,* XV, No. 59-60 (1963), 275-306. Reprinted in the Bobbs-Merrill Reprint Series in Philosophy. Indianapolis: The Bobbs-Merrill Co., Inc.*

Prichard, H. A., "Does Moral Philosophy Rest on a Mistake?", *Mind,* XXI (1912), 487-499. Reprinted in *Contemporary Ethical Theory: A Book of Readings,* ed. Joseph Margolis. New York: Random House, Inc., 1966.*

Rawls, John, *A Theory of Justice,* especially Chapter 9. Cambridge, Mass.: Harvard University Press, 1971.*

Richards, David A. J., *A Theory of Reasons for Action,* especially Chapter 14. London: Oxford University Press, 1971.

Toulmin, Stephen Edelston, *An Examination of the Place of Reason in Ethics,* Chapters 11-14. Cambridge: Cambridge University Press, 1950.*

Trigg, Roger, *Reason and Commitment.* Cambridge: Cambridge University Press, 1973.*

Wallace, G. and A. D. M. Walker, eds., *The Definition of Morality*. London: Methuen and Co., Ltd., 1970.*

An existentialist concept of an ultimate normative commitment is presented in:

Olafson, Frederick A., *Principles and Persons: An Ethical Interpretation of Existentialism*. Baltimore: The Johns Hopkins Press, 1967.*

*Available in paperback

Index

A

Absolutism, ethical, *see* Relativism, ethical
Act-utilitarianism, *see* Utilitarianism
Acts v. motives, 37-40
Analytic ethics, *see* Metaethics
Aristotle, 131
Autonomy of the will, *see* Formalism, ethical

B

Bentham, Jeremy, 55, 60

C

Categorical Imperative, *see* Formalism, Ethical
Causal explanation (cause and effect), *see* Determinism
Compatibilism, *see* Determinism, soft
Cognitivism, 190

D

Deontological ethics, 55, 82-84, 114-115
and Moral Law, 56, 83-84, 86
Derivative value, *see* Value, derivative
Descriptive ethics
defined, 5
individual, 4
and normative ethics, 6
societal, 4-5

Descriptivism:
description & evaluation in, 201
criticism, 202-204
Foot, Philippa, 200
and naturalistic fallacy, 201, 202
Determinism:
causal explanation (cause and effect), 151-152
defined, 150
and moral responsibility, 152-153
indeterminism, 152, 157
and science, 151
Determinism, hard:
and free will (freedom), 162-163, 165-166
and moral responsibility, 170-173
three propositions, 160
Determinism, hard & soft, 160-163
Determinism, soft (compatibilism), 157-160
and free will (freedom), 157-159, 160-162, 165
inescapability of, 163
in practical life, 164-165

E

Egoism, ethical
defined, 32
Hobbes, Thomas, 47-49
Leviathan, 47
obligation, concept of, 49
individual ethical egoism, 32-33
criticism, 51-52
personal ethical egoism, 33

criticism, 52
and psychological egoism, 33-36, 46
universal ethical egoism, 32, 33,
47-49
criticism, 49-51
and utilitarianism, 47, 61
Egoism, psychological:
criticism, 36-45
defined, 31-32
and hedonism, 43-44
arguments for and against, 36-45
tautology, 44-45
and universal ethical egoism, 33-36,
46
Emotive theory, see Noncognitivism
Epicurus, 33
Ethical egoism, see Formalism, ethical
Ethical pluralism, see Pluralists, ethical
Ethical relativism, see Relativism,
ethical
Ethical skepticism, see Moral reasoning
and Relativism, ethical
Ethical universalism, see Universalism,
ethical
Ethics:
analytic ethics, see Metaethics
autonomy of, 187-188
defined, 1, 11
descriptive ethics, see Descriptive
ethics
monistic ethics, see Monistic ethics
normative ethics, see Normative ethics
Ethnocentrism, see also Relativism,
Ethical
and nonnaturalism, 179
Evaluation, standards of, see Prescriptivism
Excusability, see Moral Responsibility

F

Foot, Philippa, see Descriptivism
Formalism, ethical
autonomy of the will, 89, 108-109
self-directed, 109
categorical imperative, 87-88, 91
defining of moral rule, 87
three formulations, 88-89
deontological system, 82-84
"formalism," meaning of, 92-93
and freedom, 90-91
generalization principle, see universalizability below
Good Will, the, 85
three propositions of morality,
85-86
justice, principles of, 109-111
v. utilitarian justice, 110

"kingdom of ends," see moral community below
man as end, 89, 105-108, 109
absolute value, 106
conditional value, 106
moral agent, 93-95
definition, 93
four aspects, 94
moral community, 89-90, 100, 108
moral law, proof of, 90-92
universalizability, 88, 95-105, 215
basis for moral reasoning, 96
consistency, 97
defined, 95
generalization principle, 100-101
logical universalizability, 95-98
universal acceptability, 102-104
universal applicability, 98-102
and utilitarianism, 55-57
value, absolute or unconditional, 106
value, conditional, 106
Freedom, see Determinism, hard, and
Determinism, soft and Formalism,
Ethical, and Moral responsibility
Free will, see Determinism, hard, and
Determinism, soft and Moral
responsibility

G

Generalization principle, see Formalism,
Ethical
"Good," meaning of, 193-200
Good Will, the, see Formalism, Ethical

H

Hare, R. M., see Prescriptivism
Happiness
as standard of value, 130-143
happiness assertions, 138-140
objective value, 137
three concepts:
essentialist concept, 131-133
plan-of-life concept, 133-137
self-evaluative concept, 138-142
three conditions, 133-136
Hedonic paradox, 126
Hedonism, 121-127
egoistic hedonism, 122
psychological hedonism, see Egoism,
Psychological
valuational hedonism, 121
four implications, 123-125
v. hedonistic utilitarianism, 122
Hobbes, Thomas, 33, 47-49
Leviathan, 33, 47

I

Incompatibilists and libertarianism, 156
Intrinsic value, *see* Value, Intrinsic
Intuitionism, *see* Nonnaturalism

J

Justice, *see* Formalism, Ethical and
Utilitarianism

K

Kant, Immanuel: *see also* Formalism,
Ethical
and ethical formalism, 55
*Fundamental Principles of the Meta-
physics of Morals* discussed:
Preface, 85
First Section, 85-87
Second Section, 87-90
Third Section, 90-92
list of writings, 84
"Kingdom of ends," *see* Formalism,
ethical

L

Language, moral: *see also* Noncognitivism
objectivity of, 179-181, 193
and naturalism, 181
Leviathan, see Egoism, Ethical, and
Hobbes, Thomas
Libertarianism, *see* Moral Responsibility

M

Metaethics: *see also*, Relativism,
Metaethical aims, 7, 9
v. Normative ethics, 6, 8, 9
Mill, John Stuart, 127-128 *see also*
Pleasure
Utilitarianism, 55, 60, 116
Monistic ethics, 58
Moore, G. E.: *see also* Naturalistic
Fallacy
Principia Ethica, 182
utilitarian, 60
Moral agent, 6, *see also* Formalism,
Ethical
Moral commitment, 208-209, 219-227
individual autonomy, 225
respect for, 226
individual responsibility, 227
nature of choice, 225
Moral community ("kingdom of ends")
see Formalism, Ethical

Morality:
actual and ideal, 1, 3, 4-6
case against, 210
Myth of Gyges, 209-210, 217
customary morality, 9-11
ethics as study of, 1, 4-6, 9
justification of, 209, *see also* Moral
Reasoning
and nonegoism, 211
purpose of, 78-80
reflective morality, 9-11
moral growth, 10, 11
Ultimate Question, 211
and ethical egoism, 210
Moral law: 56-57, 82-84
Categorical Imperative, 87-88, 91,
see also Formalism, Ethical
Good Will, the, 86
Moral norms, 2-3
defined, 2
Moral principle, 17, 209-211, 219-227
Moral reasoning: *see also* Noncognitivism
and Prescriptivism
deliberation & justification, 211
intersubjective validity, 213
denial of, 214
and ethical relativism, 214
and ethical skepticism, 214
moral beliefs, 213
logic of, 211-215
Ultimate Question, 208-227
absurdity of, 215-216, 226
first proposed answer, 220-222
second proposed answer, 223-225
Skinner, B. F., and, 218
three formulations, 217-219
defining oneself, 224-225
unanswerability of, 223
and utilitarianism, 215
Moral responsibility: *see also* Determinism and Determinism, hard
accountability, 166, 169-170
analysis of, 167-173
causal responsibility, 167
flaw in character, 167-169
return to moral equilibrium, 169
excusing conditions, 146-150, 168
lack of ability, 149-150
circumstances beyond control,
148-149
excusable ignorance, 147
constraint, 147-148
and determinism, 152-154
freedom, compatibilist (soft determinism), 157-160
causal explanations, 157-158
criteria of, 159

free will, 166: *see also* freedom,
  compatibilist above
future-oriented concept, 170-173
  blame justified, 170
  four criticisms of, 171-172
  rebuttal, 172
libertarianism, 154-156
  incompatibilism, 156
  moral agent, 154
  moral self (soul), 155-156
  personality, 154
  traditional concept, 167-171
Motives, 37-45, 218-219
  types of, 38-40
  and psychological egoism, 40
  self-interest, 42
  unconscious motives, 40
Myth of Gyges, see Morality

                   N

Naturalism:
  objectivist, 177
  subjectivist, 177
  value judgments, 176-177, 181
Naturalistic fallacy, 181-188
  deductive fallacy, 185-187
  definist fallacy, 182
    open-question argument, 182-184
    reasons-for-acting argument, 184-185
  descriptivism, and, 200-202
  Moore, G. E., originator, 181, 188
    and nonnaturalism, 188
  and science, 187
    autonomy of ethics, 187-188
Nature, state of, 47-48
Noncognitivism, 188-194, *see also*
  Prescriptivism
  attitudes v. beliefs, 191
  or emotive theory, 188
  and moral reasoning, 192
  v. naturalism & nonnaturalism, 190
  and objectivity of language, 193
  and science, 192
  Stevenson, Charles, 193-194
  three functions of language, 188-190
    dynamic, 189
    expressive, 189
    reportive, 188
  value judgments, 189-190
Nonderivative value, *see* Value, intrinsic
  and Value, nonderivative
Nonegoist and Ultimate Question, 211
  and psychological egoism, 37, 40, 42
Nonnaturalism:
  defined, 177
  and ethnocentrism, 179

  and intuition, 178
  and objective values, 177-178
  and self-evidence, 178-179
Normative ethics, 6, 9, 13, 175
  system of, 31, 55-58, 82-84, 114, 146

                   P

Plato, 131, *see also* Intrinsic Value &
  Myth of Gyges
Pleasure: *see also* Hedonism & Utilitarianism
  defined, 125-126
  v. happiness, 129, 142
  hedonic paradox, 126
  Mill, J. S., on, 127-128
  quantity v. quality, 127-129
Pluralists, ethical, 57-58
Prescriptivism, 194-200
  Hare, R. M., 194
  v. noncognitivism, 194-198
  principles: term analyzed, 199-200
  standards and rules, 198
    justification of, 198-200
  syllogism of moral reasoning, 199
  and universal principles, 194-197
  value judgments, analysis of, 194-198

                   R

Reconciliationism, 156
Relativism, ethical: *see also* Moral Reasoning
  absolutism, 26-29
    two meanings, 26-27
    universalism, ethical, 28
  descriptive relativism, 14
    cultural variability, 14
    ethnocentrism, 15-16
    origins of morality, 15
    supporting arguments, 16, 22, 23
    utility, 17
  metaethical relativism, 23-26
    conceptual relativism, 23-25
    ethical skepticism, 25
    methodological relativism, 25-26
  normative ethical relativism, 18-23
    criticism of, 21-22
    supporting argument, 21
Responsibility, *see* Moral responsibility
Right and Good, relationship between,
  114-115
Rule-utilitarianism, *see* Utilitarianism

                   S

Science, *see* Noncognitivism and Determinism
  and ethics, 4-5, 187

Skepticism, ethical, *see* Moral Reasoning
    & Relativism, Ethical
Skinner, B. F., *see* Moral Reasoning
Soul, the, *see* Moral responsibility
Stevenson, Charles, 193-194

T

Teleological ethical system v. deon-
    tological, 55-56, 58, 82-84, 114-115

U

Ultimate Question, *see* Moral Reasoning
Universalism, ethical, 18, 20, 23, 24, 28,
    31
Universalizability, *see* Formalism, ethical
Utilitarianism: *see also* Moral Reasoning
    and Egoism, ethical
    act-, 63, 66
        and rule-, 63-72
        extensionally equivalent, 69
        incompatibility, 68-72
        moral reasoning, 215
    agathistic utilitarianism, 60
    basic concept, 60
    Bentham, Jeremy, 55, 60
    contemporary rejection of, 72
    defense of, 78-80
    derivative value, 59, 119
    eudaimonistic utilitarianism, 60
    v. formalism, 55-57
    hedonistic utilitarianism, 60

    impartiality of, 61
    intrinsic value, 59, 73
        measured, 73-75
        Moore, G. E., 60
    justice, 72-78, 109-111
        conflict with utilitarianism, 75
        and social conflict, 76-77
    Mill, John Stuart, 55, 60, 116, 127-128
    right and wrong, 61
    rule-utilitarianism, 63-72
        defined, 64
        second-order moral rule, 70
Utility, principle of, 17, 63-64, 66,
    72-74, 215

V

Value, conditional and unconditional,
    see Formalism, Ethical
Value, derivative, 59, 119
Value and facts, *see* Naturalism and
    Nonnaturalism
Value, intrinsic: *see also* Hedonism,
    Happiness, Utilitarianism
    definition, 59
    four aspects of, 115-121
        fact v. value, 116
        natural v. nonnatural properties, 118
        nature v. consequences, 117
        nonderivative value, 59, 119-120
    Mill, J. S., 116
    Plato, 115-116
Value, nonderivative, 59, 115, 119-121